MW00581033

Brand Antarctica

POLAR STUDIES

Series editor: Michael Robinson

————BRAND ANTARCTICA

How GLOBAL CONSUMER CULTURE SHAPES OUR PERCEPTIONS of the ICE CONTINENT

HANNE ELLIOT FØNSS NIELSEN

University of Nebraska Press   Lincoln

An earlier version of chapter 5 was originally published
as "Save the Penguins: Antarctic Advertising and
the PR of Protection" in *Anthropocene Antarctica:
Perspectives from the Humanities, Law and Social
Sciences*, edited by Elizabeth Leane, and Jeffrey
McGee, 117–32 (London: Routledge, 2020).

The University of Nebraska Press is part of a land-
grant institution with campuses and programs on the
past, present, and future homelands of the Pawnee,
Ponca, Otoe-Missouria, Omaha, Dakota, Lakota, Kaw,
Cheyenne, and Arapaho Peoples, as well as those of the
relocated Ho-Chunk, Sac and Fox, and Iowa Peoples.

Library of Congress Cataloging-in-Publication Data
Names: Nielsen, Hanne Elliot Fønss, author.
Title: Brand Antarctica: how global consumer
culture shapes our perceptions of the ice
continent / Hanne Elliot Fønss Nielsen.
Description: Lincoln : University of Nebraska Press, [2023] |
Series: Polar studies | Includes bibliographical references
and index. | Summary: "In Brand Antarctica Hanne
Elliot Fønss Nielsen analyses advertisements and related
cultural products to identify common framings that have
emerged in representations of Antarctica from the late
nineteenth century to the present"—Provided by publisher.
Identifiers: LCCN 2023012608
ISBN 9781496221216 (hardback)
ISBN 9781496238245 (epub)
ISBN 9781496238252 (pdf)
Subjects: LCSH: Tourism—Marketing. | Branding
(Marketing)—Antarctica. | Nature in advertising—
Antarctica. | Advertising—Tourism—Antarctica. |
Antarctica—Discovery and exploration. | BISAC: HISTORY /
Polar Regions | SOCIAL SCIENCE / Media Studies
Classification: LCC G155.A54 N54 2023 | DDC
919.8904/00688—dc23/eng/20231012
LC record available at https://lccn.loc.gov/2023012608

Designed and set in Charter by L. Welch.

For Stephen Dodge

Contents

Illustrations

Preface

Before we begin, take a moment to consider: what does Antarctica mean to you? Antarctica is not one thing; its four syllables carry so many, at times contradictory, resonances. Today, the southern continent is a place of peace and science, but the contemporary protection offered to the continent is not a given. As this book shows, Antarctica's human history is a commercial history. Marine animals have been hunted, expedition stories have been sold, and the model for celebrity endorsement was honed in Antarctica. The materiality of the Far South is sold through modern-day tourism, while the ideas associated with the place have powerful branding allure. Antarctica's framing in advertising therefore provides a proxy for the way the continent has been valued at different points in time.

This book outlines five key framings of Antarctica—a place for heroes, extremity, purity, protection, and transformation—and argues that the conceptual framing of a place can have very real material impacts. The stories that circulate matter because they influence how we view, think about, and interact with the ice at the ends of the earth. Those stories (and a pesky appendix) are why this book is here today.

In April 1961 Soviet surgeon Leonid Rogozov fell ill with appendicitis while in the Antarctic. As the station doctor, his fate was quite literally in his own hands—Rogozov operated on his own abdomen, thereby saving his life, and going down in Antarctic folklore. Following this incident, many National Antarctic Programs required winter expeditioners to have their appendixes removed before being deployed. I heard this in passing and thought nothing of it. The story lay dormant, like a seed. Then, when I found myself struck by appendicitis in Vietnam, casting around for one good thing, my brain obliged with the thought: "At least now I can go to Antarctica." And so it all began.

I first went South with Antarctica New Zealand in 2011, as part of the University of Canterbury's postgraduate certificate in Antarctic studies. There was a lot of snow and ice, but my interest was in the human stories that are layered over the continent. I was in a place for heroes during the Scott centenary, talking to climate scientists about threats to Antarctica and feeling like I was experiencing the place incorrectly somehow because the visit did not feel "life changing." Overlapping framings of the place coalesced in an Antarctic encounter that has, in fact, shaped everything since.

Upon my return I took a job with an advertising company. Drinking coffee from my Scott Base mug each morning, my mind would wander back—I wanted to find out more about the stories that circulate about this frozen place. Somewhere between writing advertisement copy for tractors and dreaming of the ice, my PhD project was born, asking how Antarctica had been depicted in advertising and what this meant both for us as humans and for the continent. Once I started looking, the advertisements just keep coming.

Eight years have passed since I embarked on this project. Atmospheric CO_2 levels have risen from 398 ppm in 2014 to 418ppm in 2022 and are climbing. Over that time, I've come to know Antarctica in different ways: as an Antarctic tour guide, a researcher, resident of an Antarctic gateway city, and a parent acutely aware of how in the Anthropocene the futures of my child and the ice are intertwined. The word "Antarctica" now carries so much more meaning for me. It's brought friendships, wonder, ecological anxiety, academic discovery, and so many stories. And although the ice itself is far distant from Hobart's shores, Antarctica has helped me make a home.

I begin with my story of my Antarctica, and you begin with yours. Ice moves. Perspectives shift. Stories accumulate like snow, year on year. Our collective stories are what this book is about. Perhaps your own Antarctica will look slightly different by the time you reach the final page.

Acknowledgments

This book was written in lutruwita (Tasmania) on the lands, seas, and waterways of the Muwinina people. The Muwinina people belong to the oldest continuing culture in the world. They knew this land, they lived on the land, and they died on this land. I honor them. I pay my respects to elders past, present, and emerging and to the Tasmanian Aboriginal community that continues to care for Country. It is a privilege to stand on Country and walk in the footsteps of those before us.

Thank you to Elizabeth Leane, Nicolá Goc, and Julia Jabour for providing expert literary, media studies, and Antarctic input into this project and for helping me to see Antarctica from new angles. Thoughtful and thorough comments from Klaus Dodds, Leslie Roberts, and Adrian Howkins strengthened the book and helped me make my own arguments more clearly, while Marcus Haward reminded me that the perfect is the enemy of the good. Thanks, also, to Emily Casillas for guiding me through the publication process.

This project benefited from funding via an Elite Australian Postgraduate Award Scholarship and small grant support from the Scientific Committee on Antarctic Research (SCAR) Standing Committee on Humanities and Social Science (SC-HASS), the University of Tasmania (UTAS) People and Environment Research Group, and the American Geographical Society at the University of Wisconsin—Milwaukee. A big thank-you goes to Steve Christenson and Cheryl Rugg for hosting me in Milwaukee and showing me the best of the dairy land.

Colleagues at the UTAS English Department, the Institute for Marine and Antarctic Studies (IMAS), and the University of Canterbury's Gateway Antarctica have shown me that lunchtime conversations really can lead to epiphanies. Discussions with colleagues from the SCAR SC-HASS and the Association of Polar Early Career Scientists (APECS) enriched my thinking, while conversations with Renuka Badhe and Hannah Stark have made the future seem a less scary place. I am indebted to many others for comments, links to media articles, and photographs of Antarctic advertisements that have subsequently turned into fruitful lines of inquiry.

My peers have been a constant source of support, both academically and in real life. Members of Antarctic and Oceans Law, Politics, Policy, Humanities and Social Sciences (ACCLIMATISE); the Red Pen Bandits; the English Theory Reading Group; the UTAS People and Environment Research Group; and the Twitter Shut Up & Write Tuesdays community have offered comments, cake, and encouragement. Special thanks go to Robyn Greaves, Rose Walker, Miranda Nieboer, Gabriela Roldán, Valeriya Komyakova, and Indi Hodgson-Johnson. Rebecca Hingley's editorial assistance is much appreciated.

To Mum and Dad (Bronwyn and Poul), Grandma and Grandad (Greta and Ken), and Mormor and Morfar (Unni and Peter): thank you for all the stories and scintillating conversations and for teaching me to aim high. Finally, the biggest thank-you to Stephen, Elliot, and Mya Pup—for waving me off to Antarctica and warming the house on my return. I could not have come this far without you.

Brand Antarctica

Introduction

Antarctica's Commercial Connections

Tracing your finger over a detailed map of Antarctica—the supposed "last wilderness" and emptiest place on Earth—can be an unsettling experience. At the continent's coastline, you come across Mobiloil Inlet, named by Sir Hubert Wilkins in 1928 after the Vacuum Oil Company of Australia. Farther inland the Horlick Mountains, the Ford Range, and the Rockefeller Mountains are all reminders of Admiral Richard Byrd's Antarctic expeditions and official sponsors. Other names are more obscure, yet they act as the key to a rich and storied past: Sulzberger Bay (figure 1) commemorates the publisher of the *New York Times*, Newnes Land refers to the British media baron Sir George Newnes, while Hearst Land was named in honor of Newnes's American rival, William Randolph Hearst. Such media sponsors played an important role in financing early Antarctic expeditions, and modern maps do not let this be forgotten: the commercial-industrial history of the South is inscribed on the map.

Today, new Antarctic place-names must be approved by national place-naming committees before they can officially enter into wider circulation. Most committee guidelines exclude commercial names from consideration, but the commercial roots of many historical place-names remain evident. Machinery that has been used in Antarctica has acted as namesakes for mountains and glaciers, such as the Arrol Icefall, named after Shackleton's Arrol Johnston motor car; Mount Tucker, named for the Tucker Sno-Cat Corporation of Medford, Oregon, creators of the vehicles used in the Commonwealth Trans-Antarctic Expedition (TAE) of 1955–58; and the Bombardier and Havilland Glaciers, named for the manufacturer of the tracked Sno-Cat and skidoo vehicles and for the De Havilland Twin Otter, "the workhorse of Antarctic aviation," respectively.[1]

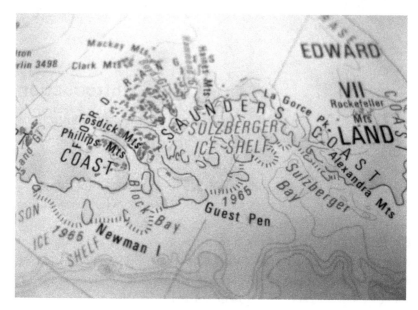

FIG 1. Close-up of a 1969 Antarctic map, showing commercial place names. From the American Geographical Society Library, University of Wisconsin–Milwaukee Libraries (070 A-1969). Photographed by Hanne Nielsen.

In the Ross Sea region, the generically named Sponsors Peak, located between Barwick Valley and the Upper Victoria Glacier, matter-of-factly honors the sponsors of the 1958–59 Victoria University of Wellington Antarctic Expedition.

Naming not only transforms space into place but ties geography to history.[2] In the Antarctic cases considered above, a transitory physical link has become permanent, with the place-names enduring long past the lifespan of the actual pistons and tracks. The brand names, dating to the mid-twentieth century when the last major Antarctic "firsts" were being tackled, add an enduring layer to the commercial history of Antarctica, which has developed from a lucrative hunting ground to a place that is valued for its symbolic connotations. It is such a history of Brand Antarctica—as showcased in print advertisements featuring the continent, commemorated on maps and packaging, and revisited and recast by modern-day companies—that this book seeks to explore.

Antarctica: A Continent Narrated, Framed, and Experienced

During a 1998 address in Christchurch, New Zealand, Kevin Roberts of advertising agency Saatchi & Saatchi outlined a series of brand values for Antarctica. The list included terms and phrases such as "clean," "untouched," "pure," "beauty," "extreme," "the last frontier," "hope," "penguins," "World Peace," and "the last stand—a chance to rectify the mistakes we've made elsewhere." He claimed such values "present a product which is relevant to today's consumer, and they support a wider code of positive Antarctic values which encourage responsible use of the continent."[3] The 1959 Antarctic Treaty sets Antarctica aside as a place for peace and science, and this cornerstone of the Antarctic Treaty System (ATS) remains in effect. However, responsible use of the continent is just one way Antarctica has been framed over the course of its human history; it has also been seen as a place for profit, a place for heroes, a place for testing men and machines, a place to protect at all costs, and a place that changes people. Brand Antarctica is—much like the ice of the southern continent—dynamic, mutable, and responsive to human activities in far distant locations.

Brand Antarctica is also a powerful cultural force for motivating interest in the Far South. Most people will never visit Antarctica, so their experience of the continent is mediated through forms of cultural production, including films, photography, books, television, art, diaries, and advertisements. When the imagined version of Antarctica most people carry in their minds is far more real than actual snow and ice, the very idea of Antarctica presents an ideal background against which to peddle fantasies. Antarctic studies scholar Erin Neufeld and her coauthors argue that "the values that people bring to the Antarctic are rooted in their experience elsewhere, at home, outside the Antarctic."[4] This makes Antarctica a fertile research ground for all those interested in values, perceptions, and human interactions with place. Lack of access need not be a barrier to understanding, or to imagining, Antarctica; indeed, as ecologist David Walton writes, "the very idea of this polar place has excited the imagination for centuries."[5] Greek philosophers posited *Terra Australis Incognita* as a theoretical counterpoint to the landmasses of the north over two thousand years ago, and the continent continues to inspire artists and writers from afar.[6] In *The Myth of the Explorer*, historian Beau Riffenburgh notes that "historians and geographers have agreed that what is perceived to exist or happen is equally important as what actually exists or happens."[7] This means that cultural production has an important role to play in shaping knowledge about and attitudes toward Antarctica and its perceived value. Whether the word "Antarctica" brings to mind images of penguins, icebergs, heroes, science, or climate change, the films, novels, and advertisements that permeate society provide a frame for perceptions of this remote, comparatively unvisited, yet hugely valuable place.

This book asks: how has Antarctica been used in advertising, and what does this tell us about human attitudes and practices toward the continent? Advertisements are useful because they showcase so patently the commodification of Antarctica. At the same time, they provide a shortcut to ideas that are already in common cultural circulation, providing a mirror for our attitudes toward the place. As cultural studies scholar Judith Williamson puts it, "Ads are the great recyclers of images: they feed off the iconography of the present, at the same time as perpetuating it."[8] Each chapter provides the historical, social, cultural, and geographic context for understanding the ways the South has been used to sell products, as well as stories, experiences, and ideas. By examining advertisements that feature the southern continent, it is possible to gain insights into how Antarctica has been constructed in overlapping and sometimes competing ways—and therefore to see how and why we have cared about the place at different points in time. A firm grasp on this past is vital for ensuring that care and protection for Antarctica continues into the future.

This book demonstrates how advertisements, packaging, and promotional materials featuring Antarctica reveal a series of cultural framings of the region that have emerged from the late nineteenth century to the present, namely heroism, extremity, purity, fragility, and transformation. These frames are not exhaustive, nor are they exclusive. Rather, they offer a loosely chronological way of understanding how and why Antarctica has been valued at different points in time, as the abstract qualities and values that have been associated with Antarctica are rendered visible through textual analysis of the case study advertisements. As new framings emerge, they add layers to existing ways of conceptualizing Antarctica—a place where the "representational practices of consumerism" are particularly stark.[9] By providing an overview of the commercial history of the Far South, I argue that Antarctica ought to be seen as a vital part of a global commercial system, rather than a continent that exists apart from the rest of the world. Capitalism brings Antarctica and its branding to our doorsteps physically, metaphorically, environmentally, and symbolically.

Advertisements Wanted: Sourcing Materials

Advertisements trace the commercialization of Antarctica but also highlight the role of commercial settings in shaping the dominant imaginaries of Antarctica.[10] The form of advertisements has shifted over the span of the study period (1895–2022), reflecting both wider developments within advertising and shifting attitudes toward relationships with the Far South. Although it can be argued that advertising dates back to the public criers of ancient Greece and Rome, the modern form with which people are most familiar appeared in the nineteenth century, alongside the Industrial Revolution.[11] It was at this time that "the corporate signature, as the embodiment of pure exchange value in monopoly capital, [found] its independent existence."[12] As markets became more readily available and large-scale production became possible, the need to differentiate one product from another became more pressing, and rhetoric became a valuable tool. Looking back over the Euro-Western history of advertisements from the 1890s to the present, we see that an early emphasis on copywriting gradually shifted toward display and illustration, with lifestyle coming to the fore.[13] Until the 1920s, information was a key component of advertisements, but this was later superseded by symbolic representations, and—post-1945—by concern for the emotional reactions of the viewer.[14] Early testimonials stressed the utility of a product, while modern examples focus on the emotional experience and satisfaction of the consumer. As social communication expert William Leiss and his coauthors explain, the product no longer stands as an autonomous object independent of the human world but rather is displayed as an integral part of the codification of human existence and interaction.[15]

Such developments are mirrored in the corpus of anglophone Antarctic advertisements examined in this project, with early testimonials exhibiting verbose qualities and more recent examples relying much more heavily on visual language and connotation to communicate Antarctic connections and their message.

Over five hundred advertisements were collected during the process of writing this book. For the purposes of this study, the word "advertisement" is understood to refer to "a notice or announcement in a public medium promoting a product, service, or event or publicizing a job vacancy."[16] The majority of Antarctic advertisements relate to tangible products rather than intangible services—it is easier to anchor the connotations associated with a distant place using a concrete item. Print advertisements and digital still images in English were drawn from New Zealand, Australia, the United Kingdom, and the United States; these alone comprise hundreds of examples from the late nineteenth century to the present. Limiting the scope of this book allows for more in-depth analysis of the case-study advertisements, while leaving the door open for future studies to be repeated in a range of other linguistic and sociocultural contexts.

Advertisements were deemed to be "Antarctic" due to the geographic markers in the imagery or text. In some cases the presence of a penguin marks an icescape as south polar, as opposed to polar bears in the north. Penguins can act as a metonym for Antarctica, regardless of their genus; it is not uncommon to come across African blackfooted or Magellanic penguins in campaigns that reference the Far South, even though neither are Antarctic species. However, penguins and polar bears meet in advertising campaigns far more often than in real life—the well-known Coca-Cola campaign that features both has a lot to answer for when it comes to geographical awareness.[17] Other Antarctic advertisements gesture to historical figures and narratives by featuring scenes reminiscent of Ernest Shackleton's ship, *Endurance*, trapped in the ice, or Robert Falcon Scott's men trekking to the pole. Such advertisements are included in the analysis, as the images incorporate the icescape, and the historical figures have meaning largely in association with the continent.

There is some overlap between Antarctic advertisements and those that feature mountains and deep oceans, as the extremity theme is applicable to all—for instance, watchmakers may use a range of extreme environments as settings for a single campaign. Deserts and the high seas are, like Antarctica, easy to project ideas upon due to their perceived emptiness (in all cases, "empty" is an anthropocentric and colonial positioning, given the non-Western human histories and range of more-than-human organisms that thrive in these places). Desert and ocean imagery is often presented in environmental campaigns alongside Antarctica, with all being framed as vulnerable to human-induced change while posing a threat to humans—further studies might examine these interactions between icescapes, seascapes, and landscapes in advertising in greater depth.

In the context of the Anthropocene, the symbolism associated with ice can collapse geographical boundaries, with frozen places standing in for a global climate system that is under threat. Advertisements featuring ice are common to both the Arctic and the Antarctic, and in many cases the poles are conflated; both the north and south polar regions are cold, comparatively featureless icy landscapes that have been constructed as remote in the Western imagination. Given the ways polar explorers, sponsors, advertisers, and the climate crisis cut across both the Arctic and Antarctic, there is potential for further cross-polar work on advertising to be developed in the future. However, the Arctic has a long human history, and Indigenous people have lived well above the Arctic Circle for thousands of years—this is in contrast to Antarctica's comparatively young human history, and means framings can resonate differently in the two contexts. This book, therefore, focuses specifically on Antarctica.

Taking a historical-diachronic approach, I contextualize advertisements and other commercial cultural products within both media and Antarctic history. Situating examples culturally and historically provides the background needed to analyze each text effectively and to bring Antarctic lenses to the fore. This is a particularly useful method to apply when working with a large body of texts because, as communications scholar Avivit Agam Dali puts it, "Diachronic analysis enables us to trace values and perceptions" in a similar way that an archaeologist might examine a series of relics from different periods. An advertisement is seen as a cultural artifact, or a reflection of elements from the daily culture that can aid the researcher "in extrapolating values and ideologies from a particular era."[18] The media chosen to exhibit such advertisements has also shifted, with the newspapers and magazines

FIG 2. Hatch's Sea Elephant Harness Oil [picture: obtainable wholesale and retail from the sole manufacturers J. Hatch & Co., Invercargill, NZ]: [Joseph Hatch & Co.], [191-]. Digitized item from W. L. Crowther Library, State Library of Tasmania.

that were dominant in the early part of the twentieth century giving way to film, billboards, online banner advertisements, and other forms of digital and social media. A number of the advertisements featured in this book were not able to be reproduced due to copyright constraints but can be accessed using the URLS provided or via the Internet Archive (http://archive.org/web/web.php). The ephemeral nature of advertising posed a particular challenge. Advertisements are designed to function within specific cultural contexts and are generally regarded as disposable specimens of popular culture rather than as valuable historical artifacts. The temporary nature of many Antarctic advertisements—that they fall by the wayside when no longer valuable in their ability to quickly convey a message—further illustrates the relative speed with which framings of Antarctica emerge and are discarded. Though Antarctica remains as a constant, the icy imagery—and the message it carries—is presented and interpreted in very different ways.

Antarctica's Commercial History

The human history of Antarctica is predominantly a commercial rather than a heroic-exploratory-scientific history. While oral histories document southern voyages of explorers such as Polynesian navigator Hui Te Rangiora as early as 650 CE, Western interaction with the region coincided with an interest in resources.[19] Sealers and whalers first encountered and mapped the continent's coastline as they headed south for their hunts in the late eighteenth and early nineteenth centuries. When Capt. Edward Bransfield (UK), Capt. Nathaniel Palmer (US), and Adm. Fabian Gottlieb von Bellingshausen (Russia) all officially logged sightings of Antarctica during 1820 and 1821, their reports "opened a brief period of exploration motivated by commercial concerns."[20] The sealing industry in the Far South hunted fur seals primarily for their skins and fur, with blubber used for oil. Knowledge about the location of hunting grounds was very valuable, so sealing captains did not always record their exact location in readily available logs and maps. Commercial sensitivities therefore mean that the true extent of exploration in the Antarctic region during the early nineteenth century is largely unknown.[21]

The captains' fears about losing exclusive access to their sealing grounds—and thereby their livelihoods—were not unfounded. By the mid-nineteenth century fears were being voiced about the sustainability of hunting practices, with this concern articulated directly in James Fenimore Cooper's 1849 novel *The Sea Lions; or, The Lost Sealers.* By the end of the century Antarctic fur seals had been hunted almost to extinction in a number of previously fertile locations, while elephant seals continued to be hunted in the sub-Antarctic region through the early twentieth century. Penguins were not immune to such commercial interest either. Macquarie Island is home to royal, king, rockhopper, and gentoo penguins, and Joseph Hatch rendered the first two species down for lamp oil on Macquarie Island between 1890 and 1920.[22] However, unlike the elephant seals—another of Hatch's target species (figure 2)—these charismatic megafauna were not prominent in the product advertising. Rather, their public appeal saw the penguins became the face of the first international environmental campaign in the 1920s when well-known Antarctic figures such as Douglas Mawson and Apsley Cherry-Garrard spearheaded a protection campaign to end the commercial harvest of the birds. Contrary to popular opinion, the penguins were not marched into boilers while still alive, but the narrative was compelling in garnering public support for a ban on penguin harvesting. This environmental campaign foreshadowed a later branding of the wider Antarctic region as somewhere with intrinsic value and in need of protection.

Products from Antarctica—seal furs, whale blubber, and krill oil included—contribute to the wider commodification of Antarctica as resource, idea, and product. Some of the earliest Antarctic advertisements related to such products, including an "Antarctic Whalebone" brand from 1895 (figure 3). Featuring a black-and-white drawing of a whale, icebergs, and two lost polar bears, this advertisement promotes the baleen from a whale's mouth, which was commonly used in the creation of undergarments and umbrellas. Here the term "Antarctic" appears in quotation marks, using the exotic location to draw attention to a product available from the local drapers and highlighting the global extent of the capitalist machine. The Southern Ocean is an important feeding ground for cetaceans such as humpback, minke, blue, fin, and southern right whales during the austral summer, making it an attractive location for whalers to operate. As the number of animals dwindled in other places, Antarctica remained "the last and greatest sanctuary of the whale."[23] Shore-based stations were active on the sub-Antarctic islands and in the Antarctic Peninsula region from 1904, followed by factory ships from 1926 onward.[24] Although pelagic whaling was dominant from 1930 onward, the shore-based whaling station at South Georgia continued operation until 1965. In addition to their baleen, whales were flensed for their blubber, which was rendered down into oil and used to lubricate machinery, manufacture food products such as margarine, and even to fuel streetlamps in distant cities such as London.[25] As a result, Antarctic products were being consumed across the world. As the "Antarctic" whalebone example shows, the continent was visibly implicated in a global system of harvest and trade.

As vintage imagery has come back into vogue, advertisements from the early twentieth century have appeared for sale as prints on online poster sites. The reemergence of the "Antarctic Whalebone" advertisement, which is now marketed on several stock photo websites, illustrates a secondary commercial use. This different sort of commodification is a reminder of the sometimes unpredictable afterlife of advertisements. Here the original need to market a product with an Antarctic link has been superseded by a demand for polar nostalgia. This is true of many

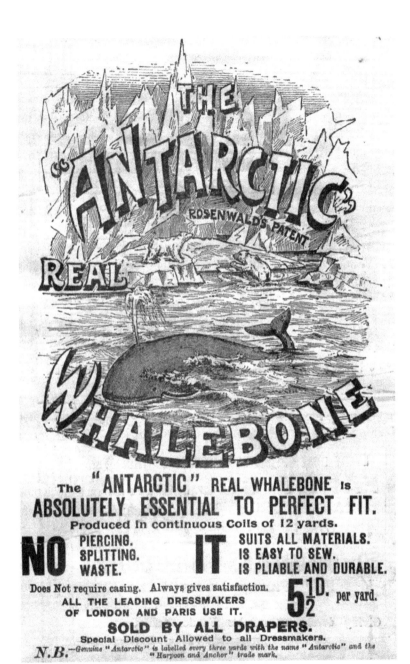

FIG 3. Advertisement for "Antarctic" brand whalebone, 1895. Retro AdArchives / Alamy stock photo.

Antarctic advertisements that date from the Heroic Era through to the International Geophysical Year (IGY) of 1957–58 and beyond; the UK-based Advertising Archives website offers prints featuring Scott promoting Oxo soup and Shackleton endorsing Bovril, while the Vintage Ad Browser website includes a 1930 Byrd endorsement for Carl Zeiss binoculars and a 1959 Ray-Ban sunglasses advertisement, complete with a link to the online marketplace eBay where polar enthusiasts can buy their own printed copy. The context of the original advertisement has often been lost; the advertisements are presented not as persuasive images to be disseminated via popular culture but as aesthetic artifacts to be admired in their own right. Commercial texts from Antarctica's past, therefore, remain valuable currency in a new forum—although they feature point-edly outmoded framings, such as in the whaling example, the nostalgia is part of the attraction. Meanwhile, the emergence of new companies such as Shackleton clothing (see chapter 2) continue to show how Antarctic images and experiences remain capable of being marketed afresh. As both technologies and attitudes evolve, the ways humans interact with—and take resources from—Antarctica also changes.

A 2012 Blackmores advertising campaign for Antarctic krill oil featuring computer-generated images of penguins and icebergs (see chapter 4) is a reminder that direct harvest of Antarctic resources has continued, albeit with new target species and the introduction of international management regimes to control catch limits. These histories of marine resource use are connected—glaciologist and polar veteran Olav Orheim writes that "it was the introduction of large-scale whaling, a much more important commercial activity, which brought forward the need for regulations [on harvest in the Southern Ocean]."[26] As of 2022, the International Whaling Commission (IWC) (established in 1946) and the 1972 Convention for the Conservation of Antarctic Seals (CCAS) control whaling and sealing activities in the Southern Ocean, with both setting an allowable catch limit of zero, demonstrating how Antarctica is now valued in different ways.

The Antarctic Treaty was signed in 1959 by twelve countries, and Antarctica is now governed by the ATS, with fifty-six parties. Over the years, new instruments have been established under the ATS to address emerging interests. The Commission for the Conservation of Antarctic

FIG 4. Reusable cups featuring the slogan "Don't Krill My Vibe . . . Protect the Southern Ocean." Distributed at CCAMLR, 2019. Photo courtesy of Antarctic and Southern Ocean Coalition.

Marine Living Resources (CCAMLR) was set up by convention in 1982 in response to increased interest in the krill fishery, and it continues to determine catch limits for fish and krill in the Southern Ocean and designate Marine Protected Areas.[27] The annual CCAMLR meeting in Hobart, Tasmania continues to be flashpoint for marketing material that promotes greater protection, with nongovernmental organizations (NGOs) such as the Antarctic and Southern Ocean Coalition (ASOC) running campaigns aimed at policy makers and the public that frame Antarctica as a place to protect rather than exploit—a message promoted by supplementary merchandise, such as the reusable cups distributed by ASOC during the 2019 CCAMLR meeting (figure 4).

REBRANDING FOR PROTECTION

What environmental historian Alessandro Antonello dubs the "greening of Antarctica"—the move toward an environmental focus in Antarctic governance—can be understood as an exercise in (re)branding with wider geopolitical connotations.[28] Anticipating interest in mining in the Far South, Antarctic Treaty Parties negotiated for a Convention on the

Regulation of Antarctic Mineral Resource Activity (CRAMRA) throughout the 1980s. However, CRAMRA never came into force, with Australia and France deciding not to accede. This was due in part to a shift in public framing of Antarctica as a place to protect and changing perceptions of the environment more generally. CRAMRA was followed by the 1991 Protocol on Environmental Protection to the Antarctic Treaty, known as the "Madrid Protocol," which includes a moratorium on mining. Nevertheless, the topic of resource extraction continues to fuel myths about the Antarctic Treaty expiring in 2048. For example, the specter of future mining continues to provide urgency to the campaigns of environmentally focused organizations, such as the 2041 Foundation (2041 marks fifty years since the signing of the Madrid Protocol). In fact, the Antarctic Treaty has no expiration date, and neither does the Madrid Protocol. Although a review conference on the operation of the protocol may be called in 2048, fifty years since it came into effect, any changes would require adoption by three-quarters of the Antarctic Treaty Consultative Parties (ATCPS) and all of those who were ATCPS at the time of adoption.[29] While the protection Antarctica currently enjoys is not inevitable, repeated rhetoric about a 2048 treaty expiration is as much a branding exercise in protection designed to create urgency and mobilize environmental action as it is a misunderstanding.

Interest in various resources has continued since the entry into force of the Antarctic Treaty and the Madrid Protocol but with a different focus. For instance, discussions have been held regarding the feasibility of using Antarctic icebergs as a fresh water source. In 2017 the National Advisor Bureau, a firm based in the United Arab Emirates, announced the "UAE Iceberg Project," in which an Antarctic iceberg would provide fresh water for the equatorial nation.[30] More recently, biological prospecting, or "bioprospecting," has put products with Antarctic roots on consumer shelves as an ingredient in cosmetics, nutraceuticals, foods, and medicines, with the Antarctic connection billed as a selling point due to connections with the idea of purity. The concept of Antarctica as a place for harvest, therefore, has a long and varied history. This provides important context for examining subsequent representations of Antarctica in commercial settings.

Selling the Stories: Sponsorship and Exploration

Physical products are not the only thing of value in the Far South—images and stories have also been a lucrative asset for explorers over the last two centuries in particular. The relationship between early explorers and the press performed an important role in shaping the way we think about Antarctica. Indeed, according to archivist and historian Robert Matuozzi, "The popular history of polar exploration is in large part the story of its promotion in the mass media."[31] Fame was a product not only of the feats that explorers could achieve but the way those feats were later sold to the public, a situation that leads cultural geographer James Ryan to conclude that "explorers, press, publishers and societies of science and empire all played a part in fermenting a complex 'culture of exploration.'"[32] They also participated in a complex culture of advertising and media. Antarctica came into view in the midst of a developing global media industry. As explorers were marching off into the unknown and sending back dispatches about their icy discoveries to headline the evening news, publishers were translating exploration into remuneration via circulation: the more copies sold, the more valuable the advertising space in the pages became.

At the dawn of the Heroic Era (1897–1922), there was huge public interest in exploration, and "newspapers strove to meet an almost insatiable demand for coverage."[33] Technological advances in printing and transport made it easier to disseminate news farther away, at a faster rate. The British press had focused on exploration as part of empire building; the notion of an empire that reached right around the globe combined with the speed of news to make the world seem smaller. Journalism history expert Martin Conboy outlines how this impression was reflected in the papers themselves: "The rapidity of social and technological change allowed the new popular daily newspapers to articulate the late nineteenth-century awareness of a shrinking world."[34] Increased literacy rates following the removal of the stamp duty helped to fuel readership numbers both locally and in colonies elsewhere. Reading the same news as peers in geographically distant places also helped to create a sense of coherence and belonging, reassuring readers that "the imagined world" beyond their own experience was "visibly rooted in everyday life."[35] People were reading the same news at approximately the same time and imagining the same scenes and events taking place. This means that the shift in media distribution also led to a shift in the way readers thought of their own relationships with one another and with the most remote corners of the earth.

The narration of Antarctic exploration occurred against a backdrop of changes in media ownership and a shift to sensational storytelling. By the end of the nineteenth century, news syndicates of periodicals and papers were being formed around individual businessmen, leading to stiff competition for lead stories between these different news empires. Changes such as centralized production, syndication, and a more personal relationship between readers and journalists meant the popular newspaper evolved into a "highly capitalized market product for a separated 'mass' readership."[36] As advertising became a growing revenue stream for publishers, advertising agencies were formed to create and place copy across a range of popular media. This period coincided with the rise of New Journalism, a populist print style that spread from the penny press of the United States to the Sunday papers in Britain. British New Journalism put the emphasis on sensationalism, with multiline headlines, increased use of imagery, and adopting a familiar tone with readers. It brought features such as display advertising, human interest, summary leads, and front-page news to a daily readership, presenting them in a way that was "more broadly accessible and therefore more profitable."[37] New Journalism saw a shift from seemingly hard facts to a more obviously subjective voice; it also made journalism more amenable to personal stories of exploration. It is no coincidence that, as Ryan puts it, "The figure of the explorer assumed its most potent form in the second half of the nineteenth century," when audiences were hungry for stories of "national heroes struggling against nature in remote and dangerous places."[38] One of the main criteria for starring in a sensational plot was to claim a "first." The polar regions, then, provided a perfect setting for compelling and sensational tales of exploration.[39]

PICTURING ANTARCTICA

Photography also played a role in the selling of stories. Unlike early imperial explorers on other continents, early Antarctic explorers had the benefit of photography to help narrate their expeditions as the first land-based Antarctic expeditions occurred at the same time as the invention of cinema and after the innovation of still photography. Humans have never known a time when their interaction with Antarctica could not be conveyed by camera or film. Indeed, photographic equipment was taken south on every expedition, from Carsten Borchgrevink's 1898 *Southern Cross* onward, and several expeditions took dedicated professional photographers and cameramen. Herbert Ponting traveled south with Robert Falcon Scott, while Ernest Shackleton and Australian expedition leader Douglas Mawson both employed the "camera artist" Frank Hurley to record their expeditions. Expedition leaders were well aware that photography was valuable "not only as a scientific record of a new environment, but also as a means of promoting and generating funds," while the photographers were valuable in their own right—Shackleton was offered funds in exchange for photographic and press coverage rights, provided that Hurley was the photographer.[40] At times the harsh conditions and the lack of visual features on the white landscape limited the use of the new technology, but the images that were successful were soon circulated widely, creating a scaffold on which the public could build their own imagined versions of Antarctica. The media played a key role in this process of dissemination, distributing written and visual narratives of the heroes and their men, and advertisements for the products they took south.

Carsten Borchgrevink—an Anglo-Norwegian immigrant to Australia— knew the importance of positive publicity and selling a story. His 1898 *Southern Cross* expedition, which was both the first private Antarctic expedition and the first to winter on the continent, was funded by press baron George Newnes. Several Antarctic expeditions had already headed south—most notably the *Belgica* expedition of 1897—but all were financed by a combination of military and scientific bodies, or other national funding.[41] Having provided the necessary funds for Borchgrevink to set sail, Newnes—who was best known for his daily newspaper the *Westminster Gazette* and his periodical publications the *Strand Magazine* and the *Wide World Magazine*—then had access to exclusive tales of exploration. These stories were accompanied by photographs from the Antarctic, thus making the continent visible to a wide audience back in England. Newnes was also the publisher of Borchgrevink's official expedition account, *First on the Antarctic Continent*, which incorporates multiple newspaper clippings. Although it was costly to fit out an expedition such as the *Southern Cross*, the stories that appeared in Newnes's media stable drew enough interest to warrant the expense.[42] They helped to sell more newspapers and magazines, making the advertising space within their pages all the more valuable and starting off the relationship between advertising and the Antarctic.

A PLACE FOR MEN WITH BEARDS

Official expedition narratives are another manifestation of the selling of Antarctic stories. These stories have endured—the volumes of early explorers such as Mawson, Scott, and Shackleton remain in popular circulation today. Exploration accounts were tailored to the mass market and, therefore, needed to be able to sell both themselves and the (heroic, masculine) reputations of explorers—struggle and excitement were, as Riffenburgh notes, "the key to journalistic hero-creation."[43] When Roald Amundsen returned from his successful expedition to the South Pole in 1912, his account failed to tap into the tropes of extremity, hardship, and endurance that an audience expected in an Antarctic story. The publisher William Heinemann had already run the polar narratives of both Fridtjof Nansen and Shackleton but was so put off by the "wretched cable interview" that Amundsen provided to the newspapers that he rescinded his offer to publish the Norwegian's narrative: "I must say I am so disappointed with the want of imagination he displays and the blindness he seems to have for a pictorial attraction in even so thrilling a thing as his achievement, that I have decided not in any circumstances to compete for his book."[44] While the explorer's achievements were more than newsworthy, the manner in which they were recounted was not; in this case, the ability to pitch yourself and sell your story took precedence over the substance of the story itself.

Given the imperative to produce a readable and compelling account, official expedition narratives were often co-written, with collaboration at times blurring into ghostwriting. Shackleton was one explorer who made use of a ghostwriter in order to better sell his narratives. Both *Heart of the Antarctic* (1909) and *South* (1919) were written with the assistance of

Edward Saunders, a journalist from New Zealand. Shackleton dictated the events of the first book during the voyage back to England, and Saunders transcribed before shaping the narrative into its published form. While the explorer was adept at oral lectures, interviews, and sound bites, he "lacked the sustained concentration necessary to write a book," and therefore turned to a journalist to assist with the vital task.[45] At the turn of the twentieth century, it was not unusual for an official expedition narrative to have been penned by many hands. Such a practice had a long history, going back to the days of explorers such as Capt. James Cook.[46] While it had previously been a common practice to acknowledge the multiple authors, the growth of the "hero business" signaled a shift in the attribution of narratives, with several well-known expedition leaders engaging ghostwriters to pen the stories under the explorer's own byline (fellow expeditioner Archibald McLean assisted Mawson in writing *Home of the Blizzard*, while Richard E. Byrd's accounts were penned by others). The official story needed to be engaging and dramatic in order to sell copies, and thus, advertising. In Shackleton's case, the story itself was promoted—the *Daily Express* carried an advertisement for the full story that was due to appear in the sister publication *Pearson's Magazine*. A successful expedition account would cement an explorer's reputation while ensuring a return on the publisher's investment and generating further publicity, which in turn facilitated fundraising for future expeditions. As Riffenburgh explains, this model was "mutually beneficial to the explorers and the newspapers"—and also very "popular with the hero-seeking public."[47] The story was therefore both a commodity and an advertisement for the explorers who headed the expeditions.

A PLACE FOR PEACE AND SCIENCE

The dominant discourse about Antarctica in 2022 holds that the continent is a place for peace and science. While both are central to the 1959 Antarctic Treaty and the wider ATS, they are not necessarily the dominant representations within popular culture. Science is the main human activity in the Antarctic, with National Antarctic Programs administering research projects and logistics. Under the Antarctic Treaty, science legitimates the human presence on the continent—and this focus also colors how some earlier expeditions, such as Scott's, are recalled today. However, literary scholar Elizabeth Leane reminds her readers that "the very designation of the Antarctic as the 'continent for science' is of course a representation—a very powerful one, which resonates with the icescape itself, a giant white laboratory coat with its connotations of objectivity and impersonality."[48] This representation has had implications for both the Antarctic continent and the species that call it home. Historian Peder Roberts asserts, "There are alternative ways of articulating Antarctica—as a space for commerce, industry, urbanization, or even militarization."[49] It is important to remember that the cultural frames through which Antarctica is viewed are grounded in particular contexts and histories and are subject to shift as values and priorities back home change. The idea of Antarctica as a place for peace and science that needs to be protected is not inevitable and should not be taken for granted.

The advertisements examined throughout this book make it clear how little traction the science framing has in popular culture. Despite the number of scientific projects that are undertaken in Antarctica each season, scientists and scientific work rarely appear in advertising material. The notable exceptions relate mainly to important events and national expeditions—for example, in a 1956 advertisement, Visco-Static Motor Oil refers to scientists on the Australian National Antarctic Research Expedition—or to products from Antarctica. Chapter 6 explains how the purity frame reveals close associations between notions of science, objectivity, and purity. Washing powders and skin care products have leveraged such associations, employing scientific language like "enzymes" and "extremophile" as a selling technique—but these are the exception rather than the rule among Antarctic advertisements. That advertisements rarely employ science is telling of wider social priorities and perceptions; with most Antarctic research funded by government agencies, science takes, rather than makes, money.

Framing Brand Antarctica

From early whaling and sealing to Heroic Era narratives of exploration to contemporary NGO campaigns calling for protection, Antarctica has been sold as a product and as an idea. Commerce and branding continue to have a powerful influence on perceptions of the continent today.

Tourist brochures promise blue-sky days and untouched icescapes, while southern rim cities promote their polar connections and their Antarctic identities. Alcohol, clothing, and vehicle makers continue to reinforce the narrative of Antarctica as extreme. Environmentalists use branding of particular species to help promote particular views of Antarctica—the inaugural World Krill Day on August 11, 2022, aimed to raise the profile of the cornerstone Southern Ocean species and promote the creation of Antarctic marine protected areas (actions included a petition calling for the creation of a krill emoji). This book does not aim to make value judgments about what constitutes "good" or "bad" use of Antarctica and Antarctic imagery. Rather, it outlines the various commercial uses of the Far South to identify and analyze common themes that have emerged in popular Antarctic discourse. Six thematic chapters examine the recurrent Antarctic tropes of heroism (past and present), extremity, purity, fragility, and transformation in depth. Taken together, these chapters help reveal the various ways Antarctica has been imagined, valued, and understood, providing a comprehensive analysis of how some humans, embroiled within the advertising-exploration-science complex, have conceptualized the ice at the end of the world. In making visible the continent's commercial connections, the book acts as a counterweight to those who peddle histories of Antarctica that champion heroism, science, and exploration. Human entanglements with Antarctica are in fact more wide-ranging, more nuanced, and more valuable—in multiple senses—than traditional framings may suggest.

The first two chapters address heroism, a theme that has been entwined with the Antarctic ever since the Heroic Era of exploration (1897–1922). These days scientists and support staff from a range of backgrounds live and work in the Antarctic, yet Edwardian explorers continue to dominate depictions of humans in Antarctica.[50] Those explorers—including Shackleton, Scott, Mawson, and Amundsen—have worn the badge of "hero" at various points in time and have been ignored or denigrated at others precisely because the definition of a hero is culturally dependent. Analysis of Antarctic heroes can therefore reveal much more about a society—and how it thinks about Antarctica as a place—than the hero figures themselves. Chapter 1 showcases the range of ways Antarctic explorers have provided endorsements for products they used in the

Far South, tracing connections between sponsorship and advertising during the Heroic Era.

Chapter 2 builds on this foundation, examining the ways contemporary advertisements have used heroic associations in order to create an imagined link with the continent. Such associations can be capitalized on directly or treated with ironic distance; the chapter includes examples of more recent advertisements that explicitly make the viewer aware of a disconnect between the sepia-toned "Antarctic hero" and the Antarcticans of today. Historical, masculine narratives continue to hold appeal: recent Antarctic expeditions have seen veterans and adventurers follow "in the footsteps of" earlier explorers, and there are many examples of leadership books inspired by the idea of Shackleton. While advertisements have moved from the endorsement format to employing the *idea* of a hero, the very concept remains valuable in its many forms. Together the first two chapters reveal the mutable character and continuing potency of the heroism theme.

The heroism theme has close links to extremity. Where the former sees man pitted against nature, in the latter it is machinery that proves its tough credentials through interactions with the ice. This framing casts Antarctica as the ultimate testing ground: as the coldest, highest, windiest, driest continent, it is a place for firsts and for superior performance. Extremity lends itself well to endorsements that suggest a product used in Antarctica will work anywhere—several watchmakers, clothing companies, outdoor equipment labels, and producers of building materials have employed this technique. Vehicle manufacturers have also used Antarctica's association with the extreme in order to prove the quality of their cars: the Hyundai Endurance expedition that had Shackleton's great-grandson drive across Antarctica in the 2016–17 summer is but one example in a long line of vehicular "firsts"—further examples are addressed in chapter 3.[51] Many of the advertisements examined in this chapter continue to feature men and to associate the idea of extremity with that of masculinity. This is partly a function of the kinds of products being advertised—including watches—and reflects what leisure studies expert Paul Gilchrist has described as "the popular coupling of manhood and mountain conquest."[52] Extremity also appears in more nuanced incarnations, whenever Antarctica is figured as an absence or as a final frontier. Antarctica may be a continent of superlatives—highest, driest, windiest—but it is also a continent of associations. This means that the extremity frame is not limited to products that are present in Antarctica. Rather, the concept can be applied to other products and brands simply by invoking Antarctic imagery and calling upon the associated theme.

The purity frame casts Antarctica as an untouched wilderness, rather than a place for people and machinery. Interestingly, this theme emerges most often in advertisements for products that physically come from Antarctica (such as krill oil). Such imagery and associations can be problematic and ironic, given that the product is taken out of the "pristine" environment that is used in its marketing. Examples analyzed in chapter 4 include advertisements for soap, alcohol, and health products. In some cases, the idea of purity is foregrounded, bringing with it natural connotations. In other instances—particularly in earlier advertisements—the related idea of "cleanliness" (and its domestic associations) is used instead. Antarctica's unique history makes it an easy place to paint as clean—unlike other parts of the globe it has no Indigenous population nor a war history (the exception is the sub-Antarctic conflict between the UK and Argentina over the Falkland Islands/Islas Malvinas, which culminated in a war in 1982). The process of bioprospecting is one recent example that is discussed, in light of advertisements featuring extremophiles from the Antarctic. Invisible influences are also at play; anthropogenic traces can be read in layers of Antarctic ice that were laid down long before any human set foot on the continent's interior. This chapter explores the cultural connotations of the purity theme, linking these to discourses about wilderness and science and setting them against the backdrop of instruments designed to protect Antarctica. The rhetoric around Antarctica and purity offers productive ground for both marketing and analysis; whether Antarctica really remains clean and untouched by human influence is a different question.

Chapter 5 shows how Antarctica has also been represented as a fragile environment threatened by anthropogenic climate change. Speaking in 2010, Judith Williamson noted that "we have a very specific and limited repertoire of imagery currently at our command to signify 'climate change'"—this includes penguins, polar bears, glaciers, icescapes, and calving ice.[53] The advent of climate change and the growing awareness of its impacts has affected the way Antarctica has been viewed. The fragility frame presents Antarctica as a symbol of vulnerability—of an environment that needs saving—and the implication is that by consuming the product in question, consumers will be helping to preserve that environment. Whether or not the suggested associations between the brand and environmentally friendly practices are legitimate is beside the point: what is important is the presence of the thematic link. Williamson has described this "ice-washing" phenomenon, remarking that the mere presence of polar imagery has come to suggest a commodity is "climate friendly," and that such connotations make a product more attractive to environmentally conscious consumers.[54] Antarctica may be located at the end of the earth, but we now know that our whole world is driven by an interconnected system. The fact that this idea is emerging in advertisements indicates that it is already in common cultural circulation, as advertisements seek to capitalize on existing cultural connections rather than creating new paradigms.

The final chapter returns to Antarctica itself, approaching the continent as a destination. Thanks to Antarctic tourism, seals and whales are of interest once again—not for commercial harvest but as wildlife to observe in the context of the "wilderness" of the Antarctic continent. An overview of the Antarctic tourism industry leads into a discussion of how the experience is advertised. Although much academic scholarship has looked at Arctic and Antarctic tourism, the advertising of the tourism product has not been the focus. Upon examining promotional material for such voyages, I found that several of the themes from the previous chapters—heroism, extremity, purity—have also been employed to sell Antarctica as a destination. Tourism is also linked to the theme of transformation. Chapter 6 therefore explores the way the journey to Antarctica can function as a metaphor, turning a voyage south into a transformational experience. Antarctica has been used as a proxy for a number of personal challenges—from stage fright to battles with breast cancer—so the *idea* of Antarctica as a place for transformation has been put to use in various situations, far from the ice itself. Whether people wish to follow in the footsteps of their heroes, participate in extreme sports in the Far South, or photograph untouched landscapes, there is a tour on offer to fit the bill.

Antarctica: Not For Sale?

Once known as *Terra Australis Incognita* and imagined but never seen, Antarctica is now very much part of the global environmental and economic system. It has been surveilled, theorized, modeled, photographed, and used as a symbol for many causes. As this book demonstrates, Antarctica is more accessible to a wider audience—physically and imaginatively—than ever before. And the cultural meanings that are mapped across the white expanse matter, both because of what they reveal and what they conceal. The human history of Antarctica includes elements of harvest—from sealing and whaling to krill oil and icebergs—but it did not end with the closure of sealing and whaling grounds, nor with the environmental protection provisions introduced in the Madrid Protocol. Instead, the continent is put to work as a symbolic force through advertising, where it is used as shorthand to call upon a range of thematic associations. Antarctica will continue to be depicted in advertising material; as journalist Mark Tungate puts it, "As long as somebody has something to sell, adland will always have a place on the map."[55] If this study were repeated at a future time, it would likely reveal new frames and tropes, based on new Antarctic advertisements and the worldviews they reflect.

So long as Antarctica continues to be regarded as an alluring place for the collective imagination, it will continue to inhabit the fringes of that map of "adland," providing ongoing insights into our relationship with the southernmost reaches of the planet. Analysis of the advertisements examined in this book reveals that Antarctica is, and has always been, very much "for sale."

Heroic Antarctica

Sponsorship and Selling a
Narrative in the Age of Heroes

It is telling that an advertisement, supposedly written by Ernest Shackleton on the eve of the *Nimrod* expedition, has endured as one of the most famous Antarctic texts (figure 5). The much-circulated recruitment notice reads: "MEN WANTED for Hazardous Journey. Small wages, bitter cold, long months of complete darkness, constant danger, safe return doubtful. Honour and recognition in case of success." Although the advertisement itself is most likely to have been apocryphal (the first printed reference dates to 1944, and exhaustive searches of period newspapers have revealed no sign of an earlier original), it continues to appear in popular culture.[1] The three lines have been reproduced across countless media—on T-shirts, posters, mugs, and even as the central conceit of an advertising campaign for the city of Detroit.[2] The advertisement has been used as shorthand for the Heroic Era of Antarctic exploration, evoking ideas and practices of heroism, masculinity, and endurance. As literary scholar Elizabeth Leane puts it, the advertisement is "a Heroic-Era fiction that has entered into communal memory."[3] Now in cultural circulation, it has taken on an identity of its own. Rather than trying to attract expeditioners, the advertisement has become a product that now sells itself—and the promise of adventure.

The "Men Wanted" advertisement has the power to conjure imagined scenes of the Far South, drawing the viewer or wearer into a rich historical and geographical tapestry of heroism and masculinity. The continued use of the text reveals much about how Antarctic history is remembered, and it reprises an imagined version of Antarctica as harsh and hostile and as the domain of the hero. Reproductions, including those on apparel, offer a way to connect with a famous story and to advertise a certain "knowingness" of Antarctic history. Whether worn ironically

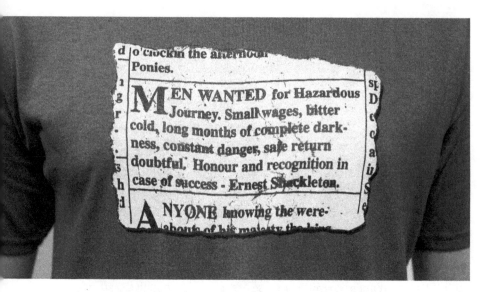

d o'clock in the afternoon Ponies.

MEN WANTED for Hazardous Journey. Small wages, bitter cold, long months of complete darkness, constant danger, safe return doubtful. Honour and recognition in case of success - Ernest Shackleton.

ANYONE knowing the were-

FIG 5. The famous (apocryphal) recruitment advertisement for Shackleton's second Antarctic expedition, as it appears on a T-shirt, 2012. Photo by Richard Williams.

or in earnest, the three sentences make a person instantly recognizable as an Antarctic afficionado.

The term "Heroic Era" or "Heroic Age" is used to refer to the period of Antarctic exploration that took place between 1897 and 1922, marking the period between the Belgian Geographical Society's *Belgica* expedition and the death of Ernest Shackleton during his *Quest* expedition when the first inland exploration of Antarctica took place.[4] The men who were exploring the Far South during that time continue to carry the "hero" label. Definitions of hero were and are culturally dependent, as heroes are intimately connected to their host societies and reputations, as historian Max Jones has noted, and subject to negotiation and contestation.[5] Nevertheless, Western folklore shares a traditional hero narrative with a predictable story arc: hero is called to action; ventures forth into a strange and supernatural world; struggles against obstacles, villainy, and adversity; is helped by "donors" along the way; and eventually triumphs, returning home transformed, bringing new knowledge and insight. This arc dates to classical Greek literature, where the hero was played by the likes of Heracles and

Achilles but is particularly pertinent when discussing colonial exploration. Jones and his coauthors explain how "the modern imperial hero emerged in Britain during the eighteenth century around such figures as Admiral Vernon, General Wolfe and Captain Cook."[6] Many permutations of the narrative have emerged since, encompassing tales of military might (Lord Nelson), political struggle (Rosa Parks and Nelson Mandela), compassion (Florence Nightingale), exploration (Dr. Livingston), and popular fiction (Batman and Katniss Everdeen). In the Antarctic context, heroism is closely linked to the battling of extreme conditions and either a heroic death or extraordinary experience of resilience and survival. As these heroes are culturally contingent, an examination of Antarctic heroes reveals much about the societies that bestowed the title upon the explorers.

The reputations of Heroic Era explorers, including Shackleton, Robert Falcon Scott, and Douglas Mawson, have been leveraged for commercial gain, both through direct endorsements and subsequent product rereleases. This chapter explores the theme of heroism within the Antarctic context by analyzing appearances of the Antarctic hero in advertisements. The idea of the "Antarctic hero" can be traced back to the first inland expeditions into the continent at the turn of the twentieth century, a time when space was being turned into place with every snowy footfall. A short overview of important Antarctic figures and events from this period helps to contextualize a more detailed interrogation of advertisements and endorsements within a particular context of exploration and conquest and establishes the connections between media, exploration, and sponsorship in the Far South. Heroes were used in advertising material as "icons of imperial development" during their lifetimes.[7] Such figures have continued to stand for imperial mindsets for decades since, even as empires around the world have been dismantled. In the Euro-Western imagination they are also emblematic of Edwardian values and a nostalgia for past expeditionary feats. By examining early Antarctic sponsorship, where heroism played a key role in the product pitch, the commercial implications of the hero trope become clear.

Heroic Era in Context

The Heroic Era of Antarctic exploration was a time when expeditions set off for the South motivated by romantic-sublime ideas of man versus nature. This model cast the wilderness as both something to inspire feelings of the sublime in the beholder and as something to be conquered by masculine feats. Expeditions were mounted by Belgium (1897 *Belgica*), Germany (1901 *Gauss* and 1911 *Deutschland*), Sweden (1901 *Antarctic*), France (1903 *Français* and 1908 *Pourquoi-Pas? IV*), Japan (1910 *Kainan Maru*), Norway (1910 *Fram*), and Australia and New Zealand (1911 *Aurora*). In the English-speaking world it is the British expeditions of Scott (1901 *Discovery* and 1910 *Terra Nova*) and Shackleton (1907 *Nimrod*, 1914 *Endurance*, and 1922 *Quest*) that have gained the most critical attention, while the British-born Mawson (leader of the 1911 Australasian Antarctic Expedition with *Aurora* and 1929 British, Australian, New Zealand Antarctic Research Expedition [BANZARE]) is well-known in his adopted home of Australia. The Heroic Era label does not mean that all explorers from the time have always been viewed as heroes. On the contrary, tracking the changing popular reputations of early explorers, such as Scott, Shackleton, and Amundsen, reveals much about shifting cultural values and the dominant discourse around heroism. That the Heroic Era is often referred to in quotation marks in contemporary scholarship indicates an early awareness that the connotations of the name should not be taken for granted.[8] Nevertheless, these expeditions drew on commercial sponsorship to varying degrees—for expedition leaders, performing the role of the hero paid the bills.

Quests for geographic priority in the Far South captured the attention of the print media and the public imagination. Notions of priority and claiming territory both manifest in the "race to the pole," a recurrent trope that dates to 1911–12, when the British Scott and the Norwegian Amundsen both led teams in pursuit of the geographic South Pole. In the aftermath of Amundsen's victory and Scott's death, it was via the media that the narratives that have cemented the Heroic Era in the public imagination first came to light. In his native Norway, Amundsen's feats were celebrated, as they helped to put the newly independent country on the world stage. The celebrations were reserved, however, due to the involvement of another local hero. The well-known Norwegian explorer Fridtjof Nansen had set aside his own plans to head South, lending his ship to Amundsen for a northern expedition instead. In England, Amundsen was cast as the villain—not only was he foreign but he had acted in an "unsporting" manner by announcing he would sail north, not south, and only informing his crew and those back home of his real intentions once the ship reached Madeíra, Portugal. It was not so much Amundsen's own actions that led to this casting, as the need to create a contrast to Scott—every hero story needs a counterpoint villain. Scott, on the other hand, was placed on a pedestal—quite literally, as his wife, Kathleen Scott, created a bronze sculpture of her husband to stand at London's Waterloo Place, opposite the Arctic explorer Sir John Franklin. Thanks to his death, Scott was revered throughout the British Empire as a symbol of the best of British stoicism and heroic sacrifice.

The Race for News: Reporting Exploration "Firsts"

Alongside Scott and Amundsen's race for the pole, there was a fierce race to be the first to publish the news back home. Conflict leads to drama, which in turn could be sensationalized in headlines and used to sell newspapers. Antarctic exploration was therefore brought into the realm of popular culture.[9] The prominence of the explorers and the currency of ideas of extreme exploration combined to create a perfect publicity storm. Scott's *Terra Nova* expedition had the support of the Central News Agency, while Amundsen had an agreement to send his first dispatch to the British newspaper, the *Daily Mail* (circulation 900,000 in 1910).[10] As it happened, Amundsen was first to reach the pole, on November 14, 1911—Scott arrived just thirty-three days later. Immensely disappointed at having been beaten, Scott was nevertheless well aware of the importance of communicating the events of the summer to those back home. Having reached the pole, he made a direct reference to news in his diary: "Now for a desperate struggle to get the news through first. I wonder if we can do it."[11] This reference was omitted from the first published versions of Scott's diaries, probably because it shines light on the explorer's consciousness of his own relationship with the media.[12] Although he had failed to reach his goal with priority, he still had a story to both tell and sell. Amundsen, too, was aware of the value of his story. Having experienced financial loss when details of his previous Gjøa expedition in the Arctic were leaked in 1905, Amundsen was particularly determined to control the release of his Antarctic narrative.[13] The Norwegian went so far as to return to the Australian port of Hobart rather than the New Zealand port of Lyttelton as planned and to confine his men to the ship when they arrived in port in order to prevent a leak to the local media. These measures helped preserve the commercial value of the news when it did break.

The amount of copy generated by the 1911 race to the pole solidified the well-established relationship between the media and explorers and led to the concept of a "race" becoming a valuable Antarctic trope. This race scenario has played out many times over the past century, both in the media and on the ice. When Australian aviator Hubert Wilkins announced plans to fly over the continent, Richard Byrd, then a captain in the U.S. Navy, was organizing an expedition to attempt to fly to the South Pole. These men had different aims, but, nevertheless, the race element was picked up by the print media in the United States and elsewhere. Recognizing the news potential of Wilkins's expedition, news baron William Randolph Hearst offered to pay $40,000 (equivalent to $693,000 today) for exclusive press coverage, with a $10,000 (equivalent to $173,000 today) bonus if Wilkins made it to the South Pole.[14] With his daily audience of twenty million people across his stable of magazines, newspapers, and radio stations, Hearst was arguably "the most influential [man] in America" at the time.[15] Although the geographic South Pole was never on Wilkins's intended itinerary, the deal was signed. Wilkins completed the first Antarctic flight, over the South Shetland islands and Antarctic Peninsula, in 1928. For Hearst, this was the first of many deals with explorers in which he dictated the terms in advance and offered an explicit financial incentive for an explorer to strive to achieve the most newsworthy feats. Wilkins's 1931 *Nautilus* expedition, which saw him attempt to sail a submarine beneath the North Pole, was another example where full payment was withheld until after the expedition's return: to earn the full $150,000 (equivalent to $2,923,000), the submarine and the airship *Graf Zeppelin* were required to rendezvous at the pole and exchange passengers. A simple meeting was worth just $100,000 (equivalent to $1,950,000) if it happened at the pole, or $30,000 (equivalent to $585,000) if it occurred anywhere else in the Arctic—both time and place played important roles in constructing the most lucrative stories of polar exploration.[16]

Heroic Era explorers' narratives were carefully curated every step of the way as they were published and sold. This curation continues today as scientific and expeditionary projects are framed in the same terms. The race trope reemerged during the 1950s when the Commonwealth Trans-Antarctic Expedition (TAE) was painted as a race between the co-leaders, Vivian Fuchs and Edmund Hillary, who were approaching the pole from opposite sides of the continent—conflict between the leaders spilled into a disagreement over who had authority to pen the official book about the expedition, again demonstrating the commercial and cultural power of narratives. The centenary of several Heroic Era expeditions saw reenactment races and expeditions organized in the Antarctic, with modern-day heroes following in the footsteps of Heroic Era figures (as detailed in chapter 2). The idea of a race has appeared in relation to scientific activity in the Antarctic, with efforts to drill an ice core that dates back one million years framed as "an international race to find the ancient time capsule."[17] The concept of an Antarctic race therefore continues to have high news value, even as scientists take the place of or are conflated with explorers. During the early twentieth century, geographical exploration was transformed, by virtue of newly developed journalistic techniques, into "a news commodity" with a strong focus on firsts.[18] The Antarctic hero—a masculine figure who strove to achieve firsts in a remote and inhospitable part of the world—was therefore a function of the interactions between exploration, sponsorship, storytelling, and the media machine.

Products In and Out of Place

Photography played a central role in financing early Antarctic expeditions, with images featuring sponsors' products a valuable revenue stream. Even while isolated in Antarctica, Scott's party was aware that distinctive visuals were an important way to assert the brand identity of the expedition and were actively creating such images themselves. The published advertisement for His Master's Voice gramophone features a photograph of "one of the sledge-dogs, listening to 'His Master's Voice'" and posed to resemble the terrier that features on the record company's logo. In the quoted telegraph message, Edward Evans goes on to explain the story behind the image: "Mr Ponting our photographer, took some photographs of the Siberian sledging dogs listening to the Gramophone, similar to your well-known fox-terrier. I am returning to London shortly, and will communicate with you then regarding these."[19] Aware of the media machine and the financial and reputation-making power of endorsements and sponsorship, Scott's men deliberately posed the dogs to recreate the scene pictured on the record company's logo. Although they were living far from civilization at the time, they were already giving thought to the future promotional uses of such photographs once they returned home.

The photograph of the dogs was not the only such staged image, and at times the photographs from Scott's *Terra Nova* expedition suggest a certain cynicism about the necessity of sponsorship and promotion. A photograph featuring Heinz baked beans stars a grinning Frederick Hooper spooning the beans toward his mouth as he perches atop a branded crate (figure 6). This image reveals the extent to which the explorers were conscious of their roles as what we would now describe as brand ambassadors. James Ryan describes it convincingly as "a playful parody of the explorer-as-advertiser."[20] The image contains all the expected elements, such as visible packaging, an Antarctic scene, and a smile, but at the same time it is staged in a way that mocks the very conventions to which it conforms: the smile is a little too wide, the product placement a little too blatant. Although the photograph was never used for advertising by the Heinz company, the existence of the image demonstrates that explorers themselves were all too aware of their reliance on advertising media.

This awareness of the complex interactions between exploration and the media is also evident in other contemporary Antarctic expeditions, such as Mawson's Australasian Antarctic Expedition on the *Aurora* (1911–14). Like many expeditions of the Heroic Era, Mawson's men produced a newspaper over the winter months that was intended for a limited distribution and audience but was later reproduced in Australia to raise additional funds. The *Adelie Blizzard* followed in the tradition of Scott's *South Polar Times* (1901–4 and 1910–12) and Shackleton's *Aurora Australis* (1907–9).[21] Upon publishing the *Adelie Blizzard* at Cape Denison in Antarctica, Mawson sent a message home to announce "the publication of the first 'real newspaper' in Antarctica."[22] This newspaper featured articles, classified advertisements, and—in an Antarctic first—news that had been received via the radio connection. Mawson sought and was granted honorary membership to the Australian Press Association. Soon afterward the liquor company Wolfes Schnapps, who was "going along with the charade," enquired about placing an advertisement in his publication,

FIG 6. Frederick Hooper, of Scott's Terra Nova expedition, photographed by Herbert Ponting. Terra Nova expedition, 1911. Scott Polar Research Institute Picture Library, P2005/5/1065.

but as "payment was not forthcoming," the newspaper editor Archibald McLean noted wryly, the advertisement never appeared.[23]

The fact that media conventions such as placing an advertisement were satirized in the Antarctic newspaper indicates the men's familiarity with the way their own exploration was embroiled within the commercialized media landscape. Explorers needed funds to mount expeditions, publishers needed exclusive content, and advertisers needed an edge over their competitors. Antarctic exploration brought all three together to sell the story, sell products, sell reputations, and build public consciousness of Antarctica as a remote, hostile, exciting place for men to survive the extremes.

What Is a Hero?

While the figure of the hero is central to the Heroic Era of Antarctic exploration, a single definition of the term is not straightforward. Writing about "This Hero Business" in 1928, Antarctic aviator Richard Byrd recounted an exchange over the definition of a hero:

"But what is a national hero, and why?" I asked a newspaper friend of mine.

"Oh, someone who's worth two columns and a front-page steamer, fireboats and a basket of medals," came the cynical reply.[24]

Heroism is closely bound up with public perceptions but also business-like judgments and is therefore—as Byrd's newspaper friend suggests—closely linked to media coverage and public recognition. While heroic recognition has its roots in greatness, and celebrity recognition is rooted in fame, the line between the two can be hazy. The question of who is afforded the designation of "hero" is culturally, geographically, and temporally dependent, so the idea of the hero has appeared in many guises over the past century. The term "hero" has even developed a specialist meaning within the advertising industry itself; in the digital era, a "hero image" is a large banner that is prominently displayed on a web page. Contemporary companies that have used the hero as a central advertising conceit include Nike's "Does a Hero Know She's a Hero if No One Tells Her"? (1999–2000), GoPro's "Be a Hero" (2021), and the Pan American Health Organization's "Every Blood Donor Is a Hero" (2012)[25]—here the hero umbrella deliberately encompasses everyday people of different genders and backgrounds in order to have broad appeal, though in other campaigns the endorsement model still reigns. The transactional qualities of heroism are therefore recognized by sponsors and heroes alike.

Although particularly prominent in the South, the use of the heroism trope in advertising during the Heroic Era period was not limited to Antarctica. Historian Max Jones and colleagues have written about how "the media revolution of the second half of the nineteenth century dramatically transformed the transmission and reception of heroic reputations, in particular through the proliferation of visual iconography."[26] This included marketing material. Endorsements were a common format, with the reputations of heroic figures such as Charles Lindbergh and Amelia Earhart being used to leverage attention for a range of products such as Mobiloil and Horlick's Malted Milk during the 1920s and 1930s (the same products appear in Antarctic advertisements).[27] Such endorsements generally took a personalized format, where attributes ascribed to the hero are transferred to the product. For instance, Horlick's Malted Milk was often associated with vigor and strength. While drawing on celebrity connections, early endorsements stressed the utility of the product in question, harnessing the reputation of high-profile people to catch the attention of the audience. Many early Antarctic advertisements took this form, whereas more recent advertisements that draw on the heroic theme tend to use the concept of a hero rather than a specific personality. Cultivating a heroic image became all the more important during this time because of its intimate connection to the success or failure of the expedition and to the ability of the leader to remain solvent rather than going bankrupt.

Hot Drinks, Biscuits, and Wine

Leveraging the public reputations of heroes has long been a successful strategy in the Antarctic context. Many products, including Horlick's Malted Milk and the Arrol-Johnston motorcar, first came to Antarctica with explorers as part of endorsement or sponsorship deals, and their presence in Antarctica was documented for commercial reasons. While these deals meant that expeditions were fitted out with necessary equipment for little cost, sponsorships were rooted in commercial advantage rather than altruism. In the case of the car, the Scottish industrialist William Beardmore, who financed Shackleton's 1907 *Nimrod* expedition, had recently acquired the Arrol-Johnston Company, so the vehicle was sent south as a publicity opportunity. Such products were often featured in advertising campaigns that drew on their expeditionary experiences. In one notable case, Mawson refused to pay the bill for the Vickers airplane used in the Australasian Antarctic Expedition, on the grounds that having the plane on the expedition was "a colossal advertisement for them."[28]

The Heroic Era is very much tied up with corporeality, associated with physical exertion and bodily feats of endurance. Although leaders such as Scott, Shackleton, and Mawson all took machinery south (to varying effect), it was images of man-hauling that typified the period. In order for man to "take on the wild" without perishing, nourishment was a prime necessity. Hence, food, bodies, and the heroism of the Heroic Era are closely linked, both in terms of enabling exploration and in terms of promotions. The following vignettes—focused on Bovril spread, Huntley & Palmers crackers, Yalumba wine, and Mackinlay's whisky—draw out these connections, tracing the brands' Antarctic connections from the Heroic Era to the present day. Hot drinks, biscuits, and alcohol were all associated with the cultivation of the body-figure of the heroic explorer, with qualities demonstrated in Antarctica projected onto the products purchased and consumed back home.

SHACKLETON SAYS, "IT MUST BE BOVRIL"

Shackleton provided several endorsements for the meat extract Bovril during his Imperial Trans-Antarctic Expedition of 1914–17. A full-page black-and-white advertisement that appeared in the *Illustrated London News* in January 1914 is typical of endorsements from the time—the bulk of the page is taken up by text and is accompanied by a small, detailed map of the Antarctic, complete with Shackleton's intended trans-Antarctic route sketched across the surface (figure 7). The eye is immediately drawn to the largest, boldest text one-third of the way down the page, which reads "it must be Bovril." This slogan, which went on to form the basis of an entire Bovril Antarctic campaign, is repeated in a large, bold font at the bottom of the page, leaving the reader no doubt as to the name of the product.[29] The third bolded section, located two-thirds of the way down the page, refers to the qualities of the product: "proved by independent scientific investigation to possess a body-building power equal to from 10 to 20 times the amount taken." Nutrition was a young field at the time, and it was common for food advertisements to draw upon narratives of strength, energy, and health alongside mentions of science. The inclusion of scientific references add weight to the claims of the product's quality, but it is the accompanying image and the smaller text that refers to Shackleton's planned Antarctic expedition that lent the product authenticity. They provide evidence to Bovril's assertions of superiority, security, reliability, and familiarity and elevate its status precisely because Shackleton was a well-known figure who was trusted by the public. His words carried (or were assumed to carry) authority, which is why, as the accompanying text explains, Shackleton himself makes the bold statement that "it must be Bovril" as opposed to any alternative drink. This advertisement is a classic example of a celebrity endorsement, using a polar celebrity to gain leverage for a product that was sold on the domestic market.

According to the advertisement, Bovril is imperative for Shackleton's survival because of the geographical extremity of the situation. The text

WRITING to the agent entrusted with the purchasing of the stores for the forthcoming Imperial Trans-Antarctic Expedition, Sir Ernest Shackleton uses these words :

" I consider the question of the concentrated beef supply is most important—

it must be Bovril"

For the first time in the history of Antarctic exploration Sir Ernest Shackleton will undertake an expedition where there will be no food depots for the return journey. The party must entirely and absolutely rely upon the food they carry with them. Therefore every ounce of food must be of the maximum food value, and every ounce must yield up its maximum nourishment to the men who carry it.

Men who trust their lives to their food take no risks, and Sir Ernest Shackleton, planning this expedition with as intimate a knowledge of stores as of ice and snow, has recognised the scientifically proved value of Bovril.

Bovril is the food which has been

proved by independent scientific investigation

to possess a body-building power equal to from 10 to 20 times the amount taken.

This was found to be due partly to its own high food value and partly to its remarkable powers of assisting the assimilation of other food. The investigation which established this unique | power of Bovril was carried out by one of the foremost physiologists of the Kingdom on behalf of a Government Department, and the results obtained applied to Bovril and Bovril alone.

That is why Sir Ernest Shackleton writes:

"it must be Bovril"

S.R.D.

FIG 7. Bovril advertisement with Shackleton's endorsement, 1914. *Illustrated London News*, January 31, 1914.

explains how "for the first time in the history of Antarctic exploration Sir Ernest Shackleton will undertake an expedition where there will be no food depots for the return journey." This focus on pushing geographical boundaries—while using Bovril to insulate oneself from otherwise insurmountable physical boundaries—also appears in other contemporary Bovril adverts. The first Bovril testimonial was provided in April 1890 by American explorer H. M. Stanley (known for his rescue of Dr. Livingstone), while an example from 1900 features Lord Roberts moving across South Africa and spelling out "Bovril" in the process.[30] Literary scholar Anne McClintock describes the South African advertisement as an overt example where "the colonial map enters the realm of commodity spectacle."[31] Shackleton, too, is undertaking a colonial conquest by exploring untouched ice for the first time. That he is doing so in the name of king and country as part of an imperial expedition is reinforced by the inclusion of the map of Antarctica. Maps are powerful geopolitical tools, but their usefulness can also spill over into the world of advertising. As historian Barbara Bush puts it, "To map was to possess, to tame and order terra nullius."[32] In the case of Shackleton and Bovril, the possessing was done not only by a nation-state but also by a brand, laying claim to a supporting role in the archetypal narrative of the conquering hero.

The brand name Bovril itself carries gendered connotations that relate to the heroism theme. While the prefix "bov" refers to an "ox"—appropriate for a beef extract product—"vril" is taken from Edward Bulwer Lytton's 1870 novel *The Coming Race*, which features a race of incredibly strong superhuman beings known as the "Vril-ya." They were said to gain their "life force" from a magical substance called "Vril."[33] Thanks to the success of the book, the word "vril" soon became synonymous with life-giving strength—the name Bovril, therefore, means "great strength obtained from an ox."[34] In the Antarctic context, the life-giving properties of Bovril are particularly important, as so little stands between the explorers and their deaths at the hands of the elements. Bovril was an everyday ration, but it was also a chief food for invalids, included in the list of "medical comforts" for both maintaining the strength of expeditioners and healing those who fell ill.[35] The connotations of both virility and masculinity contained in the word "vril" are also important in this context—as are the connotations of fragility and possible recovery. To survive in a harsh polar setting, virility and vigor—both established Edwardian-era markers of heterosexual, dominating masculinity—were essential. Bovril, which had previously been associated with strongmen, the front lines of the Boer War, and "the hardships and endurance of the fighting soldier," found a perfect match in the Antarctic explorers of the Heroic Era.[36]

Bovril marketing has since reprised the product's polar links on several occasions. An advertisement from the winter of 1956–57—coinciding with the Commonwealth Trans-Antarctic Expedition, when Antarctica was back in the news—features a young boy announcing, "I'm just back from the Pole, Mummy." The text explains: "Few Polar expeditions have gone without their Bovril. Shackleton and his men had Bovril every day—and he himself said 'I am certain it was one of the greatest helps during that long and arduous journey.'"[37] Here the suggestion is that those who play at polar exploration need just as much nourishment as the explorers who actually head south themselves. Another example from 1957—a time when several Antarctic bases had just been established for the International Geophysical Year—links explorers at the pole with the housewives at home who shopped for their families and were thus the very market for which Bovril advertising was tailored. Man-hauling figures are depicted, with the text explaining that Bovril has been used everywhere "From the North to the South Pole, from the snows of Everest to the firesides of Britain." Drawing upon the history of the product—specifically the way it helps hold bodies together—the advertisement suggests that the life-giving properties of the beef extract beverage have both domestic and exotic applications. It goes on to address the theme of heroism directly, claiming, "Bovril is indeed a drink for heroes. And a drink for families too."[38] In doing so, it links the male-hero figure to the support network back home—and to the domestic environment in which products such as Bovril were bought and used. The deployment of the polar hero trope in a domestic context fifty years after the first Bovril endorsements by polar figures appeared indicates that it continued to carry weight as a symbol for survival in extremity.

HUNTLEY & PALMERS AND THE POWER OF NOSTALGIA

At times the producers of goods have created special editions of their products to commemorate expeditions or to accompany them south. The

Huntley & Palmers Polar Biscuits are one such example. Eight different varieties "were specially designed to commemorate the British Expedition to the Antarctic," with biscuits featuring images of the *Terra Nova*, British flag, the names and dates of four polar expeditions (Scott 1901, Shackleton 1902, Peary 1908, and Scott 1910), and men dressed in thick polar clothing.[39] Four of these are prominently featured in a full-page advertisement from 1912, the year Scott and his men reached the geographic South Pole and perished on the return. The advertisement appeared prior to news of Scott's death reaching the outside world; it was not until February 1913 that the world learned of the expedition's disastrous ending. It must therefore be read as appearing during an in-between time, after it was known that Amundsen had been first to reach the pole in February 1912 but before the fate of Scott's party had reached the outside world. This accounts for the very small font at the foot of the advertisement that explains "it may be interesting to record that Huntley & Palmers Biscuits were also supplied to Captain Roald Amundsen"—the company was hedging its bets by mentioning both parties involved in the race to the pole. In the British context where this advertisement appeared, discretion was required, as Scott was the national hero. The biscuits were marketed and sold in the context of the British Empire, and therefore it was more useful for Huntley & Palmers to advertise their connection with the British party than with their demonstrably successful Scandinavian counterparts.

"Antarctic" products sold on the domestic market were not always the same as those that traveled south with explorers. In the case of the 1912 Huntley & Palmers example, text explaining that these biscuits "were taken, with many other of Huntley and Palmers Specialties, by Captain Scott on board the 'Terra Nova'" offers legitimacy to the product's polar associations.[40] An image of the biscuits takes up almost a third of the total advertisement space, with the polar imagery that has been stamped onto the biscuits highlighting the link to Antarctica. The polar imagery also presents a variation on the original staple; while Huntley & Palmers biscuits were consumed in Antarctica, those specimens were not as detailed as those on the domestic market. Instead, the polar biscuits used by the explorers were much plainer in appearance, as the focus was on their function as a source of much-needed calories. This became clear as early tins of the biscuits were discovered in Antarctic huts by both expeditioners in the 1950s and the New Zealand Antarctic Heritage Trust (NZAHT) in the 2000s and conserved—along with other branded crates of food products—as part of the ongoing maintenance of "heritage" (figure 8).

Biscuit tins were a powerful marketing tool in their heyday; they acted as a symbol for the global reach of the British Empire in much the same way as Oxo stock and Pears soap. Historian Tom Griffiths describes Huntley & Palmers biscuits as "a wonderful symbol of empire for Scott to take to the end of the earth," because of the brand's thoroughly English history.[41] Founded in Reading in 1882, the company had already sent its wares with Dr. Stanley to central Africa and to many other English colonies all over the globe.[42] At the time, branding was an important way of asserting control over the British Empire, with British-made products in use everywhere. As Anne McClintock puts it, "Empire was seen to be patriotically defended by Ironclad Porpoise Bootlaces and Sons of the Empire Soap, while Stanley came to the rescue of the Emin of Pasha Iaden with outsize boxes of Huntley and Palmers Biscuits."[43]

In this context, Antarctica was the final commercial frontier, and thus imagined as a powerful magnet for such products and brands. Indeed, it can be argued that the biscuits themselves, via associated advertising campaigns, acted to bring Antarctica into the fold of this empire. Publicity photographs of Huntley & Palmers packing crates in situ on the ice, augmented by an endorsement from Scott himself (quoting a letter from Scott to Huntley & Palmers), proved the biscuits' worth to empire and exploration.[44]

SCOTT'S LAST BISCUIT

In September 1999, the Huntley & Palmers brand name was propelled into the limelight once again, thanks to the auction of an historic biscuit from the Antarctic. Billed as "Scott's Last Biscuit," it was supposedly removed from alongside the three bodies in Scott's tent in 1912, before being returned to Scott's wife, Kathleen. According to Griffiths, this "last biscuit was [Scott's] metaphor for heroism in extremity," two themes that continue to be associated with Antarctica.[45] Sarah Moss's 2006 book on the literature of polar exploration appeared under the same title, because Moss saw the fascination with the biscuit as "strangely symbolic of the modern fascination for writing about polar travel."[46] Thomas Keneally

FIG 8. Huntley and Palmers crate in situ in Scott's hut. Photo by Chris Rudge, 1989 © Antarctica New Zealand Pictorial Collection, https://adam.antarcticanz.govt.nz.

also reflected on "Captain Scott's Biscuit," in a 2012 Granta piece. The biscuit therefore has relevance across multiple periods of Antarctic history, from exploration to modern-day tourism. Far more than a stale cake of calories, for the men in Scott's tent the biscuit came to stand for hope and a potential future that was not to be. As well as extensive media attention, the biscuit attracted almost £4000 when it was purchased by the renowned polar explorer (and defender of Scott's reputation) Sir Ranulph Fiennes. Fiennes, who wished to keep as many Scott relics in England as possible, later discovered that he had likely "fallen for one of the many Scott myths," as the provenance of the biscuit proved impossible to verify.[47] The fact that such myths exist and continue to pervade modern British culture is testament to the power of heroism's association with Antarctica since the earliest days of exploration.

Scott's last biscuit may not have been found with the explorer, but it did date to his expedition. The biscuit has since been analyzed and found to contain less vitamin B and thiamine than other varieties, thanks to the use of white flour and sodium bicarbonate, rather than rolled oats and wholemeal flour (as used by Amundsen).[48] Investigations into the contents of the biscuits invariably lead back to the arguments over the reasons Scott's expedition ended so disastrously. For those on the side of historian and Scott detractor Roland Huntford, the poor nutritional planning feeds into the narrative that Scott was an ill-prepared bungler, while for those on the side of Fiennes, it seems unfair to hold a century-old recipe, created when "the science of nutrition was in its infancy," to the same nutritional standards we understand today.[49] Here, thanks to its entanglement in a century of narrative, a humble biscuit becomes more than a relic of expedition sponsorship, transforming instead into a flashpoint for historiographic debate and arguments over the science of nutrition.

The connection between the Huntley & Palmers brand and Antarctica was revisited on a larger scale during the centenary of Scott's *Terra Nova* expedition, with a limited-edition replica series going on sale across the UK. Branded as "Capt. Scott's Expedition Biscuits," the "High Energy Low Cholesterol" snacks came in handy packs of four, encased in a cardboard carton that told the story of Scott's dash to the pole: "When Capt. Robert Falcon Scott and Roald Amundsen had their Great Race to be the first to reach the South Pole in 1911/12, Huntley & Palmers baked the biscuits that the British team used to sustain them on their arduous journey."

Consumers are then offered the chance to take on the role of Scott by consuming the biscuits that the packaging claims have been created to "the exact same recipe, only substituting vegetable oil for lard as a concession to today's tastes." While the change in ingredients is remarked upon, the aesthetic change is not. Instead of intricately stamped biscuits, these are roughly cut squares of grayish oatmeal—a far cry from the appealing biscuits featured a century earlier. These aesthetics appeal to a contemporary audience, however, as the rough appearance sits well with narratives of Antarctica as a tough place, where survival takes precedence over everything else. The survival-giving energy contained within the biscuits—470kcal per 100g of product—is key. The rereleased biscuits, therefore, need not be pleasing to look at (or even to eat)—instead, the symbolic link that they provide to the narrative of a national British hero is what lends these biscuits an air of desirability to the target market.

The promise of a link to history is additionally reinforced on the packaging of the modern-day product, where the famous story of Captain Lawrence Oates's sacrifice during Scott's *Terra Nova* expedition is reprised. Realizing he was holding back his companions, the unwell Oates left the tent, telling his companions, "I'm just going outside and may be some time." The biscuit packaging calls upon this story: "So next time you feel like leaving the tent in the middle of a blizzard and uttering the words 'I'm just going outside and may be some time,' don't forget, as the gallant Capt. Oates obviously did, to take an EXPEDITION BISCUIT or four with you!" This tongue-in-cheek reference to Captain Oates's suicidal sacrifice illustrates the shift that has occurred over the intervening century—a diversifying cultural engagement with the legacy of the Scott expedition. Where initially Scott, Oates, and their three companions were painted as tragic heroes, changing views of the expedition and the definition of hero over the intervening years have led to the situation where the maker of a product uses Scott's name to associate their product with Antarctica and with historical prestige but at the same time recognizes alternative interpretations of the traditional narrative, including Scott as bungler. Such wording enables the consumer to both partake of the original qualities—such as heroism and stoic masculinity—and to put themselves at an ironic distance from it. Making this concession allows space for the consumer to mock the received narrative while joining it, thus opening the potential audience to a much wider market than if the biscuit packaging had simply repeated the now outdated myth of Scott as untouchable. Extremity, heroism, and historiography are all drawn upon to create a modern-day wrapper for these recreated biscuits that are, as the packaging proudly states, "perfect with cheese or on their own."

SOUTHWARD HO! YALUMBA'S ANTARCTIC TIES

Britain was not the only place where endorsements from polar explorers were used to market products. Mawson's 1929 BANZARE Expedition attracted support from a range of Australian businesses, including the South Australian Yalumba wine. The product's name features in a number of songs written by Heroic Era expeditioners, with the closing stanza of the sea shanty "The Intrepid Explorer" reading:

Put me down on the first bit of
Pack ice

With Yalumba uncorked near my mouth
And leave me to die unmolested
For I see we'll never get south.[50]

A photograph from the Christmas dinner at Cape Denison was subsequently used in advertising material back home, in a campaign described by Barossa Valley wine merchants as "the most famous Yalumba 4 Crown Port advertisement."[51] The image, which appeared in advertisements throughout 1930, is taken from the point of view of an expeditioner sitting just to the right of the head of the table, inviting the viewer into the scene (figure 9). That scene consists of a table laden with food, gifts, and four bottles of Yalumba port wine, all of which are turned to face the camera so the branding is clearly visible. Seven expeditioners named in the advertisement in small text above the image as Sir Douglas Mawson, Prof. T. Harvey Johnston, B. Child, H. Fletcher, R. A. Falls, R. G. Simmers, and Dr. W. W. Ingram are visible around the table, occupied reading letters or gazing upon the port and gifts. The black-and-white photograph has been tinted so the background appears orange, while the text "Southward Ho! with 'YALUMBA'" has been superimposed across the top of the image. The caption, united with the image by a red border that bounds the entire advertisement, reads "Christmas dinner at the Antarctic: To guard the health of the party Sir Douglas Mawson naturally chose Yalumba Port." This is a typical endorsement-style advertisement that uses a celebrity (and their well-known feats) to promote a product. It also carries connotations of extremity, suggesting, much like earlier advertisements for Bovril, that if Yalmuba could guarantee health in the harshest of conditions, it would also be able to work wonders back home in Australia.

One of the bottles of port that traveled to Antarctica with Mawson in 1929 worked further wonders in 2011, when it was put up for auction in support of an Antarctic Heritage organization. The ninety-two-year-old bottle, which was created by Yalumba for Mawson's expedition, was one of only four remaining from the original batch; the other three were to remain at the Yalumba Museum in South Australia.[52] It was auctioned at a centenary dinner, marking a hundred years since Mawson set off from Hobart on his first Antarctic expedition. Hosted by the Mawson's Huts Foundation, the event was intended to raise funds for the preservation

FIG 9. "Southward Ho! with Yalumba." A Yalumba port wine advertisement featuring a scene from Mawson's Australasian Antarctic Expedition, 1930. Courtesy of Yalumba.

of Mawson's huts at Cape Denison, Antarctica—the very setting of the photograph in the 1930s Yalumba advertisement. The same bottle of port therefore had implications for both the heroism theme and the modern-day heritage business and was valuable for the company through these two lenses. Yalumba had already supported a 1997 expedition dedicated to the restoration and upkeep of Mawson's huts and supplied wine to the Mawson's Huts Foundation Expedition 2000–2001.[53] Ten years later the historic 1929 bottle of port that bore the company's name served another purpose, raising almost AUD$15,000 (equivalent to US$12,000) for the foundation and thus contributing to both the upkeep of the physical hut in the Antarctic and to the legacy of an Australian Antarctic hero. This legacy also proved useful for the modern-day owners of Yalumba; as the company continued to maintain both physical and narrative links with the Antarctic via the heritage association, the brand name was featured in contemporary media coverage of events.

Antarctic-hero-themed packaging is another way Yalumba has reprised and reinforced the brand's Antarctic links. Wine labels featuring woodcut-style images of Mawson's Far Eastern Party (Cabernet Sauvignon 2010), Cape Denison (Sauvignon Blanc 2010), and Douglas Mawson's face (Wrattonbully Range, 2011) brought Antarctic history to the shelves of consumers. While some alcohols, including vodka and whisky, are culturally associated with cold-climate environments, wine is by contrast linked with the temperate regions in which it is produced (such as the Barossa Valley, in an Australian context). When it comes to cultural connotations, wine is not a particularly masculine or stoic drink—it is more likely to be enjoyed in comfortable surroundings, with associations of sociality and urbanity, or linked to psychological welfare. So how does a beverage from balmy South Australia—using an Aboriginal word meaning "all the country around" and usually enjoyed at a room temperature that is well into double digits—continue to find value in an association with Antarctica?[54] The link is Mawson, both as Antarctic explorer and as a well-known South Australian and national hero. Mawson's heroic reputation only continued to grow once he returned to his homeland from his Antarctic adventures—his face even appeared on the Australian $100 note. As the Yalumba labels demonstrate, the notion of Mawson as hero is still in popular circulation. Ongoing associations with contemporary Antarctic heritage activities continue to lend an air of authenticity to the packaging of the Mawson's range, while adding a layer to stories of Antarctic heroism within Antarctica.

Shackleton's Whisky

The story of Shackleton's whisky, which spans three centuries, further demonstrates the value of heroism for the heritage business. In January 2010 the NZAHT excavated three cases of Mackinlay's Rare Old Highland Malt under Shackleton's hut at Cape Royds.[55] The whisky, which had been bottled in 1896, was taken south during Shackleton's *Nimrod* expedition and was rediscovered in 2006 during maintenance work. After almost a century in the Antarctic ice, the bottles had become highly newsworthy artifacts that also acted as a gateway to Antarctic heritage. One case was removed to New Zealand and, in an event dubbed "The Great Whisky Thaw," the gradual warming of the bottles over several weeks was live streamed so audiences around the world could enjoy the spectacle. Owners of the Mackinlay's brand, Whyte & McKay Ltd., flew to New Zealand for the event. With the centenary celebrations of several Heroic Era expeditions, including the *Nimrod*, coming up, this was too good a marketing opportunity for the whisky makers to pass up. When Whyte & McKay enlisted master blender Richard Paterson to recreate the blend, he was well aware of the symbolic value of the discovery and the way his new blend would offer the imbiber a connection to Antarctic history; Paterson noted that he "wanted to capture the essence of Sir Ernest Shackleton within this whisky."[56]

The attention to detail that went into the reconstruction and rerelease of the whisky demonstrates the value of heroism for the heritage business.[57] The presentation of the replica whisky echoed the old crates and straw packaging found under the historic hut, and to mimic the imperfections in the original glass, the bottle manufacturer had to disable quality control.[58] Alongside the bottle, each box contained memorabilia related to the *Nimrod* expedition, including small photographs, a map, and a facsimile letter. The rerelease of Shackleton's whisky was not just about the whisky; rather, they were consciously creating an artifact that could connect consumers to Antarctica via Shackleton. The first edition whisky was followed by a general rerelease, in simpler packaging but further emphasizing the Shackleton link. Here Shackleton's name appears in large font on the label and embossed into the bottle glass, while Richard Paterson's signature is used to lend authenticity to the blend. This packaging also featured augmented reality, with photographs, a computer-generated model of a ship, wind sounds, and a recording of Shackleton's voice, which were accessible when the label was scanned using the Shazam app. The new technology contrasts with the historical details of the original replica, but both examples offer the consumer a sensory connection to a Heroic Era narrative. The accessibility of the general release in terms of price, packaging, and availability was beneficial to both the whisky producer and those conserving Shackleton's Antarctic hut, as 5 percent of funds from the whisky sales went back to the NZAHT—this arrangement continued for over a decade. Shackleton's whisky was therefore a valuable opportunity for raising awareness of Antarctic history and funds.

Heroic Antarctica

From heroism to heritage, Heroic Era stories have been retold, reimagined, and recommodified for vastly different audiences and purposes. During the Heroic Era of Antarctic exploration it was not enough to accomplish heroic acts. Rather, explorers needed to narrate these in ways that captivated audiences and sold the story, as selling the story was an important funding stream for explorers and sponsors alike. Making use of celebrity status to garner donations or raise funds by providing endorsements to companies was one way of ensuring an Antarctic expedition was financially viable and of ensuring a brand name attracted wide exposure. These endorsements also provided companies with material that showcased key attributes of their products, such as fortification of the (heroic) body. Endorsements are therefore another example of selling the story, this time with a more explicit link to advertising practices. In the case of recent rereleases of products such as Huntley & Palmers biscuits, Mawson-branded Yalumba wine, and Mackinlay's Rare Old Highland Malt, the classic advertising strategy of "retreat into the past" has been "ideologically used to sell the product."[59] A romantic harkening back to the Heroic Era occludes the ways alcohol has been a problem on contemporary Antarctic stations and appeals to those with an interest in Antarctica's past. Giving packaging an aged appearance, echoing the poses in famed photos of Antarctic explorers, and naming historical figures in modern-day advertisements gesture to a particular time in Antarctica's history, lending products an air of authenticity. The reprised historical links between each product and the Antarctic have continued to be useful precisely because of the lingering narratives of heroism that surround explorers such as Shackleton, Scott, and Mawson—"man-hauling" figures are heroes at a glance.

The Antarctic hero continues to be in commercial circulation today, including in advertisements for companies with no existing Antarctic connection; but now the focus moves from physical links with Antarctica (such as endorsements of products in situ) to the very idea of the hero, and the ways that idea has been reprised over time within the commercial context. While public perceptions of well-known Heroic Era figures have shifted over the course of the past century, the range of advertisements (both past and present) show that heroes are still wanted, after all.

In the Footsteps of Heroes

Reprising and Rethinking
Antarctic Histories

In early 2015, a most unlikely character made her way to the South Pole. Dressed in her trademark pink jumper and accompanied by Boots, her monkey sidekick, Dora the Explorer was there to welcome the band of weary, weather-beaten explorers with an enthusiastic "Bienvenidos— Welcome to the South Pole!" As if the presence of the young, Latina, and geographically underdressed cartoon character were not enough to disrupt the explorers' envisioned glorious arrival, Dora topped it all off with the punch line, "What took you so long?" A more pertinent question might be, "What was Dora doing there in the first place?"

Aside from subverting traditional ideas of the masculine hero who conquers the Antarctic wilderness, she was the star of a TV advertisement for the insurance company Geico. "If you're Dora the Explorer," the narrator concluded, "you explore—it's what you do." If you want to "save 15 percent or more on car insurance," on the other hand, "you switch to Geico."[1] Dora's presence in this Antarctic advertisement raises questions of masculinity, nationalism, and construction of place (the South African black-footed penguins, which feature in the composite "South Pole" shot, are a good 4,000 miles away from home). A South American girl embedded in a digitally constructed icescape meant to represent a place first claimed by British men—who goes by the name "explorer" to boot—subverts the trope of Antarctica as a place for masculine heroes with a stiff upper lip. The advertisement demonstrates that the idea of Antarctica as a place for explorers, for firsts, for testing human limits, and for heroes still lingers as recognizable but can be combined with ironic, postmodern distancing. Dora the Explorer's presence neatly encapsulates the way the concept of the Antarctic hero has evolved over the past century, as audience values and expectations have changed. Brightly colored Dora, the explorer heroine of millions of contemporary children, shows up the sepia-toned "heroes"—"driven nearly mad from starvation and frostbite"—as relics of a time long past.[2] Here, advertisers are cashing in on a "knowingness" of the dominant polar narratives—poking fun, being ironic, and turning a profit by recasting the heroes of old in newer, modern guises.

As Dora's appearance shows, the concept of the "Antarctic hero" remains commercially valuable, even as the meaning of the term has shifted. A 2017 survey of women in Antarctica elaborates upon the ways the hero framing can exclude those outside the category of able-bodied white men (this has implications for clothing sizes, access, and safety).[3] Advertisers can unsettle this association by subverting expectations and appealing to a market segment for whom traditional hero narratives are not attractive. In other instances, those more traditional narratives can be called upon to appeal to consumers who have a particular interest in Antarctica's past. This is becoming easier, as an existing Antarctic connection is not a prerequisite for activating the hero framing. As the examples in this chapter show, companies with no existing Antarctic links can use narratives about Antarctic heroes to brand and market their products—be they warm coats or the promise of change. Ernest Shackleton's name has been used metaphorically in a range of settings in recent times, including in climate-controlled boardrooms, while modern-day expeditions continue to use the sponsorship strategies familiar from the Heroic Era in order to attract the funding required to go ahead. An examination of the 2013 Walking with the Wounded South Pole expedition reveals how the term "hero" has shifted in meaning over the past century to become more inclusive, while also demonstrating the continued power of Heroic Era imagery, including photographs of people "man-hauling." The image of the bearded explorer may have been superseded by the likes of intrepid Dora in modern incarnations, and today's hero may look and feel different. However, contemporary advertisements demonstrate how the Heroic Era of Antarctic exploration continues to circulate throughout the Euro-Western cultural imaginary as an easily recognizable shorthand for challenge and hardship at the ends of the earth.

Heroes Recast

In the century since their Antarctic expeditions, the stories of Robert Falcon Scott and Roald Amundsen have been recast many times. As cultural historian Stephanie Barczewski puts it, "Real men become archetypes when filtered through popular memory, and real events become myths."[4] Historian Max Jones and his coauthors note that "heroes mark both the limits of permissible memory and the immutability of certain values," and this means the study of their reputations can be instructive, telling us about culture more broadly.[5] While the pendulum of popular opinion swung firmly away from Scott as national hero during the 1960s and 1970s, there have been defenders of his reputation. The explorer Ranulph Fiennes, who has himself spent multiple seasons in polar regions, published a comprehensive biography, *Captain Scott*, defending Scott's decisions and arguing that unless one has experience in extreme landscapes one cannot comment on decisions made. In more recent years, the pendulum has swung toward the middle, with recognition that Scott was neither flawless nor completely inept. Amundsen, too, has been the subject of renewed interest, with Roland Huntford's *Scott and Amundsen* highlighting the positive qualities of the Norwegian that had long been ignored. His dedication, focus, efficiency, and planning have since been lauded as examples to follow. Importantly, the actions of both men have stayed the same—it is the interpretations of those actions, considered through a range of lenses at different points in time, that have led to different retellings of the stories and to the designation or revocation of the hero label from each of the Heroic Era explorers. This has also led to the branding of each leader being perceived as more or less valuable in different contexts.

ON BRAND WITH SHACKLETON

Ernest Shackleton is a Heroic Era figure who has come to stand for strong leadership in the modern context. His exploits have shaped the mythology of Antarctica. Born in County Kildare, Ireland, in 1874, Shackleton trained in the merchant navy before heading south for the first time in 1901 with Scott's *Discovery* expedition. He would go on to lead several of his own Antarctic journeys, coming within ninety-seven miles of the South Pole in 1909 during the *Nimrod* expedition, watching his vessel *Endurance* be crushed in the ice of the Weddell Sea in 1915, and finally dying en route to Antarctica during his *Quest* expedition in 1922. His journey across ice floes and in whaleboats to Elephant Island and then South Georgia following the wreck of the *Endurance* has since gone down in history as one of the most impressive feats of survival in extremes. Shackleton has recently been lauded for never losing a man under his direct command (although three of his support crew in the Ross Sea party perished during the *Endurance* expedition) and for his ability to build a rapport in his team. At the time, however, Scott's recent death had "elevated him to the status of martyred national hero who far eclipsed Shackleton in the eyes of the British public."[6]

It was not until the late twentieth century that Shackleton came to be seen as the more effective leader and described as "a hero for our time."[7] Cultural studies scholar Rebecca Farley has observed that "Shackleton became popular at precisely the moment when the popular media were bemoaning twin crises of masculinity and whiteness"—Shackleton offered a model for both, and it was largely among the ranks of white men that his story gained new currency.[8] The reputation revival in the late 1990s and early 2000s saw Shackleton's leadership style used as the basis for business seminars and his name used as a "synonym for courage, bravery and most of all, leadership."[9] He became particularly popular post-9/11 as a model of leadership and endurance in times of crisis and enjoyed widespread popularity in the U.S. context.[10] The recent rise in Shackleton's popular reputation also parallels a shift in focus from a single hero to a leader supported by a team. This model finds far more uses in the modern-day business environment than the authoritarian model associated with other Heroic Era figures, such as Scott. This opinion shift can be attributed to changing cultural values and expectations: it is not the figures themselves but rather our own interpretations of their actions and achievements that have changed. In the contemporary context, Shackleton's perceived teamwork is very on-brand.

Shackleton's popularity exemplifies how the dominant narratives about Antarctica continue to be both masculine and very white. For instance, Nobu Shirase's 1910 Japanese Antarctic expedition is regularly left out of Heroic Era accounts. The literal whiteness of Antarctica has been used by white supremacists when propagating Nazi survival myths about the Far South, while access to Antarctica does not immediately change the dominant narratives about the place.[11] Historians Lize-Marié van der Watt and Sandra Swart note that in post-apartheid South Africa, it was not Black scientists and station personnel who were celebrated "but rather the exploits of black men who fit into the mold of the white explorers of the Heroic Age through a series of firsts—including the first to the South Pole, first to do an unassisted trek and so on. They literally had to walk in the footsteps of white men to prove their worth."[12] These "in the footsteps of" expeditions also bring the question of nationalism to the fore, as Heroic Era expeditioners were often tasked with claiming territory for their home nations—nations that already had long histories of colonization in other parts of the world. As historian Ben Maddison puts it, "Antarctic exploration was saturated in colonialism from start to finish"—the location may have been different, but the sentiment about acquiring territory remained the same.[13] Antarctica was, therefore, "the last locality, where fantasies of white masculinities could be played out."[14] It is also the last locality where the hero narrative continues to circulate—and be accepted—in an earnest rather than ironic manner. This allows the Antarctic hero to have afterlives that would not be possible in other geographic locations.

BYRD AND THE HERO BUSINESS

The business of heroism, centered on the trope of the hero, played an important role in facilitating expeditions well past the Heroic Era and into the Mechanical Age of exploration. Richard Evelyn Byrd was an aviator, American naval officer, and polar explorer who "understood the machinery of celebrity better than he understood the machinery of aeroplanes."[15] His privately funded expedition of 1928–30 has been called "the first 'million dollar' Antarctic expedition," and pilot Dean Smith portrayed it as "Byrd's own show: he was producer, director and star."[16] Recognizing the value of his role as a public figure, Byrd dedicated a chapter in his 1928 book *Skyward* to "This Hero Business"—a phrase encapsulating the performativity and commercial transactions associated with being a professional explorer. Byrd was no stranger to medals or media coverage or to playing the role of hero. Like earlier explorers, he recognized that the sale of books and stories defrayed the costs of previous expeditions and provided money for supplies and equipment for the next. His second Antarctic expedition (1933–35) was also characterized by the cult of celebrity as he used modern media to capitalize on his Antarctic exploits. Byrd used this media candidly and skillfully, working with radio and print outlets to orchestrate newsworthy events in high latitudes and deliberately construing himself as a media personality. Byrd himself explained, "Once you enter the world of headlines you learn there is not one truth but two: the one which you know from the facts; and the one which the public, or at any rate a highly imaginative part of the public, acquires by osmosis."[17] That public self was useful for attracting sponsorship and further media coverage; archivist and historian Robert Matuozzi has described Byrd's public career as "an expression of the cultural and economic energies that defined American society in the twentieth century, especially large-scale consumer capitalism and advertising."[18] By building on his success as an aviator in the Arctic in 1926 and in flying across the Atlantic in 1927, the media industry helped to construct Byrd—and other contemporary aviator-explorers such as Hubert Wilkins—as a celebrity figure. Both publishers and sponsors continued to benefit from carrying news stories throughout Byrd's private Antarctic expeditions—and from presenting the familiar figure of the polar hero in a new, technologically assisted, and American guise.

UNSUNG HEROES

While the names of leaders like Scott, Shackleton, and Amundsen are the ones that have gone down in history as the heroes of the Heroic Era, the efforts of their men are now recognized as crucial. In recent years there has been a shift of focus to the crews and workers of the expeditions who made the exploration possible. Maddison argues that the "heroization" of Antarctica is problematic because it hermitizes Antarctic exploration, focusing on the heroes rather than putting exploration events within the context of the rest of the world. In recent years there has been growing acceptance that the Heroic Era is not all about the heroes who have stood at the center of the seminal narratives of exploration. For instance, Mawson's Huts Replica Museum in Hobart has sought to profile all the members of Mawson's team, rather than focusing solely on the expedition leader.[19]

In Ireland, the shift away from heroes has manifested in renewed interest in Tom Crean, an Irish seaman who served on three Antarctic expeditions (*Discovery*, *Terra Nova*, and *Endurance*). An extremely popular one-man show by Aidan Dooley that dramatizes Crean's life has been touring the world since 2004, while the pub that Crean opened in Annascaul upon his return (aptly named The South Pole Inn) is a highlight of the Tom Crean Trail that sees tourists visit sites of significance related to the expeditioner's life.[20] As Crean's story has gained in popularity, it has also gained commercial value. In 2017 Crean was featured on the tailfin of a Norwegian Air airplane that ran transatlantic routes from Ireland, with the airline's chief commercial officer declaring, "Tom Crean is an unsung hero and a truly inspirational figure" and therefore a good candidate for the first Irish tailfin hero in the fleet (figure 10).[21] Ireland's new marine research vessel, delivered in 2022, was also named RV *Tom Crean* in the expeditioner's honor. Such recent examples show that "hero" is a term that is broadening out to include not only the leaders of expeditions but also those who worked hard each day to make the expedition possible—and that these minor figures also have commercial value for Brand Antarctica.

In Heroes' Footsteps: Centenary Reenactments

As the centenaries of Heroic Era voyages approached, both modern-day expeditioners and sponsors showed renewed interest in commemorating exploration narratives. Sponsorship plays an important role in modern-day reenactment expeditions, much as it did for the original explorers. As Rebecca Farley puts it, invoking Shackleton (or any other Heroic Era figure) "legitimates corporate sponsorship of these adults' expensive play. . . . They are professionally obliged to record their adventures, leaving public traces that are not only more durable, but also more widely accessible than individual childhood fantasies."[22] Just as the explorers of the Heroic Era were obliged to sell their stories back home, modern-day adventurers are expected to create a record of their endeavors. This record is of value for the corporate sponsors who make possible such expeditions. Jack Wolfskin, for example, provided support for Arved Fuchs's Shackleton 2000 expedition: the outdoor outfitter hosted a website offering customers the chance to meet the explorer and to win a limited edition

FIG 10. Norwegian tailfin hero, picturing Tom Crean. Norwegian Airlines, 2017. Creative Commons.

"authentic Arved Fuchs outfit."[23] Writing in 2013, consumer behavior expert Nancy Spears and her coauthors concluded that "regarding celebrities as modern-day heroes is positively associated with using them in ads," and this principle holds true in the Antarctic context.[24] It also carries echoes of Byrd's "hero business" of some seventy years before. The opportunity to wear explorers' clothing has other contemporary parallels; with the centenary celebrations of many Heroic Era expeditions on the horizon, companies such as Jaeger and Gieves and Hawkes reprised their earlier Antarctic links by offering limited edition replica clothing for sale.[25] That there is a market for these reprised artifacts indicates a desire for a tangible link to Antarctica's past among audiences familiar with the canonical narratives of Antarctic exploration. It also signals an ongoing opportunity for both expedition sponsors and companies wishing to capitalize on modern-day Antarctic links and themes.

Ancestry is another connection to Antarctica that has been drawn upon to invoke the hero theme in recent years. Commercial Antarctic tour operators have offered special centenary voyages, taking descendants of Heroic Era explorers south as both guests and lecturers on special "in the footsteps of" expeditions. Other descendants have taken the "footsteps" idea much more literally; the 2008–9 Matrix Shackleton Centenary expedition, which followed in the tracks of Shackleton's 1907–9 quest for the pole, included five descendants of Heroic Era figures: the modern-day expeditioners were related to Frank Wild, Frank Worsley, Jameson Boyd Adams, and Shackleton himself. Henry Worsley, an army officer and a descendent of *Endurance* skipper Frank Worsley, was the expedition leader; he then went on to guide the Amundsen team during the 2013 Walking with the Wounded expedition, and in 2015–16 attempted the first solo crossing of Antarctica, as envisaged by Shackleton a hundred years earlier. Worsley published an account of his modern-day journey entitled *In Shackleton's Footsteps: A Return to the Heart of the Antarctic*. This official account juxtaposes the modern expedition alongside the original push for the pole, drawing parallels between funding challenges, sponsorship, weather, and the route itself.

Several sponsors of the 1907 expedition offered support to the reenactment, with Worsley explaining that because of "the eye-catching plan 'Descendants Completing Unfinished Family Business by Retracing Shackleton's Route Across the Antarctic in the Centenary Year'" the party garnered interest from companies seeking an association with "the powerful Shackleton ethos."[26] Sponsors were also attracted by the prospect of displaying their logos in publicity images from the expedition. The 2008–9 In the Footsteps of Shackleton expedition was a success commercially and geographically and in terms of generating an ongoing legacy: the Shackleton Foundation was founded in the wake of the expedition, ensuring that "Shackleton's name lives on as a synonym for courage, bravery and most of all, leadership."[27] Such rhetoric gestures toward the recent transformation of Antarctic Heroic Era names from historical figures into concepts that can be applied more broadly, both within and outside of the Antarctic context.

The name Shackleton continues to hold allure for those who head south. In 2015 Henry Worsley mounted a solo expedition across Antarctica "in the spirit of Shackleton" to mark the centenary of the *Endurance* expedition and to raise money for the Endeavour Fund. This fund was established by the Royal Foundation in 2012 to "inspire servicemen and women to explore new physical challenges as part of their recovery; rebuilding their confidence and looking forward with optimism to the next chapter of their lives."[28] After traveling 913 miles (1,469 km) in sixty-nine days, Worsley fell ill with peritonitis and radioed for help. He was flown to Punta Arenas, Chile, but died in hospital on January 24, 2016.[29] Worsley's death was narrated in heroic terms not unlike those used when Scott's fate was reported by the press a century earlier: He was described as "a man who showed great courage and determination" by Prince William to the BBC, while the *Daily Mail* claimed, "Henry Worsley lived and died like a hero from another age."[30] His final message also carried echoes of Heroic Era language, with the explorer noting "my summit is just out of reach," while the acknowledgment that "I too have shot my bolt" is a direct reference to Shackleton's own words when he turned back from the South Pole in 1909.[31] Worsley's ashes were subsequently taken to South Georgia, to be buried in the vicinity of Ernest Shackleton in the cemetery at Grytviken, during the summer of 2017–18.[32] Aware of the heroic connotations associated with the modern-day explorer, Ice-Tracks Expeditions advertised berths on "Henry Worsley's Final Voyage South" (November 30–December 18, 2017), allowing members of the public to follow the explorer to his final resting place. This eighteen-night trip, billed as a "special commemorative voyage," transformed Worsley from the one following in heroes' footsteps into the hero others sought to follow. It is also a stark and somewhat grotesque reminder that there continues to be money in polar tragedy. The key pillars of the contemporary hero business in Antarctica—nostalgia, genealogy, and reenactment—come together in a tour product to create ongoing value from the concept of the Antarctic hero.

Reenactments are particularly interesting in the era of the Antarctic Treaty. Signed in 1959, the treaty provides for the non-militarization of the continent. While weapons testing and military exercises are not permitted, military logistics regularly support Antarctic science, and ambitious expeditions that echo the goals and routes of Heroic Era can and have been undertaken by military personnel. When the Antarctic is used as a platform to figuratively and literally link veterans from wars to heroic explorers, the continent is drawn into militaristic cultures. However, the established hero narrative in the Antarctic allows for the feats of individual military personnel to be celebrated in a way that does not inflame geopolitical tensions. Focusing on sponsorship and altruistic outcomes is another way to legitimize reprisals of the hero theme.

As the vignettes in the next section detail, stories from the past are reprised and at times reinterpreted. Descendants of Heroic Era explorers, women, people of color, and other historically marginalized groups add their own layers to polar history by visiting a century later, and minor figures step into the hero role. However, the concept of achieving a "first" remains attractive. In January 2022 Captain Preet Chandi became the first woman of color to undertake a solo expedition to the South Pole. She attracted sponsorship from dozens of companies, including the technology firm Cognizant, and the successful expedition made headlines as "Polar Preet" demonstrated that "nothing is impossible."[33] The captain was given a hero's welcome upon her return to the UK.[34] The visibility of Chandi's achievement is important—she is a far cry from the bearded men of the Heroic Era, and her success suggests the Antarctic continent is a place for a much wider range of people than the hero framing might suggest.

Sponsorship, Heroism, and Adventure

Reenactments of Heroic Era feats provide an opportunity for the original sponsors to gain renewed commercial leverage from their historical Antarctic connections. Huntley & Palmers (now owned by a larger corporation) reassociated their brand with Antarctica in 2012 by becoming the official biscuit supplier to both the International Scott Centenary Expedition and the British Services Antarctic Expedition. The former expedition was a type of pilgrimage to pay homage to Robert Falcon Scott, with the aim of holding an honorable commemoration service in Antarctica on the centenary of Scott's death. This type of expedition sees participants quite literally follow in the footsteps of Heroic Era figures. The focus on honor and "scientific legacy" indicate that Scott is a figure still held in high regard by those taking part and, therefore, still considered to be a powerful—and valuable—brand.[35]

The British Services Antarctic Expedition (BSAE2012) was somewhat different: British Armed Services members traveled "in the Spirit of Scott, but not in his tracks," and aimed to raise £10,000 for the Help for Heroes charity.[36] Founded in 2007, the charity's aim is to provide "direct, practical support for those affected by military service."[37] Such association with an organization that supports heroes is also a reenactment of past fundraising, as the BSAE2012 website explains: "After news of Scott and his team's demise reached the UK, funds were contributed by the public to look after the families of the heroic explorers. In keeping with this sentiment, the BSAE2012 aims to raise money for modern day military heroes."[38] These two expeditions differ in their goals, with one representing a literal reenactment and the other drawing upon the "Spirit of Scott" and the heroic resonances of his story. Nevertheless, both share a sponsor that has Heroic Era links—the reprisal of Huntley & Palmers support for these Antarctic expeditions indicates that the Scott narrative and the associated idea of the polar hero have ongoing commercial currency.

WALKING WITH THE WOUNDED: CHARITY AND INSPIRATION

The 2013 Walking with the Wounded South Pole expedition involved three teams of wounded war veterans from the UK, U.S., and the Commonwealth undertaking a race to the South Pole. Antarctica is now heavily surveilled, with satellites collecting data about ice sheets, shelves, and sea ice year-round. Nevertheless, in this instance the ice was cast as the "other" against which these heroes had to pit themselves. This was the third Walking with the Wounded event, following the inaugural North Pole trek in 2011 and Everest climb in 2012.[39] All three events took place in frozen environments that carried similar connotations of extremity; the cold-polar branding was therefore not unique to Antarctica. Such expeditions are used to raise the profile of the Walking with the Wounded charity, to "provide inspiration to those coping daily with injury and disability" sustained in the line of duty, and to demonstrate to both employers and those who have been wounded how injured veterans are still "able to achieve at the very highest level."[40] Like the BSAE2012, donations from the public go directly to the charity, as each expedition is financed by commercial backers. The backers, in turn, gain exposure for their brands, much as Huntley & Palmers and Bovril did some hundred years earlier. The Antarctic setting makes the expeditions newsworthy through a combination of its extreme environment and the explicit historical parallels with hero narratives.

Walking with the Wounded veterans take the place of Heroic Era explorers—literally as they walk in their footsteps, metaphorically as they take on the role of hero, and commercially as they attract sponsorship to undertake Antarctic endeavors. In Euro-Western cultures, explorer-heroes have traditionally been depicted as being white able-bodied men. This is particularly true in the Antarctic context, where the stories of British explorers such as Scott, Mawson, and Shackleton have saturated the narrative landscape throughout the Western world. The Walking with the Wounded expedition challenged the notion that Antarctica is the domain of white able-bodied men, with both male and female soldiers with various disabilities and from a range of ethnic backgrounds taking part. Importantly, the figures pictured in advertising material—both for the expedition and for sponsors—still look the same as the explorers of the Heroic Era; swaddled in thick clothing that masks any signs of gender or race, they mimic their counterparts from a century earlier. Such imagery allows the role of the hero to be recast, while drawing on the rich symbolism associated with the image of a figure struggling across an icescape; their difference is allowed only to then be disguised so that the stereotypical male-hero figure—and all its attendant cultural and commercial associations—can be recognized.

The Walking with the Wounded South Pole expedition had several sponsors: Virgin Money took title rights, while nutrition and weight loss company Noom Coach (U.S.), veteran support organization Soldier On (Commonwealth), and whisky producer Glenfiddich (UK) took on naming rights for each of the teams (relationships with both Virgin and Glenfiddich were managed by marketing consultancy firm Captive Minds, an agency that has since gone on to coordinate other polar promotions, including Manon Ossevoort's 2014 trek to the South Pole aboard a Massey Fergusson tractor). Sponsorship provided funds for the expedition to go ahead, and in return each company was provided with positive media coverage and photographs of its brand name or product in situ in the Antarctic. This was not any version of the Antarctic, however. The "Antarctic ice" depicted was, ironically, in Iceland—a far more accessible northern near-polar location. Rather than being characterized by photographs of charismatic penguins and the brilliant contrast of white ice to blue sky, the promotional photographs feature a series of figures, dressed in the thickest protective clothing, leaning forward into their harnesses as they haul their sleds across sastrugi-strewn plateaus and through snowstorms. The image depicts a tough landscape—freezing, unforgiving, embodying concepts of the sublime as described by the first explorers to venture into the Antarctic interior during the Heroic Era of exploration.[41]

It was such promotional images that formed the basis of domestic UK advertising campaigns for both the expedition itself and the naming sponsors; the campaign run by the whisky company Glenfiddich—a newcomer to polar sponsorship—demonstrates the contemporary power of the hero trope.

SPIRIT OF A NATION: GLENFIDDICH AND THE ANTARCTIC

In November 2013 Glenfiddich ran a £600,000 London-based advertising campaign that drew directly on the brand's newfound Antarctic association. The campaign, which ran as posters, broadsheet adverts, radio slots, online, and as signage in the London underground, included a partnership with the Telegraph Group media company, which featured exclusive human-interest advertorials related to the expedition in the *Sunday Telegraph*.[42] Glenfiddich advertisements displayed images of people on skis towing sledges and trekking through a polar landscape, under the tagline "Spirit of a Nation." In each rendition, the sledge-hauling figures are depicted in motion, walking in single file toward the vanishing point on the horizon or toward the viewer. This kind of physicality and movement through the landscape was central to the iconography of the Heroic Era, and in echoing the imagery of a hundred years earlier, the advertisements also invoke ideas of conquering and firsts. As the marketing company Captive Minds describe in their project showcase, the "key to the campaign was an image that conveyed determination, leadership, teamwork and the freezing conditions that team Glenfiddich would face in Antarctica."[43] The polar landscape in question is actually Iceland, but in the context of the adverts, the heroic figures pictured, and the well-publicized expedition, it is intended to be read as the "Antarctic." The campaign brings to the surface ideas of heroism, nationalism, and nostalgia, pitting man against nature, with a decent whisky at his side.

Glenfiddich sponsored the expedition because, as Senior Brand Manager Sarah Harding explained, it was "mutually beneficial" for both the charity and brand: "The stories [the expeditioners] tell, the inspirational people and how they have overcome challenges, has a spirit which matches our heritage."[44] Whisky is, according to author Neville Peat, the quintessential explorer's drink, "steeped in history, maturity, endurance, character, and edgy technology," making the Antarctic trek an ideal fit for the brand.[45] Whisky also has a long association with the idea of masculinity, much like Antarctica. Such associations continue today, as brought to the fore by journalist Emma Barnett in a 2013 article for the *Telegraph*, entitled "Why Is Whisky Still a 'Man's Drink'?"[46] Although around a third of whisky drinkers in the UK and U.S. are now women, Barnett details how her "personal tipple still continues to raise eyebrows."[47] The Glenfiddich advertisements do feature women, but participants are pictured in poses that echo Heroic Era photographs of men man-hauling over the ice. Differentiating features such as gender, race, and physical ability are occluded by bulky polar clothing, so the images evoke the hero theme without overtly challenging assumptions that the hero must be white, male, and able-bodied, thus perpetuating existing stereotypes. Other links to Antarctica that appear in the Glenfiddich campaign are very subtle and relate to the continent itself. Ice cap satellite imagery was used to create the textured typography in the adverts, with the project description noting this attention to detail as paralleling "the craftsmanship and attention to detail that makes Glenfiddich the world's most awarded single malt."[48] The links between whisky and Antarctica, drawn out by narrative, are powerful precisely because they reinforce existing tropes.

The Glenfiddich advertisements that formed part of this campaign play on themes of nationalism both in the product's name ("Spirit of a Nation"—not specifying the UK, but appearing in that national context) and by visually reminding a British audience of earlier expeditions into the South that resulted in the claiming of the British Antarctic Territory (Falkland Islands Dependencies). These early British expeditions also resulted in claims to the areas now known as the Ross Dependency

(New Zealand) and the Australian Antarctic Territory, but the Common-wealth connection is not foregrounded in this domestic campaign. In this sponsored reprisal, the veterans who have fought for their nations continue to follow in the tradition of the early Antarctic explorers, who also carried their national flags and claimed territory for their monarchs. Prince Harry's patronage of the Walking with the Wounded expedition is very much tied up with ideas of empire and sovereignty, even at a time when the 1959 Antarctic Treaty has put all claims "on ice" via Article IV. Such narrative reinforcements of sovereignty are part of a larger effort to maintain symbolically the British claim, which is formally contested in the Antarctic Peninsula by Chile and Argentina: all three claimants continue to send their Royal Navy vessels to patrol the Antarctic Peninsula region each season while providing logistical support to scientists via National Antarctic Programs. Walking across Antarctica in the footsteps of earlier explorers is one way of reinforcing Britain's physical links to the conti-nent—in this case, the link is also associated with the whisky sponsor.

Antarctica may have provided a dramatic setting, but the target market for the Glenfiddich campaign that ran concurrently with the expedition was people back home. Alongside the figures in polar dress, the Glen-fiddich advertisements feature an image of a limited-edition whisky that was created for the event. This product was created as a solution to the Captive Minds brief to "Inspire the nation to get behind the Glenfiddich Team." A special cask was toured around the UK, gathering over two thou-sand signatures and messages of support for Team Glenfiddich, before being filled with a twenty-nine-year-old single malt Scotch whisky—the "Spirit of a Nation."[49] Scratching the surface of the Glenfiddich adver-tising campaign reveals how the connotations of the hero have changed over the last century, even as the idea has retained commercial value. Glenfiddich had no particular Antarctic link prior to the expedition but saw the opportunity to create one by building a physical link via sponsor-ship, augmenting existing associations between whisky and masculinity. The sponsorship also added to the company narrative in the process. By sponsoring the Walking with the Wounded expedition, the Glenfiddich brand tapped into and reproduced the myth of the Antarctic hero that continues to circulate in public discourse.

Leading from the South: Shackleton as Brand

The reputations of Antarctic leaders have proven valuable in recent years, as the heroes have been reprised and their actions translated into a corporate setting. Rebecca Farley has written how the 1990s "saw the emergence of a significant industry (mostly business management consultants) teaching Shackleton's leadership 'methods,'" and this pattern is evident in books such as Margot Morrell and Stephanie Capparell's *Shackleton's Way: Leadership Lessons from the Great Antarctic Explorer* and Dennis N. T. Perkins et al.'s *Leading at the Edge: Leadership Lessons from the Extraordinary Saga of Shackleton's Antarctic Expedition.*[50] Perkins and his coauthors use Shackleton's *Endurance* expedition as a model for a leadership system. Each chapter provides an example of a strategy the authors recognize in Shackleton's expedition before explaining how to apply it in a corporate setting; they draw parallels between the boardroom and Antarctica, equating the business arena with Antarctic landscapes, and managers with Shackleton. Although Antarctica and the boardroom may be far removed geographically, they are metaphorically linked by challenge: the man against nature trope is reprised, with the market taking the place of the icescape.[51] This framing has proved lucrative, but it is also problematic. When writers resort to pitting humans against the environment, the opportunity to see Antarctica as part of a world ecosystem is excluded, and an anthropocentric worldview is reinforced.

The continued focus on Shackleton has implications for how both heroes and the Antarctic continent are conceived. Farley argues that "'Shackleton,' although naming a real historic person, also describes a subject position that others may occupy, provided the rules of the discourse itself do not exclude them."[52] For modern-day explorers like Henry Worsley, that subject position proved attractive. When speaking of Shackleton, Worsley raised him onto the pedestal of heroism: "It is impossible to find reference in his writing of the fear of the unknown."[53] This perceived fearlessness and the ability to manage risks has attracted those in business to Shackleton. The narratives that have been built around his legacy hold allure—as an explorer who pitted himself against the extreme Antarctic elements and survived, Shackleton acts as an "idealized model of white masculinity."[54] Given that positions of power in the business world are still overwhelmingly dominated by white men, Shackleton remains a good fit as an idol. However, the focus on a single figure, at the expense of all others who made possible his expeditions (Frank Wild, Frank Worsley, and Frank Hurley among them) excludes a range of other brand role models, thus reinforcing structural inequalities through the deployment of a selective narrative. Farley claims that "in invoking Shackleton, these institutions draw on a strongly raced and gendered discourse of leadership. A model of white male hegemony is adopted to strengthen positions that have traditionally been and remain dominated by white men."[55] A continued focus on individual figures from the Heroic Era—such as Shackleton—therefore has implications for everyday interactions and shuts down alternative possibilities for showcasing a range of role models from different backgrounds. As Ben Maddison puts it, the working class "lacked both the means of publicity and the self-regarding subjectivity of the middle class to write themselves into Antarctic history."[56] The repetition of the same heroic narratives has the effect of repeatedly locking out these alternative perspectives of Antarctica—and occluding new, more inclusive ways of branding the place.

Abstractions and Echoes: Invoking Branding Challenges

Homage has been paid to Heroic Era explorers in a range of other ways, including the manufacture of contemporary goods that are associated with historic Antarctic tales. One such manufacturer is the UK-based Shackleton Company. Inspired by tales of Leonard Hussey's music on the *Endurance* expedition, branding and advertising professional Simon Middleton founded the company in 2013 to produce British-made banjos. The company later expanded to offer everything from replicas of Shackleton's sweater and mohair socks, to hand-made journals and handcrafted beer.[57] The website explained that the link between the disparate goods in its range is Shackleton himself: "Everything we do is inspired by the great Antarctic explorer Ernest Shackleton, his *Nimrod* and *Endurance* expeditions, and in fact the whole of what is known as The Heroic Age of Polar Exploration."[58] The question "What would Shackleton do?" also appeared on company merchandise, alongside an image of the explorer. While the links between the wide range of products offered may at times seem tenuous, according to the company the two themes that unite all the

FIG 11. Shackleton store shopfront, 2020. Photo by Ian Holdcroft.

products in the Shackleton Company's range are "the spirit of adventure of Ernest Shackleton, and a commitment to genuine British making."[59] This focus on British-made goods brings back the theme of nationalism albeit in a new way. Rather than manifesting itself in treks across charted territory, as in the case of "in the footsteps of" expeditions, this nationalism is concentrated more locally back in the UK. In the wake of the global financial crisis, when the job security of many was under threat, audiences were more receptive to narratives of conquering adversity and to the concept of supporting local-made goods. The financial, social, and temporal landscape may have changed over the past hundred years, but the fact that nationalist ideas are made to be associated with a Heroic Era Antarctic explorer indicates the power of these early narratives, and the way different elements, such as masculinity, nationalism, and leadership, are foregrounded as useful at different points in time.

The Shackleton name continues to be valuable for businessmen Ian Holdcroft and Martin Brooks's range of high-end winter clothing. The brand uses Shackleton's name as a core identity, while the nine-pointed star on the company's logo comes from the engraving on Shackleton's gravestone. Despite the visual link to a final resting place, the company uses the hero's name to evoke notions of survival in polar conditions and triumph in the face of challenge. Narrative connections to the Heroic Era are augmented by modern-day collaborations with people who work in and visit Antarctica. For example, a 2018 partnership between the Shackleton brand and the Polar Latitudes tour company resulted in specially designed expedition jackets for tourists and staff and added a further layer of Antarctic connection to the brand's own story. The 2019 release of the Frank Hurley Photographer's Jacket, developed in partnership with Leica Camera AG, saw Antarctic history come to the fore again; here the Heroic Era camera artist's name was used to market a cold-weather jacket designed for modern-day photographers—the garment features extra internal pockets for storing batteries.[60] The theme of endurance and overcoming adversity gained particular contemporary relevance in 2020 with the global COVID-19 pandemic resulting in closed borders and lengthy lockdowns across the UK and the rest of the world. A pop-up shop selling Shackleton-branded "expedition-grade apparel" appeared in the central London suburb of Chelsea in December 2020, complete with a life-size replica of the *James Caird* and projections of interviews with modern-day Antarctic expeditioners (figure 11). The large Shackleton quote on the wall, "Difficulties are just things to overcome, after all," seemed particularly apt in the pandemic context—although the difficulties associated with COVID-19 were not distributed equally. At a time when international borders were closed and the Antarctic tourism season was cancelled, it was more important than ever for the Shackleton brand to appeal to the domestic market. It did this both through conjuring up imagined future journeys (in expedition-grade apparel) and offering a tangible link to a key historical moment from Antarctic history—a message about triumph in the face of adversity was an attractive prospect for the subset of affluent consumers familiar with the Shackleton story who were 'stuck' at home during this period.

Finding the *Endurance*

In March 2022 the remarkably tangible discovery of Shackleton's vessel *Endurance* brought the Heroic Era of Antarctic exploration back into the spotlight. Impressively intact, the wreck, which sunk in 1915 after being crushed in the pack ice, was found 10,000 feet (3000 m) under the surface of the Weddell Sea. So, too, was the hero business that generated value from the story. TV historian Dan Snow was on board, as were a film crew creating a documentary for National Geographic, while the expedition had a comprehensive social media campaign; rather than in the pages of the evening paper, breaking news about the discovery was shared via the social media platform TikTok. The Endurance22 expedition set out with the aim of locating, surveying, and photographing the wreck of the famous ship. It was organized by the Falklands Maritime Heritage Trust, again highlighting the role such trusts play in raising the profile of Heroic Era stories and sites. In a financial arrangement that echoed the private sponsorship of the earlier era, an anonymous donor financed the expedition to the tune of US$10 million, allowing the South African polar research and logistics icebreaker, SA *Agulhas II* to be chartered for the voyage.

The location where the *Endurance* was last sighted is difficult to access, and a lower than usual sea ice extent facilitated access. Gesturing to this, Director of Exploration Mensun Bound noted the discovery was an important milestone, but one that was "not all about the past; we are bringing the story of Shackleton and *Endurance* to new audiences, and to the next generation, who will be entrusted with the essential safeguarding of our polar regions and our planet."[61] This suggests that there are new ways of finding meaning in old stories. The story of the *Endurance* has a different emphasis when viewed as a black-and-white photograph as compared to the full-color underwater images that highlight the diverse marine life on and around the wreck. Sea ice scientists, oceanographers, meteorologists, and marine engineers were all involved in the expedition, while the Endurance22 website prominently displayed links to the initial environmental evaluation and permit for the activities. Looking forward, the challenges faced by and in Antarctica are environmental rather than geographical. The context of a low sea ice season situates the expedition firmly in the Anthropocene, when the impacts of anthropogenic climate change are felt around the globe, and when melted ice is used to make visible a warming planet. The discovery of the *Endurance*, therefore, demonstrates that there is ongoing interest in Antarctic heroes—but also how the hero narrative can be connected to the more modern framing of Antarctica as a place for science and protection.

The Changing Antarctic Hero

The heroism trope continues to be associated with Antarctica, where it manifests in a range of different ways. Dating back to the dawn of the Heroic Era in the 1890s, the theme has been repeated, reprised, subverted, and revisited. Representations of the Antarctic hero have also shifted along with public attitudes. Where once Scott's death in the heart of whiteness was held up as an example of supreme sacrifice for one's country (the dominant narrative in Britain prior to World War II), in the later part of the twentieth century it was Shackleton's leadership skills that were seen as the most useful relic of the Heroic Era. This shift in public perception has been paralleled in advertising material, as seen in the recent examples that venerate Shackleton. As consumer behavior scholars Nancy Spears, Marla Royne, and Eric van Steenburg put it in their exploration of the links between heroes, celebrities, and advertising, "The traditional heroic model is evolving and is gradually being re-configured within a contemporary society."[62] Chapters 1 and 2 have shown how a hero can provide a direct endorsement for a brand (Bovril, His Masters Voice), offer narrative links between a product and Antarctica (Huntley & Palmers, Yalumba, Glenfiddich), or furnish inspiration for merchandise with no prior south polar links (Geico, Norwegian Air, the Shackleton Company). The continent and its history are accessible via narratives and metaphor, allowing a wide audience to experience both Antarctica and the Heroic Era from afar.

Focusing on the well-known leaders of Heroic Era expeditions, however, can be problematic, as invoking the hero theme directs the gaze toward the past. While the trope of the hero is easily recognizable when figures such as Scott, Shackleton, or Mawson are deployed, it is also exclusionary in that it shuts out other representations, including women and workers. The examples considered in this chapter, including sponsorships of reenactments and the Tom Crean tailfin, illustrate how "hero" is not a static concept, and how the definition has shifted over time. In the Antarctic context, advertisements have moved from featuring heroes themselves in endorsement format to employing the *idea* of a hero, typified by Glenfiddich's unidentified figures walking into the whiteness. The hero trope has come to stand in for Antarctica, masculinity, and wider cultural narratives of "man versus wild." At the same time, modern-day feats have been recognized as "heroic," adding further layers to the Antarctic hero discourse. The sepia-toned days when Antarctica was, as writer Sara Wheeler puts it, "a testing ground for men with frozen beards to see how dead they could get" may appear to be over.[63] However, the specter of the hero continues to loom large over the Antarctic ice, influencing who has access when and bringing in money for the brands that deploy it back home.

Cold Weather Branding 3

Superlatives and Survival
on "Continent 7"

In the winter of 2014, an unusual visitor took to the slopes of New Zealand's Mount Hutt Ski Field to showcase its extreme credentials (figure 12). Dressed in a crash helmet, with a snowboard under one arm, the Magellanic penguin looked quite at home on the chairlift barrier arm; the South American bird was depicted undertaking an extreme sport to promote Resene's new range of Extreme Paint (another iteration of the advertisement shows a penguin skydiving). Resene has a long-standing connection with Antarctica as a sponsor and enabler of Antarctic activity.[1] New Zealand's Scott Base is well known for its Chelsea Cucumber (Resene 6-071) color scheme, which has become integral to the branding of the station. The distinctive green also features in the planned rebuild, with Jon Ager of Antarctica New Zealand asserting that "the colour will link two eras of New Zealand science" in the Antarctic.[2] This Antarctic connection for the brand extends back home; featuring the International Antarctic Centre in Christchurch as a case study, the Resene website explains that "painting the Antarctic Attraction is nearly as much of a challenge as living on barren ice planes."[3]

The 2014 advertisement brings the idea of Antarctic extremity to the fore, using a penguin and the species' association with the Far South to sell white paint on the domestic New Zealand market. Penguins of all varieties have been used to conjure up Antarctica on many occasions, instantly situating any ice in the advertisement in the Far South and often calling upon the continent's associations with extremity. In this case, the icy positioning of the advertisement was important; when viewed against a backdrop of snow and ice, the Antarctic landscape depicted in the image blurred into the viewer's own surroundings. Such an icy white background also echoed the Resene product itself. The paint is white,

FIG 12. Chairlift advertisement for Resene's Extreme Paint at Mount Hutt Skifield, New Zealand, 2014. Photo by Hanne Nielsen.

like the Antarctic, and helps to cool down a house by virtue of reflecting the sun's rays. The association with toughness in the face of extreme weather conditions is also paramount. So it was that on an unassuming mountain face in New Zealand's Southern Alps, a lost penguin, a helmet, several paint tins, and the word "extreme" conjured up Antarctica as a potent publicity device.

This chapter interrogates the intersection of penguins, heroes, and the pursuit of polar firsts to explore how the theme of extremity has functioned in a range of Antarctic advertisements. The term "extreme" is defined here to refer to exceptional limits, which can be spatial, temporal, or understood in terms of physical feats: to take a product to Antarctica is to take it to its material extremes, quite literally. The advertisements examined here all employ the idea of Antarctica as an extreme environment to market a range of products—those with existing links to the Far South, those forging imaginative links, and those that are conspicuously absent. Looking back over the history of cold weather engineering and technology in the Far South, cold-weather branding plays an important role. The extremity theme casts Antarctica as the ultimate testing ground: as the coldest, highest, windiest, driest continent, it is a place for firsts and for superior performance. The advertisements in this chapter reinforce the idea that Antarctica is not only a place for tough people but also a place for tough things. In many instances, the two ideas go hand in hand. Extremity as a theme differs from heroism, however, in that the focus is less on people and more on machinery and equipment. A common thread running through the advertisements examined in this section is the idea that if a product works well in Antarctica, it will work absolutely anywhere. This is true on a range of scales, whether the product is an item of clothing, a mechanical lubricant, a building material, or a paint. If Antarctica is cast as the ultimate in extreme environments, then any products that function there must also, by association, be extremely robust.

The use of extremity in advertising campaigns is not limited to the Antarctic but has wider appeal. In investigating the risk associated with extreme sports, sociologist Catherine Palmer has highlighted how "previously 'on the edge' behavior now features in a whole range of media," where it is used to sell "mainstream commodities such as sunglasses, soft drinks, watches, alcoholic beverages and clothing."[4] Watch manufacturers, energy drink producers, and alcohol brands have long made use of elemental environments, such as mountain peaks, deep oceans, and extreme sports in the marketing of their products. Energy drinks, in particular, "rely extensively on imagery associated with extreme sports."[5] Companies like Red Bull have built their brand around the twin concepts of extremity and risk, and their logo has appeared on everything from parachutes, racing cars, and expedition sleds to the deep sea and the stratosphere.[6] Red Bull even sent surfer Ramón Navarro to the Antarctic to catch some waves in 2013, complete with camera crew to document the feat.[7] The common thread through all such examples is the notion that if a product performs under such difficult conditions, it will have no issues under everyday circumstances. In the case of products like Red Bull, this positioning also says something about the identity of the consumer, associating them with risk-taking, limit-pushing behavior. If pushing the boundaries of the possible is the aim, taking products to Antarctica is a logical commercial progression.

The extremity frame has been associated with Antarctica since the Heroic Era and continues to be deployed in modern-day advertisements and branding exercises. It peaked in popularity during the mid-twentieth century, when wooden huts and bearded men were still emblematic of the continent and environmental concerns had yet to come to the fore. Human activity in the Far South through the 1950s saw a renewed wave of interest in the Antarctic, thanks to high-profile events such as the heavily sponsored Commonwealth Trans-Antarctic Expedition (TAE) of 1955–58, the 1957–58 International Geophysical Year, and the negotiation of the 1959 Antarctic Treaty. The presence of women—the United States allowed women to work in Antarctica in 1969, while the British Antarctic Survey finally allowed women to winter over in 1996—and the sense of greater "cushiness" from the 1970s onward decreased the connection of the continent with extremity and masculinity and allowed more nuanced framings to emerge.[8] The rise of environmental concerns in the decades following the 1950s and 1960s has also made it problematic to advertise products such as oil (BP was an official sponsor of the TAE) and motorized vehicles using Antarctic scenery.[9] While this does not mean such advertising has ceased altogether, depictions must now be tempered by an acknowledgment of other framings, including that of environmental protection. The extreme frame therefore manifests in different ways at different times.

Midcentury Antarctica: Exploration, Claims, and Treaty

The 1950s were a particularly busy time in Antarctica's human history, thanks to high-profile events such as the U.S. Navy's Operation Deepfreeze (1955–56) and the TAE (1955–58). While such large-scale activities were new, the rhetoric of extremity that surrounded them was not. The associations between polar regions and extremity were imported, to some degree, from the male-dominated field of mountaineering, which emerged as a sport in the mid-nineteenth century—writing in 1903, climber Elizabeth Le Blond noted there was "no manlier sport in the world than mountaineering."[10] Associations between mountaineering and masculinity became particularly important following the world wars, as returning soldiers sought ways to repair their damaged manhood and reposition a more domesticated masculinity.[11] Arguments about the importance of mountaineering as a recuperation of masculinity following the world wars also apply readily to the Antarctic; immediately after World War II the U.S. Navy mounted Operation Highjump (1946–47), sending men, many of whom had just returned from war, to set up the base Little America IV and to map the coastline of Antarctica. Operation Deepfreeze followed, and thirty-four hundred men from the U.S. Navy headed to Antarctica in order to create facilities that included a base at the geographic South Pole and logistics for the upcoming IGY.[12] The period is interesting historically as it saw ex-service personnel pave the way for science in the region; science has since come to be seen as central to Antarctica's political and diplomatic value, together with the notion of peace.

During the mid-twentieth century, a strong interest in attaining "firsts" remained. The TAE, which sought to claim a continental crossing as a first, was a particular focus for Britain and New Zealand during this period. Expedition leader Vivian Fuchs aimed to complete Shackleton's planned 1914–17 journey across Antarctica from the Weddell Sea to the Ross Sea, via the geographic South Pole (his party also called their base "Shackleton"). The Ross Sea support party, tasked with laying depots for Fuchs, was led by the New Zealander Edmund Hillary. Hillary had already gained "extreme" credentials when he became the first to summit Mount Everest in 1953, along with Sherpa Tenzing Norgay. He would soon dominate headlines again, with his support party becoming the first to reach the South Pole overland since Amundsen and Scott in the Heroic Era. With Fuchs and Hillary approaching the pole from opposite sides, the media sought to represent the expedition as a modern rerun of the 1911 race to the pole rather than as a scientific expedition or collaborative international undertaking.[13] Such a depiction horrified Fuchs, but it clearly illustrated how strong the Heroic Era narratives remained in Antarctic discourse.[14] The value of the story also remained high: the official film of the TAE, *Foothold on Antarctica* (1956), was funded by BP, while Kodak provided photographic materials to ensure the expedition was well documented.

The TAE also sparked a new discourse around the use of technology in facilitating modern-day exploration. Images from the TAE put Fuchs's Tucker Sno-Cats and Hillary's Massey Ferguson tractors in the spotlight.

Both companies loaned machinery to the expedition for use on the trek. In analyzing the fundraising streams associated with the expedition, Antarctic studies scholar Peter Talbot concluded that "the biggest gifts in kind were related to the transport, the oil/petrol/lubricants from the British Petroleum Company (New Zealand), and also the five tractors loaned from Massey Ferguson Ltd."[15] Images of these products in-situ highlighted the importance of machinery in the period following the Heroic Era of Antarctic exploration. Geopolitics expert Klaus Dodds reflected on these attempts "to create and sustain an Antarctic culture, which built on earlier 'Heroic Era' connections with the polar continent"—this culture is now valuable in its own right.[16] A Tucker Sno-Cat and a Massey Ferguson tractor are now a local attraction, with Christchurch displaying these artifacts from the TAE in the Canterbury Museum and using them to opportunistically support its brand identity as a "Gateway to Antarctica."[17] Massey Ferguson has also reprised its earlier Antarctic connections. In 2016 a Massey Ferguson tractor was driven the length of New Zealand in order to raise the profile of the New Zealand Antarctic Heritage Trust (NZAHT) and to raise funds for the restoration of the TAE hut on Ross Island.[18] This journey was a useful marketing opportunity for the tractor manufacturer as both old and new images of the machine appeared in media coverage of the domestic expedition. Such resurrective branding work demonstrates the commercial value of key expedition anniversaries.

Following the Trans-Antarctic Expedition, facilities on Ross Island were adapted for use during the International Geophysical Year—this saw international scientific cooperation happen around the globe on an unprecedented scale, as scientists from all over the world took part "in a series of coordinated observations of various geophysical phenomena."[19] These observations also took place in the polar regions, and as a result, forty-nine stations were built in the Antarctic.[20] Many sites, including the geographic South Pole, are still operational today. (Amundsen-Scott South Pole Station has been replaced several times, most recently in 2009, but research continues on the same site.) The IGY also had lasting implications in the international policy arena. The international cooperation that had been fostered by the project—even in the midst of the Cold War—was harnessed, both in order to encourage future cooperation and to ensure security in increasingly unstable times. By the late 1950s there were seven countries with territorial claims in the Antarctic (Argentina, Australia, Britain, Chile, France, New Zealand, and Norway), and the twin superpowers of the U.S. and the USSR were also eyeing a slice of the ice. Conflict was headed off with the signing of the Antarctic Treaty in Washington DC on December 1, 1959—Article IV put claims to one side, and the treaty has been in force since June 1961.

The Creative Revolution in Advertising

Changes were also afoot in the advertising industry during the 1950s and 1960s. In the 1950s there were a series of mergers and consolidations in advertising agencies, as customers came to expect a full package of research, package design, publicity, and sales analysis. While advertising was considered a glamorous profession at the time, it was also competitive—and repetitive.[21] According to advertising expert Stephen Fox, in the U.S. context, "a typical 1950s ad repeated a simple theme."[22] This lead the industry magazine *Advertising Age* to lament in 1952 that "too many people are imitating too many other people . . . too many advertisers are 'adapting' instead of creating."[23] The old model of matching copy with an image was about to be disrupted, however, with art and advertising coming together to be celebrated in new ways. As the affective nature of advertising became more apparent, the question of what a product could do or how it might make one feel gained importance.[24] Such changes would usher in advertising's coming of age, as the industry sped toward the baby boomer market and the rise of the consumer movement in the 1960s onward.

In the 1950s, however, there was also a shift in focus from research to instinct-based advertisements, and from baroque and Romantic designs to modernist conventions, marking "a clear break from the kind of selling techniques that had been around since the birth of modern consumer culture in the late nineteenth century."[25] Up until this point, superlative-laden copy had taken precedence over visuals, and the usual process for creating an advertisement resembled an assembly line, with the copywriters completing the text and handing it to the art department for illustration. Bill Bernbach, who was both president and creative director of the 1949 start-up DDB, was central to this change; together with Ned Doyle and Maxwell "Mac" Dane he introduced an innovative new approach that would become known as "new" advertising. Bernbach insisted that copy and image be considered together, with the functions of art and copy integrated into the creative process, and that each advertisement should contain only one main idea. DDB operated on the adage that less is more; this new style of advertisement—one "based in surprise or interruption" that used something unusual to make the viewer stop, look, and take notice—would later see Bernbach credited with being the father of advertising's so-called creative revolution.[26]

The advertisements examined below span this period of revolution and the modern era, with early examples featuring large amounts of text and more recent cases giving precedence to a single image and message. They invoke the theme of extremity in a range of ways, with specific examples examining vehicles, watches, and clothing in situ in the Far South, followed by examples where Antarctica features as an absence.

Going to Remote Places: Braving Antarctica's Chill

Machinery is central to the extremity theme. It is the ability to travel across and over the Antarctic ice at much faster speeds that marks the Mechanical Age—when the extreme endurance and spatial reach of machines came to the fore—from the earlier Heroic Era. Many companies have sent their vehicles down to the coldest, highest, driest, windiest place on earth to prove themselves and their products, and they continue to do so today. In the summer of 2014–15 the Czech car manufacturer Skoda sent a group of Chinese Skoda owners on a cruise to the Antarctic to see the Yeti model (named for the mythical Himalayan snow monster) in action at China's Great Wall Station, while in March 2017 Hyundai sent Ernest Shackleton's great-grandson on a journey across Antarctica in its Endurance model to mark the centenary of the *Endurance* expedition—both instances of placing products in situ in the Antarctic were part of wider advertising campaigns for the brands. There are also a wide range of domestic advertisements for the sorts of servicing products required to keep machinery healthy under extreme conditions. These include Kilfrost antifreeze used in the 1949–52 Norwegian-British-Swedish Antarctic Expedition and the 1955–58 Trans-Antarctic Expedition, as well as the Eveready Preston antifreeze used by Richard Byrd during his expeditions in the 1930s. The branding of extremity is evident where any type of machinery has an Antarctic link; the products were used first in Antarctica, then in advertising.

A 1933 example for Veedol Motor Oil is typical of advertisements for machines used in Antarctica during this Mechanical Age period. The double-page spread includes a large portrait of Byrd on the left and an illustration of the Veedol can on the right, with a link between the Antarctic and America in the title text: "In Little America with Byrd. In Big America with You." The audience is offered the chance to make a connection with the well-known explorer by using the same product—the same strategy used in endorsement advertisements for other products such as the His Masters Voice gramophone and Huntley & Palmers crackers during the earlier Heroic Era. Here, the question posed is "How can you choose more wisely than to choose the identical VEEDOL Motor Oil that Admiral Byrd picked?" Having established the Antarctic credentials of the oil, the advertisement urges viewers to "change today for your winter protection." Safety is also a quality that is sought by automobile owners and is highlighted here via an Antarctic link. The advertisement also draws on an association between Byrd and the oil company around competency, reliability, and trustworthiness. This is a classic example of an advertisement that straddles two themes, calling upon both heroism and extremity to sell a product on the domestic, in this case U.S., market.

Antarctic heroes are not the only figures to feature in Antarctic advertisements for oil and machinery—scientists have also made appearances. In March 1956 an advertisement for Special Energol Visco-Static Motor Oil appeared in *Wheels: Australia's Motor Magazine,* under the headline "The Men of Mawson." This advertisement is unusual as it is one of few examples to feature researchers rather than explorers—the men pictured were all part of the Australian National Antarctic Research Expedition (ANARE). According to the ANARE Club, the picture of the men at Mawson Station was taken on Sunday, January 30, 1955, at the Vestfold Hills. This advertisement is also an early example of a company associating a technical product with a National Antarctic Program—an advertising technique that continues to be used today.

The ANARE men were not public figures, so the heading "Men of Mawson" is useful as a hook, given Douglas Mawson's prominence within Australia. In this case, the endurance and versatility of the product—

Visco-Static Motor Oil—are highlighted thanks to visuals and text that call upon the oil's Australian Antarctic links (the large Australian flag is prominent). The top half of the page is dominated by a photograph of six men and their tent, shown against a backdrop of snow and ice, and the bottom half contains several paragraphs of explanation about both the expedition and the tough conditions under which the oil has performed, as well as a map showing the Australian Antarctic Territory (similar to Shackleton's Bovril endorsement). Given that this advertisement appeared in a motoring magazine, the assumed audience had an existing interest in vehicle maintenance and motoring. They did not need to be told why oil was important but rather convinced that this particular brand of oil was tough and reliable, having been "proven" in the Antarctic.

Like Antarctica, Australia is a continent of desert-like extremes. "The Men of Mawson" advertisement is aimed at an Australian audience, and it assumes the viewer has prior knowledge about both ANARE and the country's previous links to Antarctica. Mawson was, and still is, a well-known figure in Australia, and it was for him that Mawson Station—the first postwar Australian building in Antarctica, built in 1954—was named. In 1956 the station was still very new, and therefore any mention carried novelty value. ANARE was also underway, so there was domestic interest in the topic, and this was intensified by public interest in the scientific activities undertaken by Australia in the lead-up to the IGY. The advertisement coincided with coverage of the upcoming internationally coordinated event but called upon very Australian links to the Antarctic to market the oil. This Australian link is visually reinforced by the fact the men are depicted beneath a fluttering Australian flag positioned at top center, while the advertisement text also bridges the gap between Australia and Antarctica by announcing that the oil advertised is "equally suitable for use in extremes of cold in the Australian Alps, or the very high summer temperatures experienced in Central Australia and Northern Australia," thus naturalizing linkages between two extremes. The advertisement appeals to the domestic Australian market by harnessing two narratives of Antarctica—those of the explorer Mawson and the ANARE at Mawson Station—and translating extreme performance and extreme environments into the domestic Australian context.

VOLKSWAGEN BEETLE: "FIRST CAR AT
THE BOTTOM OF THE WORLD"

During the 1960s a Volkswagen campaign ran in Australia under the headline "The first car at the bottom of the world." This series of advertisements, which appeared when ANARE was looking for cheap, mechanized transport solutions, highlights several elements of the branding extremity theme. First, there is the fact that an Antarctic first was worthy of media attention—even many decades after Scott and Amundsen first reached the geographic South Pole. This attention can in turn be translated into high-profile advertising. In 1963 a Melbourne-made Volkswagen Beetle was taken south to Australia's Mawson Station, becoming "the first production car in the Antarctic."[27] The car, which was dubbed "Antarctica 1" by vw and "The Red Terror" by local scientists, spent one year at Mawson.[28] A reel of 16mm film that was sent south with the car was later edited to make a short film called *Taxi to Rumdoodle*, and the vehicle itself was returned to vw Australia and used for publicity purposes after its season south.[29] The iconic vehicle toured around Australia, and advertisements featuring the car appeared in the pages of newspapers and magazines, such as *Life* and *Women's Weekly*. One such advertisement includes a photograph of the polar Beetle heading off toward an icy horizon along with the caption "First car in Antarctica." Here, ideas of precedence met those of toughness: man vs. wild transforms into machine vs. wild, and the vehicle's survival under tough and icy conditions became a strong endorsement for the product; this is despite the fact that the Australian target consumers were regularly driving in conditions a good fifty degrees warmer. The in-house *vwA Review* explained in June 1963 how "Antarctica proves once again the known Volkswagen reputation for quality, reliability, and durability."[30] Extremity is key here; given that extreme machinery is needed in an extreme environment, vw used an Antarctic theme across all advertising platforms in order to "bring home the point that the Volkswagen is, of course, the only car that can handle Antarctica."[31] The vw was not the first car in Antarctica at all—other motor vehicles taken south included Ernest Shackleton's Arrol Johnston Motor Car in 1907 and Hubert Wilkins's Baby Austin in 1927—but because vw was the first to publicly claim this honor in an advertising campaign, the accolade has stuck.

At the time these advertisements appeared, any negative connotations of a car (and therefore pollution) intruding into the pristine wilderness of Antarctica were not widespread. Even today, media studies experts Gill Branston and Ray Stafford remind readers that "television car ads often work by showing speeding cars in pristine natural landscapes—pristine because they're devoid of other cars and their polluting results."[32] This idea of a place devoid of vehicles proved valuable for Chrysler in 1994 when a satellite view of the continent allowed the car manufacturer to reference the ozone hole and, as cultural studies scholar Elena Glasberg explains, to "[extract] value from Antarctica without leaving a single step on the continent itself."[33] Advertisements that show icy backgrounds, however, are scrutinized more these days, in the age of the Anthropocene, when the human contributions to climate change are better understood. The 2015 Volkswagen emissions scandal that erupted when it became apparent that CO_2 emissions from general vehicle use differed from the emissions measured in official tests is an example of the high-profile nature of any environmental damage by corporations—direct or indirect.[34] In an era where environmental protection is paramount, the contemporary juxtaposition of machinery with an Antarctic landscape carries echoes of the extremity theme but can also evoke a different response, bringing environmental questions to the fore. This accounts in part for the gradual diminishment of these kinds of car-related advertisements after the environmental movement gained prominence through the 1980s. That Antarctica remains an attractive setting in some cases, such as for Skoda or Hyundai, links to both wider advertising trends, such as advertisements showcasing suvs in "spectacular and remote locations," and shows how the various framings of Antarctica overlay rather than replace one another.[35]

Antarctic advertisements do not necessarily need to include images taken down south—in many instances the language used is enough to place the image's supposed location. This is particularly true in the twenty-first century, when stock images mean polar scenes are only ever a mouse click away. The use of north polar scenes to stand in for the south has a long history, however. The most circulated images of Amundsen after his return from the South Pole depicted him not in the Antarctic but posed for publicity purposes in a fjord near his home outside Oslo.

A similar geographic shift is also present in the 1960s vw campaign: the original Antarctic scenes that first appeared in right-hand drive Australian vw advertisements were later recreated in the Arctic, to provide imagery for advertisements in the left-hand drive context of the United States. These advertisements also ran under the tagline "first car at the bottom of the world," alluding to the Antarctic vw, and made no mention of the fact the photographs were staged.[36] Indeed, it is minor details such as the orientation of the roof racks that give away the fact that the car in the U.S. advertisements is not the same vehicle as that used in both the Antarctic and the Australian advertisements.[37] Nevertheless, these versions had widespread penetration across the United States, illustrated by a passage in VW enthusiasts Dave Long and Phil Matthew's *Knowing Australian Volkswagens*: "In 1969, when a party of American scientists first visited the Australians at Mawson, they admitted to their hosts that, but for the international Antarctic vw publicity, they would not have known Australia maintained a scientific base there."[38] This anecdote demonstrates the power of advertising to permeate popular consciousness and shape the narratives about Antarctica and the various activities that are undertaken on the continent—even when the images shown are not from the continent at all.

While vehicles have played an important role in making Antarctica accessible for humans, smaller-scale technologies have also assisted with exploration and commercial development. Appliances such as typewriters and sewing machines made domestic life easier for early explorers, and their ability to withstand the cold of the South proved to be a lucrative marketing strategy. In 1912 Singer, which was then the world's seventh largest company, placed a sewing machine advertisement in the *Strand* magazine under the headline "The 'Singer' in the Antarctic." With no women in Antarctica at this point, the men took on tasks that were traditionally coded as feminine, such as cooking, cleaning, and sewing. The layout of the photograph that dominates the advertisement carries echoes of a familiar domestic scene, with the accompanying text all that places it on the faraway continent. According to the advertisement, the machines were selected for such a remote expedition "because they are the best."[39]

Out in the field, binoculars, radios, and voice recorders have helped expeditioners record data and to uncover and disseminate new information about the continent itself. The makers of such products were often eager to capitalize on this Antarctic connection, as Byrd's appearance in advertisements for Carol Zeiss binoculars and the General Electric All-Wave Radio can attest. Watches, too, are of particular interest in the Far South, both for their practical use and for advertising purposes. Watch advertisements in particular have drawn upon their polar connections; the links between ice, time, extremity, and Antarctica go far deeper than any explorer's simple desire to know the hour.

Freezing Time: Watches and Extreme Environments

Antarctica is often described as a timeless place, where the history of the planet remains "frozen."[40] Recent drilling missions, such as the Australian Aurora Basin drilling project, have shown how the thousands of years of ice layers in the Antarctic hold traces of past atmosphere and can act as an archive of the past.[41] In a tale that would be at home inside the pages of science fiction novel, tardigrades from Antarctica have defied time by thawing and coming back to life after having been frozen for over thirty years.[42] On the personal level, time can take on a different dimension for those who find themselves in the Antarctic. Literary scholar Elizabeth Leane has written about the unique spatiality of Antarctica, noting that "its isolation, its position on the 'bottom' of the world, its seemingly limitless icescape—produces a complex and contradictory temporality."[43] As an accurate clock is needed to correctly ascertain longitude, losing track of time can also result in losing track of space when out on the vast polar plateau. Phenomena like whiteouts and twenty-four-hour daylight can make it difficult to keep track of time, and there are many reported cases of insomnia or changes in circadian rhythms.[44] Under these conditions, it is particularly important to be able to tell the time accurately. Luckily there has been no shortage of watch manufacturers eager to see their brands ticking through the seconds and days among the snows of the South.

Watch advertisements regularly feature imagery of extreme environments such as alpine summits and activities such as deep-sea diving, flying, and polar exploration. In many cases, watch manufacturers seek a link with the polar regions because of their associations with extremity, heroism, and masculinity. A June 8, 1957, advertisement in the *New*

York Times for the Croton Nivada Grenchen Antarctic watch leverages its south polar links, with the headline, "This is the watch that went to the Antarctic." The watch itself is pictured on the right side, while the left half of the advertisement is dominated by an image of a bearded man, in polar clothing, lighting a cigarette with his watch-adorned right hand. The advertisement copy goes on to specify that its Antarctic link came through Admiral Byrd and Operation Deepfreeze, and it describes how the watch was "snowed on, rained on, sleeted on. It was never wound. It was dropped, hit and knocked against ice. It lived in zig-zagging temperatures—from 100 above to 40 below. *And it never lost a second.*" This is a classic case of a product being advertised through the "as used in Antarctica" trope; the extreme nature of the Antarctic environment is invoked as an ultimate testing ground, and the fact that the watch continued to tell the time accurately throughout the expedition is used as a testimonial to its quality.

The Croton advertisement associates the watch with the Antarctic and masculinity, thanks to the image of the bearded explorer and the language used. The text concludes with an assertion, "We don't know a father or son who wouldn't be proud to own it." Watches often become family heirlooms, passed down the paternal line from father to son. This advertisement is selling not just a watch, then, but a way to maintain the patriarchal status quo by continuing such an inheritance tradition. It also offers the promise of a particular image—one characterized by toughness and resilience. The Antarctic watch becomes a badge of manhood, thanks to its associations with Antarctic exploration and its performance in the extreme conditions of the south polar region. Those who purchase the timepiece are not only buying a watch, they are buying into a mythology of masculinity and extremity cemented by the product's Antarctic name and links.

The luxury watch brand Rolex and its long association with the polar regions and other extreme expeditions further demonstrates the trans-geographical economy of coldness and highness. A Rolex timepiece accompanied Hillary to the summit of Mount Everest in 1953 and was advertised in the November 17, 1954, issue of *Punch Magazine* under the heading "Everest Leader's Tribute to Rolex." Modern-day watches have traveled to both the South and North Poles with explorers Erling Kagge,

Rune Gjeldnes, and Alain Hubert, who subsequently appear in advertisements for the brand. These associated advertisements, such as the September 1987 *National Geographic Magazine* full-page spread "Where to spend the worst winter in the world" call upon both the extremity of the polar conditions encountered and the tough nature of the men who triumphed under those conditions in order to craft a similar image for the Rolex watches. Such advertisements employ words like "impossible," "rugged," and "explorer," and the language is complemented by images of ice and of lone figures man-hauling sleds across crevasses or white expanses. This imagery immediately evokes the Heroic Era narratives discussed previously—as does the advertisement's title, which refers to Apsley Cherry-Garrard's account of the *Terra Nova* expedition, *The Worst Journey in the World*. Rather than focus solely on man versus nature, however, this example sees the battle between the technologically advanced chronometer and the extreme conditions of the Antarctic take center stage. The advertorial style layout adds weight to Rolex's Antarctic connection, while the inset map adds a scientific air to the promotional piece.

Antarctic branding tropes are employed to weave a mythology around the Rolex product and imbue it with similar qualities to those associated with explorers who traverse the unexplored ice of Antarctica: extremity, toughness, hardship, reliability, tradition, loyalty, and survival.

Surviving the Ice: Clothing and Shelter

With monthly mean temperatures falling below -60° Celsius (-76° Fahrenheit) in winter in the continent's interior, cold weather is a key challenge that must be overcome to ensure survival.[45] The presence of a building, or provision of appropriate attire, can easily mean the difference between life and death. There are many straightforward examples of clothing and building products that have been used in Antarctica and subsequently marketed as being hardy. From jackets to tents to insulation and fiberboard, these follow a branding narrative similar to the vehicles and oils in the previous section. In other cases, companies have created either a physical or a symbolic a link with Antarctica because of the continent's extreme connotations. Whether a product's initial Antarctic link is physical or conceptual, the fact remains that in a subzero context, bodily extremities must be protected. Therefore, building materials and clothing used in Antarctica have subsequently appeared in advertisements back home: a product's physical presence in Antarctica can serve as testimony to its extreme credentials and highlights the importance of expeditionary endorsement.

FROM HOMASOTE TO HOLLAND'S:
CONSTRUCTION IN ANTARCTICA

A 1935 advertisement for Homasote "all-weather all-purpose building board" used its presence in Antarctica during Admiral Byrd's first and second Antarctic expeditions to highlight the tough nature of the material. The headline "And after six years" leads into a paragraph about Byrd returning to Little America on his second expedition, where he "broke thru the ice and snow and found his former houses as good as the day they were built." The advertisement is pinned on the claim that "Homasote withstands the most extreme weather conditions, high winds and hard rains." Three images in the top half of the advertisement—one of men excavating snow from around old structures and the other two of buildings in the Antarctic—visually support the narrative of returning and of toughness in the face of extreme conditions. Such connections to Byrd and the Antarctic are still used today by the Homasote company, whose website includes a copy of a 1947 letter from Radio Engineer Amory H. Waite Jr., who exclaimed "when other wallboards would have pulped, cracked or dissolved, Homasote remained firm and trustworthy insulation against blizzards and temperatures of minus 75!"[46] The ability to withstand polar conditions is an accolade that continues to carry weight and capture the imaginations of customers.

Antarctica has become more accessible over the intervening decades, and technology has advanced considerably, but the need for infrastructure for human habitation remains. For the companies that construct such buildings, mention of the Antarctic can be a point of interest for investors, employees, and the public alike. In August 2015 the Hillary Field Centre, located at New Zealand's Scott Base on Ross Island, was the focus of a promotional piece that appeared in the Firth Industries New Zealand staff newsletter under the headline "Holland's Solves the Problem in Antarctica." The full-page advertisement—targeted specifically at internal staff members—aimed to showcase the company's work in the unusual and difficult conditions of the Antarctic and included a large color image of "pavers being laid in the hangar—quite the task at -40 degrees." Much is made of the low temperatures throughout the text, with the opening line explaining "construction in temperatures of -40 degrees is never easy." In preparation for the polar conditions, "sands were kiln dried to provide the lowest moisture content possible." This process also had the effect of sterilizing the sand, "therefore protecting the Antarctic environment." Unlike the earlier advertisements for building materials that focused solely on the tough and technologically advanced nature of the product, this example also mentions the minimalization of environmental impacts; indeed, the rhetoric of extremity and that of environmental protection are presented hand in hand. The ability to complete a refit of the Hillary Field Centre in -40°C temperatures and without causing harm to the surrounding environment, becomes a triumph of logistics that speaks to the ability of the contracting company to find innovative solutions to extremely difficult problems. With a number of National Antarctic Programs currently undertaking research station renewals, this dual branding rhetoric of extremity and protection could be expected to make further appearances in marketing materials from the companies associated with the new builds and to be picked up by sponsoring states keen to showcase their environmental credentials.

THRIVING IN EXTREMES: CLOTHING FOR THE COLD

New Zealand has a long history of involvement in Antarctic expeditions, thanks to its location directly north of the much-explored Ross Sea region. A number of local companies have used such links in domestic advertising campaigns. The Christchurch-based clothing company Earth Sea Sky, which has drawn upon both past and present Antarctic connections in order to raise the profile of the brand, is one example. The company was started in 1990 by David Ellis, whose father, Murray Ellis, was a member of the 1957–58 TAE, in the party led by Sir Edmund Hillary. David Ellis's grandfather, Roland Murray, began the family's association with the manufacture of cold-weather equipment when he started to make down-filled sleeping bags in 1927. Upon being awarded a contract to supply the National Antarctic Program, David Ellis was quoted in an Antarctica New Zealand 2009 press release as saying, "Our family has been involved in supplying polar clothing and equipment to Antarctica New Zealand for the past 50 years. Having the opportunity to continue the association is a great honour for us."[47] Earth Sea Sky has drawn upon these gencrational and historical connections to Antarctic exploration in several advertising campaigns. These include a full-page advertisement from 1997 that features Hillary, a 2014 display-stand image profiling "56 years hands-on experience," and a 2014 in-store poster under the header "We've got history." In this case, the use of an Antarctic narrative serves to back up the company's tagline: "Made in New Zealand to perform in Extremes." The link with Hillary makes this advertisement similar to earlier examples of endorsements, but the company's association with Antarctica is not only a thing of the past.

Earth Sea Sky has more recent links to the southern continent, as it has been the official clothing supplier for the New Zealand's National Antarctic Program since 2009. A 2014 poster, displayed in the store and at the Antarctica New Zealand conference highlights this connection. Assertions in the text showcase the brand's track record in the Far South and call strongly upon Antarctica's associations with extremity: the advertisement opens with the line, "From years of experience we have found there is no better place in the world to test outdoor clothing than the frozen lands of Antarctica" (figure 13). That a National Antarctic Program chooses this clothing is used here as an endorsement of quality. This is an example of the modern-day scientist, or science agency, taking on the role of the Heroic Era explorer. Rather than a single celebrity providing an endorsement, it is Antarctica New Zealand's decision to use the brand that speaks to the quality. This Earth Sea Sky advertisement closes with the line, "The new Antarctica New Zealand wardrobe is at the cutting edge of Extreme Cold Weather (ecw) clothing design." The familiar implication is that if the clothing stands up to the Antarctic conditions encountered during Antarctica New Zealand's expeditions, it will be more than capable of performing well in all other circumstances.

While companies like Earth Sea Sky and Homasote called upon existing Antarctic connections to market their products, other brands have forged an association with the continent precisely because of its evocation of all things extreme. In late 2012, The North Face sought to create a connection between its new Steep Series clothing line and Antarctica

PERFORMANCE DRIVEN DESIGN

From years of experience we have found there is no better place in the world to test outdoor clothing than the frozen lands of Antarctica.

It took over 12 months to redesign and modify Antarctica New Zealand's latest wardrobe. Seven garments create a functional layering system to give the wearer the versatility required to cope with varying physical activities, low ambient temperatures and extreme wind chill factors.

There are three main layering zones - next to skin base layers for comfort and hygiene, mid layers for warmth and outer layers for wind protection. For maximum comfort and thermal efficiency the layers must transfer moisture away from the body and for ease of movement they must be able to slide unimpeded.

The new Antarctica New Zealand wardrobe is at the cutting edge of Extreme Cold Weather clothing design.

Earth Sea Sky Specialised Outdoor Clothing
MADE IN NEW ZEALAND
DESIGNED TO PERFORM
BUILT TO LAST

EARTH SEA SKY

Antarctica New Zealand

www.earthseasky.co.nz

FIG 13. Earth Sea Sky banner, 2014. Courtesy of Earth Sea Sky.

for this very reason. In preparation for the product launch, the company sponsored a monthlong expedition (November 21–December 21, 2012) to the Antarctic in which snowboarders Xavier de La Rue and Lucas Debari took to the slopes of the Antarctic Peninsula. Their exploits were extensively filmed for the *Mission Antarctic* movie, which was sponsored by The North Face and Swatch, and photographed for use in The North Face's Fall 2013 advertising campaign. The final 2013 campaign featured a series of images of extreme snow sports, with athletes pictured in both Alaska and Antarctica. All three advertisements have the same layout, with a product foregrounded on the left-hand side, an athlete dwarfed by surrounding ice on the right, and the caption "Conquer the Unknown. Never Stop Exploring." In one example, de La Rue is shown hurtling down the face of a glacier in Antarctica. Overshadowed by the wall of ice, the diminutive de La Rue is positioned three-quarters of the way across the advertisement and stands out only because of his yellow trousers. The image echoes both the yellow in the Steep Series jacket that is pictured on the left of the advertisement and the yellow font used for the tagline "Never Stop Exploring." The sport of snowboarding may be a far cry from the man-hauling ski marathons of a hundred years earlier, but the idea of attaining a "first" still holds allure, and the concept of pushing the body to extremes in an extreme environment remains similar. All three advertisements boldly urge viewers to "Conquer The Unknown," with the help of The North Face technical gear.

The story behind this North Face advertisement is just as important—if not more so—than the final image that was used in the advertising campaign. Traveling to the ends of the earth to partake in the extreme sport of snowboarding under the most extreme conditions is one way of creating a narrative association between a brand and the ideas of toughness and extremity. It also offered a way to engage potential customers, as the expedition blog was hosted by The North Face and regular updates and images from the Antarctic were posted under the company's branding. The theme of extremity also comes through in the advertisement's very minimal text: the line of clothing was dubbed the "All new steep series. Trusted technical gear for extreme mountain riding." Nestled in the bottom right-hand corner, beneath The North Face logo and Steep Series stamp, the fine print reads: "Extreme can't be tested in a lab. That's why the roughest possible conditions of Antarctica were necessary to perfect technology in the Sickline Jacket." Antarctica is understood to offer the epitome of cold, icy, dangerous, and extreme conditions. So, too, is Alaska—in the two Alaska examples, "Antarctica" is replaced with "Alaska," but the messaging remains the same. Only extreme athletes can manage such conditions, but—as the advertisement makes clear, thanks to the foregrounding of a technical jacket—they did so with the support of "trusted technical gear" that is also available to consumers back home.

What is for sale is gear, but also, implicitly, de La Rue's narrative of adventure, extremity, and exploration. By purchasing a Summit Series item, the consumer is also buying into a mythology of extremes and of going where no one has gone before—or so one is lead to think.

Continent Number 7: Collecting the Set

Antarctica's remoteness and inhospitable climate make it a difficult place to reach, putting it out of the grasp of most. For those who have the time, means, and desire to travel to Antarctica, however, the opportunity exists to visit the seventh continent and "collect the set." After Africa, Asia, Australia, Europe, North America, and South America, Antarctica is all that remains. The phenomenon of Antarctic tourism is examined in more detail in chapter 7, but the desire to create a tangible association with the far-flung reaches of the world has manifested itself in other, more unexpected ways. In 1961, Abbott, manufacturers of the anesthetic Pentothal, expanded their global postcard campaign to the Antarctic. Having decided that the Australian Wilkes Station represented an exotic destination from which to advertise the worldwide availability of their drug, the company addressed 280,000 postcards to doctors around the world and sent them south on the ship *Magga Dan* to be "cancelled" at the Antarctic station. While the postcards may seem innocuous on a smaller scale, the large workload they created (280,000 of 286,000 items mailed from Wilkes that year) resulted in mailing restrictions being put in place from Australian Antarctic stations and limiting any similar campaigns in the future.[48]

One side featured a photograph of the station, while the other explained that "doctors here demand—and get—the utmost in dependability and safety in their medical supplies." The idea behind the campaign was to "send cards from faraway romantic places, to reinforce the idea that Pentothal was the world's best intravenous anesthetic."[49] Antarctica was an ideal location from which to send such postcards because it was both remote and unexpected—the presence of Pentothal on the continent created an association that made the brand name worth remembering. The postcards have since become collectibles, with anesthesiologist David Lai's 2005 collection, *Pentothal Postcards*, showcasing the range of exotic locations where Pentothal was available. This collection puts Antarctica alongside Copenhagen, Kuala Lumpur, and Punta Arenas; Antarctica is caught up in an international network of exotic places and drawn into a world of global commerce.

This notion of Antarctica as "the last continent" has also been used to market events and concepts. Each year there are expeditions that head south with the specific goal of summiting Vincent Massif, the tallest mountain in Antarctica, which allows climbers to join the 7 Summits Club. For those who prefer distance running, there is always the option of joining the 7 Continents Marathon Club by running a race south of the Antarctic Circle; in the 2019–20 season 317 tourists traveled to Antarctica for this purpose.[50] Around the fringes of the continent, it is not uncommon to see Antarctic tourists posing for photographs in front of a hand-made sign bearing the number 7. For many adventurous world travelers—particularly those involved in extreme sports—the prospect of climbing, running, camping, skiing, or even just setting foot upon the Antarctic continent continues to hold allure.

PERFORMING THE BRAND: METALLICA AND COKE ZERO

On December 8, 2013, Metallica became the first band to perform on all seven continents within a twelve-month period. The Antarctic concert, entitled Freeze 'Em All, took place in a heliport at the Argentinian Carlini Base on King George Island and was attended by a select audience of 120 revelers.[51] The Metallica concert in Antarctica links to the theme of extremity, with the band collecting a full set of continents—the musicians sought to be "the first and only band in history to perform concerts on all seven continents in under a year!"[52] The performance also speaks to the theme of fragility, because in order to achieve the band's aim, it was necessary to travel to Antarctica before it became politically unpopular to do so on account of the human impact. An awareness of this element is demonstrated by the band's use of solar panels during the performance as an eco-friendly gesture. Concertgoers also wore silent disco-style earphones to create minimal disturbances for the wildlife, including nesting penguins. Responding to the demands of the Madrid Protocol, a 180-page environmental impact assessment (EIA) was carried out prior to the concert. In a nod to growing public concerns over impacts, this EIA was also highlighted in the Metallica press release, "Journey to the Bottom of the Earth."[53]

The idea of striving to have zero impact on the Antarctic environment was reinforced by the brand of the main sponsor—Coke Zero. The concert was known as the Musicá Zero project, while promotional images depicted the iconic Metallica brand name superimposed over an icy scene, with the Coca-Cola Zero logo in the bottom center. In this instance, the zero refers to a particular line of Coca-Cola products containing zero sugar. In the context of the polar imagery, however, the word "zero" also elicits associations with cold temperatures and frozen ice. Partnering the Coke Zero brand with the Metallica concert was therefore a carefully considered decision, carrying connotations of zero temperatures, zero sugar, zero impact, and zero precedent.

While Metallica fans were enjoying the band's southernmost concert, Oceanwide—the company that carried that audience south on board the *Ortelius*—was busy highlighting the positive implications of the tour. Oceanwide's CEO Michel van Gessel spoke of the concert as "a fantastic opportunity to create awareness for Antarctica as one of the very last, pristine wildernesses on our planet." Employing the protection-through-knowledge rhetoric of many tourism providers, he claimed that the concert would "promote the uniqueness of the Polar Regions and Metallica and their fans will become ambassadors of Antarctica."[54] The view that tourism creates ambassadors for a place, and that "operators can educate tourists regarding issues important to the conservation of Antarctica" is widespread throughout the tourism industry.[55] Indeed, the International Association of Antarctica Tour Operators (IAATO) lists creating "a corps of ambassadors for the continued protection of Antarctica by offering the opportunity to experience the continent first hand" as one of its objectives.[56] The icy continent is therefore a place for education, wildlife, and protection and a place of extremes, where "firsts" continue to be prized. Antarctica carries numerous symbolic resonances and can be employed in support of diverse messages and agendas; indeed, it is a place where contradictions thrive.

Value in Absence: Where Airlines Don't Go

Most people will never travel to Antarctica, but this fact is valuable in its own right because it allows companies and brand managers to use the ice as an absent counterpoint to their extensive offerings. The idea of Antarctica as an absence has been used to market several airlines; Alitalia, Pan Am, and British Airways have all invoked Antarctica as the one place they do not go. For instance, British Airways ran a 1990 campaign under the headline "Our apologies to the inhabitants of the one continent we don't serve" to promote the wide range of destinations they did service. The headline of a 1965 Alitalia advertisement reads similarly: "The only continent Alitalia doesn't fly to." The Antarctic link is created by the accompanying image, which shows a colony of Adélie penguins on the shore with a background of ice. Penguins function as shorthand for Antarctica, ensuring that the viewer understands which continent is referred to at first glance. For those who read further, the small print under the image makes this link explicit, while contrasting the offering of other destinations with the cold, uninhabited, and extreme environment of the Far South: "It isn't that we don't like Antarctica. But we Italians have always been interested in warmer things. Like good food. Comfort. And travelling in style to far-off places." The extreme inhospitality of Antarctica is used as a counterpoint to the comfortable, warm experience promised by the airline Alitalia. The target audience of this advertisement is affluent, as the advertisement appeared in *Fortune* magazine. They are expected to want to travel to places like London, New York, and Hawaii, not to the frozen ends of the earth. As a result, the final line of the advertisement urges the viewer to "Ask your travel agent about Alitalia service, but don't ask us to take you to Antarctic. It's too cold."

The American airline company Pan Am ran a similar Antarctic campaign ten years after Alitalia. An example from 1976 features a remarkably similar image of Adélie penguins against an icy backdrop and carries the tagline "It's easier to remember where we don't go." The campaign

appeared on television and in magazines and newspapers and was promoted on flights via flight attendants' badges.[57] Although this advertisement also uses Antarctica as the exception to the available routes, the
Pan Am advertisement includes commentary on the fluid demands of
its customers. The small print begins with a tongue-in-cheek offering of
"Our apologies to the Antarctica Tourist Board" for the fact that there
was still one continent to which Pan Am did not fly. It also carries a caveat
that "Of course, tastes may change radically. In which case, we'll open
Antarctica to air travel . . . And take the apology back and start taking
tourists." Commercial Antarctic tourism was still in its infancy in 1975—
the launching of the Lindblad Explorer in 1969 is seen by many as the
start of commercial Antarctic visits—but the inclusion of this statement
in the airline's advertisement indicates a willingness to change routes
to suit consumer tastes. Antarctica also featured in the Twitter feed of
budget air carrier Ryan Air during the 2020 U.S. presidential election.
In response to Donald Trump Jr.'s electoral map prediction that colored
Antarctica red for Republican, Ryan Air quipped, "If any penguins need to
be flown to Antarctica to vote, please let us know, we can open up a new
route and we're aware you can't fly."[58] In each of these cases Antarctica
figures as an absence but not necessarily a permanent one.

Pan Am's use of penguins, Antarctica, and the tagline "It's easier to
remember where we don't go" is somewhat surprising, given that Pan Am
was one of the only airlines that had actually flown to Antarctica in the
past. On October 15, 1957, a Pan Am Boeing 377 Stratocruiser became the
first commercial aircraft to fly to the continent when it landed at McMurdo
Station, commissioned by the U.S. Navy as part of a resupply mission.[59]
Rear Adm. George J. Dufek suggested that the flight could "provide a
great PR coup for Pan Am" thanks to the element of a first.[60] It did indeed
attract much media attention, not so much because of its status as the
first commercial flight but because of the presence of two female flight
attendants on board—the first women ever to visit McMurdo Station.
Ruth Kelly and Patricia Hepinstall were on the ice for only a matter of
hours, during which time they went for a dog sled ride, enjoyed coffee
in the mess, and judged a beard-growing competition (with prizes for
longest, blackest, reddest, and sexiest), but their presence was contentious.[61] Prior to the visit, Rear Admiral Dufek had been adamant that any

flight attendants would be male, as Antarctica was at that time a bastion of masculinity—a "he-man's world, with beards and toughness."[62] This framing of the place drew strongly upon the theme of extremity, with the assumption that only the hardiest men would be capable of enduring the extreme weather conditions of the Far South, making it harder for Pan Am to take advantage of the flight for branding purposes.

Instead, the allure of Kelly and Hepinstall lay in the human-interest element of their story, which added novelty to the first. In 2009, polar historian Lisbeth Lewander recorded that, when talking of her work on gender and the poles, she was often met with the comment "but there are no women in Antarctica."[63] Women are, in fact, present and have broken records in the Far South to attain their own firsts—for example, in 2013 Maria Leijerstam became the first person to cycle a recumbent bicycle to the South Pole.[64] Despite this, gender politics continues to accompany risk-taking, particularly in the context of extreme sports or polar exploration. Catherine Palmer explains how the discourse of extremity is unquestionably highly gendered, which makes it culturally unacceptable for women to dramatically (or fatally) distinguish themselves from the crowd.[65] In the case of the 1974 Pan Am advertisement, mentioning the Antarctic flight would have been a useful tactic if the airline was trying to capitalize on its history of firsts (or indeed to market itself as a diverse and inclusive brand), but in the context of a target audience with no Antarctic experience, highlighting Antarctica as an absence or lack was a way of creating resonance with a much wider audience.

While Antarctic advertisements that emphasize the frames of heroism and extremity usually feature male figures, there are occasional exceptions. An advertisement for Ray-Ban sunglasses that appeared in June 1959 issue of *National Geographic*, during Operation Deepfreeze is a prime example. The headline gestures both to the tough nature of those sunglasses, and to their desirability beyond Operation Deepfreeze itself; it reads "Proved in the Antarctic—smartly styled for you." In this case, the "you" is represented by a fashionable young woman, dressed in a pink dress and jacket and wearing horn-rimmed sunglasses. She is photographed against the black-and-white background of—as the image caption itself explains—an "Antarctic photograph of man wearing Ray-Ban Sun Glasses, courtesy of the United States Navy." Ray-Ban supplied specially designed sunglasses to the U.S. Navy for the operation to protect men from snow-blindness, but this advertisement adds another layer to the straight "as used in Antarctica" endorsement.[66] It encourages consumers to adapt new technologies that have been proven in the Antarctic and to use them in their own lives at home: "Ray-Ban Sun Glasses give *your* eyes the same fine glare protection, plus the season's most fashionable frame styles and colors." Glare protection is associated with Antarctic extremes—such as the twenty-four-hour daylight experienced on Ross Island during the summer—while the range of fashionable colors and styles are tailored for use back in the States. The female model doesn't belong *in* Antarctica—at this point, the continent was still, as Admiral Reedy put it, a "womanless white continent of peace"—yet she is shown to benefit from technology that has been tested in the extreme environment, then aesthetically altered for the domestic setting.[67] This advertisement therefore opens the door for the trope of Antarctic extremity to be put to a wider range of uses; no longer is value limited to products with an Antarctic connection, but rather the *notion* of extremity can be evoked to market products that differ from their Antarctic predecessors in both style and design.

Antarctic the Extreme

The frame of extremity casts Antarctica as the ultimate testing ground, layered with stories of firsts, of superior machinery, and of masculine endeavor. Many advertisements examined have called upon firsthand links with Antarctic expeditions to market their products—from watches, to clothing, to building materials. These advertisements are predicated on the assumption that—as The North Face puts it—"extreme can't be tested in a lab." Instead, spending time in Antarctica lends an authenticity to any product. Consumers do not need a personal link to Antarctica to be interested in a product advertised in this way. Indeed, communications expert William Leiss and his coauthors note that the "stock-in-trade of advertising is the process of invoking a chain of associations to enchant audiences."[68] In several cases associations with heroism have been used to supplement—and to grant legitimacy to—extremes, with reference made to Heroic Era figures or expeditions. The two ideas are linked, both historically and through a common tendency to call upon tropes of masculinity. Extremity reframes the idea of man versus wild into one of machine versus wild, however, with cars, oil, and sunglasses being used to help expeditioners overcome the harsh conditions of the southern continent. Where any type of machinery has an Antarctic link, the theme of extremity is not far away, and neither is the claim that if a product works in the far southern environment of Antarctica, it will excel under any other circumstances.

This continual drawing on and reinforcement of ideas of extremity has an impact on people's understanding of Antarctica, as it reprises and legitimates notions of the superlative—highest, driest, coldest, windiest. This framing also cements ideas of Antarctic exceptionalism, where the southern continent is set apart from other global systems. This is particularly apparent in the advertisements that play on the absence idea: the gap between Antarctica and a particular product can be used as a selling point. Highlighting Antarctica as an absence or lack creates resonance with a much wider audience, but it has also functioned to reinforce ideas of exclusivity (such as the notion that the continent is off-limits to women). As of 2022, the rapid acceleration of anthropogenic climate change, which has a particularly strong impact on the polar regions, has, as literary scholar Hester Blum observes, "rendered the atmospheric state of the planet itself extreme."[69] Extremity is therefore a complex and multifaceted theme that has manifested itself in a range of ways over the past century. Companies that activate this theme in advertising do so to offer their customers the chance to buy into a mythology of extremes; they offer the chance to become part of boundary-pushing product innovations or—vicariously—record-breaking expeditions, and all from the comfort of their home countries. These advertisements, therefore, illustrate how it is possible to buy into Antarctic narratives of the extreme without risking frostbite or heading to the ends of the earth oneself. After all, Antarctica is—as Alitalia put it—"too cold" for that.

Purifying Antarctica 4

Clean, Wild, and
Untouched

How do you halt time to a glacial pace in order to maintain a pure and fresh complexion? Look no further than the glycoprotein antarcticine, the key ingredient in the skin care cream Antarctilyne. The cream, which was promoted in Australia by Skin Doctors throughout 2005, contains a glycoprotein produced by the bacterial strain *Pseudoalteromonas Antarctica*.[1] Discovered at the bottom of a glacier in Admiralty Bay in 1988 by scientists from the University of Barcelona, the bacteria has gone on to have a commercial life of its own far from the ice. The skin cream is a prime example of a commercial product that both has its roots in biological prospecting and calls upon its Antarctic associations by activating the purity theme. Promotional material for the cosmetic product focuses on this connection, describing how "Antarcticine is produced by an extremophile—a 'survival' molecule which actually thrives in extreme conditions. And it doesn't get more extreme than Antarctica. Yet Antarcticine has survived for millions of years. If Antarcticine is so resilient, so powerful that it can survive in such extreme conditions—just imagine what it could do for your skin!"[2] This advertising pitch speaks directly to the myth of purity, endurance, and the cult of youth, evoking ideas of glacial beauty and of time standing still, thus implying that this product can halt time, preserving unblemished youth.[3]

Antarctilyne is not the only skin cream product to use Antarctic purity as a selling point; Kiehl's Ultra Facial Cream uses penguin and iceberg imagery to advertise the cryoprotective properties of Antarcticine; Pure Altitude's Pure Antarctica Serum also includes Antarcticine for "protection against dehydration and the cold" while Leejiham's Antarctic Cream, which has also been advertised against a backdrop of penguins and ice, contains the microorganism *P. Antarctica*.[4] Promotional material for these skin care products draws upon existing symbols and connotations to market a product by both highlighting a physical Antarctic link and capitalizing on existing Antarctic marketing tropes, including that of Antarctica as a pure and untouched frozen wilderness, unsullied by human interference.

The cultural resonances of the term "pure" demand further investigation, especially as they have been applied in the context of Antarctica. The word "pure" carries a range of meanings—it can be used to denote that something is unmixed, free of contamination, or untainted by immorality; to refer to a pedigree; or to describe the study of abstract concepts, rather than practical applications—and all these have been applied in the Far South.[5] While Antarctica is often depicted as a tabula rasa, it has a complex and often murky human history, including elements of nationalism, exploration, geopolitics, commercialization, and environmental protection. Constructing Antarctica as clean or pure therefore intersects with the continent's exclusionary history and notions of race, gender, and science; for much of its documented history, Antarctica has been the domain of able-bodied white men. In framing the polar regions as clean, untouched, and ripe for claiming, Heroic Era attitudes to exploration were underpinned by the notion of purity in precedence. As essayist Annie Dillard notes, this purity was attractive to the early polar explorers who "set out to perform clear tasks in uncontaminated lands."[6] When the Heroic Era gave way to the post–Antarctic Treaty idea of a "continent for peace and science" the idea of knowledge-driven purity translated readily into the new branding frame, with scientific inquiry replacing geographical exploration. Science itself is implicated in debates about purity, with the term "pure science" used to differentiate between theoretical and applied research. The purity frame also elides the dubious waste management practices of Antarctic science, including leaving rubbish on the sea ice.[7] Much Antarctic research is characterized as "pure science," but this label is misleading, as neither the work nor the ice of Antarctica where it is conducted exist in a cultural vacuum. Rather, the protection that is currently afforded to the Far South was negotiated within a context that places particular value on wilderness values and minimal human impacts.

It is a paradox that many products that have been taken from Antarctica—including proteins, krill, and ice itself—are promoted using the notions of the place as an untouched landscape. This chapter outlines key protection instruments under the Antarctic Treaty System (ATS), contextualized within wider environmental movements. It then examines advertisements from 1933 to 2016 to demonstrate how Antarctica's association with purity has been co-opted to promote everything from soap to alcohol. Notions first of cleanliness and then purity have been used in advertising material to market products with an Antarctic association. The distinction is important: "clean" suggests a domestic or human context, while "pure" has natural connotations and is closely linked to the idea of wilderness. The idea of cleanliness is more prevalent in the earlier years of the twentieth century, emerging in several advertisements related to Admiral Richard Byrd's second expedition, while purity has been used extensively in the twenty-first century, often in conjunction with the idea of environmental protection. Representation also depends on the available technology.

Thus, in the first half of the twentieth century, the emphasis was on efficiency in cleaning, but color photography and computer-generated imagery have allowed the purity theme to be used very easily in a symbolic way as polar landscapes can be conjured with the click of a button. Branding products as "Antarctic" and transferring connotations of "pure" onto these has become easier, even as the actual purity of the continent has come under question.

Protecting and Branding Antarctica as Wilderness

The framing of Antarctica as a pure and untouched wilderness owes much to the ATS and the way it has responded to challenges over its six-decade history. New instruments have been negotiated as concerns have been raised over various human activities in the Far South. These include the Agreed Measures for the Conservation of Antarctic Fauna and Flora (1964), which was the first attempt at prioritizing environmental protection within the ATS, and the Convention for the Conservation of Antarctic Seals (1972), which provided specific protection for a species that had previously been heavily impacted by sealing. In the marine realm, the 1982 Convention on the Conservation of Antarctic Marine Life (CAMLR Convention) was established in response to commercial interest in the krill fishery, with the objective to conserve Antarctic marine life south of the Antarctic convergence. This convention established the Commission for the Conservation of Marine Living Resources (CCAMLR), which oversees catch limits in the convention area and is advised by the scientific committee (SC-CAMLR). Although CCAMLR recognizes that the term "conservation" includes rational use; the conservation aspect is intended to protect the "pure" environments of the Far South and place limits on human use. However, that very protection can make commercial connections with the place all the more valuable; as examples in this chapter show, the association of several marine products with the perceived purity of the Far South where they are harvested becomes a key selling point.

The Antarctic continent has also been the subject of debate about wider human use of the region. During the 1980s, there was both a growing push for exploitation of Antarctica for the benefit of all nations and a counter push to see the continent set aside as a World Park. Anxieties over the imminent use of mineral resources, including chromium, nickel, gold, and coal, led to the drafting of the Convention on the Regulation of Antarctic Mineral Resource Activities (CRAMRA).[8] Concluded on June 2, 1988, CRAMRA was intended to provide a framework for the future extraction of such resources while ensuring "that Antarctic mineral resource activities, should they occur, are compatible with scientific investigation in Antarctica and other legitimate uses of Antarctica" and noting "the unique ecological, scientific and wilderness value of Antarctica and the importance of Antarctica to the global environment."[9] The same anxieties that led to the initial discussions, however, meant that the convention was never ratified. As a result of both growing political interest and publicized activism on the ice—the Greenpeace World Park Base 1987–1992 is one example—more people became aware of the importance of the continent.[10] The turn away from CRAMRA can therefore be attributed in part to the efforts of NGOs and other key actors to brand Antarctica as somewhere wild and untouched—and unmined.

Writing in 1991 about his trek across Antarctica, explorer Reinhold Messner articulated his desire "to demonstrate the wilderness of Antarctica, its beauty [and] to point to the problems of its development, exploitation and division." At the time, he saw the desire to mine mineral resources as the greatest threat to Antarctica, claiming "so long as no one really knows the commercial value of the continent, a world park can still be enforced."[11] There had by this time been multiple calls to establish a World Park in Antarctica, administered by all nations rather than the ATS. This World Park concept was championed by the Antarctic and Southern Ocean Coalition (ASOC), which formed as an amalgamation of over two hundred environmental groups, including high profile organizations such as Greenpeace and the World Wildlife Fund.[12] At the same time, political support for an alternative Antarctic governing system was being voiced, spearheaded by developing nations unhappy with the status quo. This faction wanted to see Antarctic resources used "for the benefit of all mankind," rather than a privileged few—this notion of "common heritage of mankind" is also present in the 1982 United Nations Convention on the Law of the Sea (UNCLOS) and 1962 Declaration of Legal Principles Governing the Activities of States in the Exploration and Use of Outer Space, placing Antarctica in a similar category to the high seas and space.[13] In a 1982 speech to the United Nations General Assembly, Malaysian prime minister Dr. Mahathir bin Mohamad argued that the existing ATS privileged a small number of states and suggested, unsuccessfully, that the United Nations should take over the administration of the continent.[14] While Antarctica remained a hot topic at the UN for the next twenty years, the question of resource extraction was settled much more quickly. By 1988 a convention that would allow mining under strict conditions was not deemed compatible with the environmental values of public opinion, particularly in Australia and France. Instead, fears of resource exploitation and environmental degradation led to the drafting and signing of the Protocol on Environmental Protection to the Antarctic Treaty (Madrid Protocol) in 1991. As historian Andrew Jackson details in Who Saved Antarctica?, "a regime regulating hypothetical activities," CRAMRA, was "replaced by a regime prohibiting hypothetical activities."[15] Antarctica was therefore rebranded as a pure wilderness, apart from the rest of world—a place in need of protection.

The Madrid Protocol, which has no expiration date, came into force on January 14, 1998, and brought protection to the fore of Antarctic discourse and practice. The protocol includes a prohibition on mineral resource activities, except scientific research (article 7), unless and until any review of the protocol is undertaken and a new convention to permit mining is established and in force. The Madrid Protocol, which foregrounds protection of the "Antarctic environment and dependent and associated ecosystems," also introduced the requirement for Environmental Impact Assessments (EIA) to be undertaken prior to activities commencing in the Antarctic, prevented the introduction of non-native species, and established the Committee for Environmental Protection (CEP), which meets annually alongside the Antarctic Treaty Consultative Meeting (ATCM) and provides specialist advice on matters of environmental protection. Although it is relatively recent, the Madrid Protocol and its explicit protection for Antarctica's wilderness, aesthetic, and intrinsic values continues to shape human activity in the Far South today. The development and implementation of the Madrid Protocol can be understood as a political rebranding that marks a particularly visible shift in attitudes to the Far South—from the hypothetical mining of Antarctica to comprehensive environmental protection for the place.

Connotating Purity and Wilderness

Although the Madrid Protocol explicitly protects the wilderness and aesthetic values of the continent, there is no consensus among Antarctic Treaty parties about what these actually are. Understandings of wilderness vary between people from different language and cultural backgrounds. Antarctic scholars Tina Tin, Rupert Summerson, and He River's 2013 survey of Antarctic tourists revealed that "absence of human impact" was a key factor in their understanding of the concept, but noted that the Chinese visitors they surveyed preferred the designation "pure land" to "wilderness" as in China the term "wilderness" carries connotations of desolation and lifelessness.[16] The term wilderness can therefore alienate some audiences even as it conjures notions of purity for others. In the context of the ATS, where documents are routinely translated into the four official treaty languages (English, French, Spanish, and Russian), word choice is particularly important, and the cultural associations of particular terms must be carefully considered.

The English concept of "wilderness" is deeply implicated in colonial practices. Contending the wilderness is a human creation, environmental historian William Cronin's 1989 essay "The Trouble with Wilderness," drew attention to the way "the myth of the wilderness as 'virgin,' uninhabited land had always been especially cruel when seen from the perspective of the Indians who had once called that land home."[17] As Antarctica has such a young human history, the idea of untouched innocence continues to hold particular allure. This manifests in the designation of Antarctic Specially Protected Areas (ASPA) and Antarctic Specially Managed Areas (ASMA), where human activity is severely restricted. Antarctica has no Indigenous human population but does feature in the oral histories of Indigenous people from the Southern Hemisphere. In New Zealand the story of Polynesian navigator Hui Te Rangiora venturing south to a land of ice far predates European exploration, while the southern lights, or nuyina, were well-known to the traditional owners of lutruwita/Tasmania and provided a connection to the Far South.

The implications of language choice continue to have an impact on how the continent is cast, particularly when it is presented as a pure place, separate from the rest of the world. This framing of Antarctica as untouched erases Indigenous perspectives and is but one example of how wilderness can privilege dominant perspectives and reinforce inequalities. Despite their dominance across popular culture, it is not just the leaders of the Heroic Era who have a stake in Antarctica's stories.

Constructing Antarctica as Pure

Alongside other framings, Antarctica has been constructed as pure for a range of reasons over the course of its human history. This purity has been linked to the literal whiteness of the continent, its young human history, environmental protection, race, and commercial value. Kevin Roberts of the advertising firm Saatchi & Saatchi listed the values of "clean, untouched, pure," and "beauty" as core brand values for Antarctica.[18] Such ideas can also be found in other forms of cultural production, including literature, film, and advertising. Literary scholar Elizabeth Leane has described Antarctica as "an environment which has become synonymous, in the public imagination, with 'pristine nature,'" where pristine can be understood as that which is "unspoilt by human interference."[19] In the introduction to his literary anthology *The Wide White Page*, poet Bill Manhire notes how purity, cleanness, and perfection are recurrent themes in writing about the southern continent. He argues that this purity relates not only to the whiteness of the snow but also to "purity of motive and behaviour," thus inviting reflection upon the human history—and historiography—of the continent.[20] Such an approach elides the messy commercial history of sealing and whaling in the region, wiping the slate clean.

That the color white "has become almost metonymic" for Antarctica invites analogies between the ice and notions of purity—including in relation to race.[21] Historians Lize-Marié van der Watt and Sandra Swart have analyzed this in the South African context, where they show how "in apartheid South Africa, Antarctica was constructed as a white continent, particularly a white continent of and for men." They argue that this whiteness "extends beyond merely being descriptive of an achromatic mixture of all visible frequencies—it is often imbued with cultural connotations of purity, fragility, and even [racial] superiority."[22] Antarctica's whiteness, therefore, presented a political branding opportunity for the Republic of South Africa during this period. Polar historian Peder Roberts has further explored this notion of supremacy, examining how Antarctica became a space for Nazi survival mythology and analyzing the cultural fabric that made myths about Hitler fleeing to Antarctica possible. As Roberts puts it, Antarctica "presents an extreme example of a universal truth: that perceptions of novel environments are always framed by personal experience."[23] Antarctica has therefore been used to stand in for purity in a range of different national and temporal contexts, and the type of purity alluded to can differ depending on context.

PURITY AND CONTAMINATION

The 2020 emergence of the COVID-19 pandemic saw the framing of Antarctica as a pure place reprised, with media outlets describing it as "Earth's one virus-free continent."[24] As the virus spread around the globe, the isolation of the Antarctic winter offered a protective factor, with no one coming or going. National Antarctic Programs scrambled to create protocols to prevent the introduction of the virus to the Far South (including predeparture quarantine) and procedures to follow should it arrive at a base.[25] When the SARS-COV-2 virus was detected at the Chilean General Bernardo O'Higgins Base in late December 2020, it had already had a big impact upon Antarctica, thanks to a cancelled tourist season, scaled-down or cancelled National Antarctic Program activities, and the cancellation of the 2020 Antarctic Treaty Consultative Meeting.[26] The discovery was widely reported, with particular concern focused on the risks of reverse-zoonotic transmission from humans to Antarctic animals such as whales (higher risk) and seals and birds (lower risk).[27] The pandemic brought the purity frame to the fore, with concerns over contamination taking center stage around the world and in the Far South. Such alarm about the contamination of Antarctica goes hand in hand with the notion of the continent as pure, untouched, and in need of a range of forms of human protection.

A rhetoric of purity—and an associated fear of corruption—is also apparent in the discourse around frontier Antarctic science, such as the drilling of subglacial lakes. When researchers came close to breaking through into subglacial Lake Vostok (Russian project) and Lake Whillans (WISSARD [Whillans Ice Stream Subglacial Access Research Drilling] project), with their drills during the 2012–13 summer season, the events were surrounded by anxiety about contamination and damaging untouched environments. Russian researchers described how "one of the most complicated problems was the need to test the ecological purity of the Russian technology under field conditions" because "equipment must not contaminate relict waters of this water body."[28] John Priscu, a microbiologist at Montana State University and part of the WISSARD project, explained, "The stakes for maintaining Vostok's purity are high" because the lake is "a prime analog site in our search for life on other icy worlds in our solar system."[29] The 2007 discovery that many of Antarctica's subglacial lakes are in fact connected to each other further raised the stakes, as it meant that any introduction of outside material into one lake could affect the others. Samples were eventually taken from Lake Vostok on January 10, 2013, and from Lake Whillans on January 28, 2013.[30]

The same fear of contamination—or loss of purity—leads people to argue for parts of Antarctica to remain untouched by human expeditions and investigations and to advocate for the setting aside of "untouched" parts for future research, or so they can retain their "wilderness aspect." The ATS enlists tools such as Antarctic Specially Protected Areas (ASPAS) and Antarctic Specially Managed Areas (ASMAS) to this end.[31] In truth, even the Antarctic surfaces where no human has ever set foot have been touched by human presence on this planet. We live in a time recently termed the Anthropocene, when human activity has become the dominant influence acting upon the environment and climate.[32] Antarctica is not immune to such influence. The organochlorine pesticide DDT has been detected in populations of Adélie penguins, while traces of material from radioactive testing elsewhere in the world have been found in the layers of ice cores, as has evidence of the Industrial Revolution, which took place long before any inland exploration of the continent.[33] This has implications for the perception of wilderness, as human impacts on Antarctica go much further than the footprint of any base or the line of human sight. Vestiges of human presence in the Antarctic raise questions of their own, relating to the need to clean up sites of past activities, though any clean-up must consider wider environmental impacts. While remediation of the environment is not an explicit legal obligation under the ATS, there are "definite legal obligations to prevent negative impacts on the Antarctic environment."[34] Although Antarctica is not untouched by humans, a contemporary focus on reducing impacts foregrounds notions of purity and contamination alongside conservation.

Antarctica and the Cult of Cleanliness

The idea of cleanliness in the Antarctic context ranges from the scale of the human body to that of the continent itself, and beyond. Upon returning from Robert Falcon Scott's ill-fated *Terra Nova* expedition (1910–13), Apsley Cherry-Garrard famously asserted, "Polar exploration is at once the cleanest and most isolated way of having a bad time which has been devised."[35] This Antarctic cleanliness is both literal and metaphorical. For those who travel to Antarctica, cleanliness is of utmost importance—though different attitudes have been associated with it at different times. At Antarctic bases, it is particularly important to follow strict hygiene procedures and wash hands regularly to help prevent the spread of germs—an outbreak of any communicable disease in such as remote outpost could be crippling for the station. Ship-borne tourists are also indoctrinated with the need to clean; prior to arrival in Antarctica, all tourists must attend a mandatory briefing from the International Association of Antarctica Tour Operators (IAATO), which underscores the need to protect the "pristine" Antarctic environment.[36] This is followed by a cleaning session where clothing is closely inspected by field staff, pockets are vacuumed, and boots are scrubbed clean and sprayed with biocide. The boot cleaning ritual is repeated every time guests return to the ship to prevent the spread of disease between different landing sites and penguin rookeries. On the practical side, it helps to prevent the ship from developing the odor of digested krill. On the symbolic side, Antarctica is cast as a clean place, and there is a real sense that one must be clean, too, in order to visit; the scrubbing and vacuuming are a rite of passage en route to the ice itself. In *Purity and Danger*, anthropologist Mary Douglas writes that "the sacred needs to be continually hedged in with prohibitions" and requires rituals of separation.[37] In the case of Antarctic tourism, the voyage over the Drake Passage (or any other stretch of the Southern Ocean) acts as a barrier, separating the perceived purity of the ice from the rest of the everyday world; the ice is "clean," and must be kept so at all costs.

Antarctica is also perceived as clean because of its unique colonial and war history. Whereas narratives of conquest in all other parts of the world have been revealed as highly problematic—not least because of the large numbers of Indigenous people who were negatively affected by colonial actions—Antarctica has largely remained immune to such critique. Human geographers Klaus Dodds and Kathryn Yusoff note that "polar historians have tended to view Antarctica as 'empty space.'" They argue that this does not make Antarctica immune to developments in the rest of the world; in fact, "the displacement (or lack of disruption) of colonial narratives in Antarctic colonies implicates those spatialities in a discussion of the postcolonial."[38] The Antarctic narratives that continue to circulate the most are those about well-known white European explorers from the Heroic Era, including Scott, Amundsen, and Shackleton. Europeans are not the only ones with Antarctic connections; Nobu Shirase's Japanese Antarctic Expedition (1910–12) dates to the Heroic Era, and the Council of Managers of National Antarctic Programs (COMNAP) now includes thirty-two member-nations and five observers from six continents, and the grassroots organization Polar Impact is working to raise the profile of minorities in polar research.[39]

Still, the perception that Antarctica is an exceptional place, set apart from the colonial history and politics of the rest of the world, remains, making it attractive for brands that seek to invoke associations of purity or cleanliness.

The advertising campaigns that most obviously draw on and amplify the discourse of purity and cleanliness attached to Antarctica are those promoting cleaning products. Soap advertisements play an important role in the history of advertising itself; literary scholar Anne McClintock outlines how between the 1870s and 1900, "soap became one of the first commodities to register the historic shift from myriad small businesses to the great imperial monopolies," a shift that was also apparent in the media sector in the late nineteenth century.[40] Soap advertisements also have a long history of association with imperialism, race, and purity. In her article "Soft-Soaping Empire," McClintock explains how, in the context of Victorian cleaning rituals, "soap offered the promise of spiritual salvation and regeneration through commodity consumption."[41] This consumption happened not only at home but also at the very edges of empire, as explorers carried goods into the unexplored areas of the map. Antarctica is used to offer similar salvation in more recent advertisements for cleaning products. These range from soaps for the body to those for clothing and for washing dishes. Antarctica's whiteness and associations with freshness, cleanliness, and purity enabled soap and cleaning product sponsorship and science to comingle with one another.

BYRD'S CLEANING PRODUCTS

When Admiral Byrd's second Antarctic expedition set off in 1933, they took with them "A Year's Supply of Cleanliness for the South Pole."[42] Publicity photographs show crates of Lux, Lifebuoy, and Rinso piled high on the docks in front of the ss *Jacob Ruppert*—a well-placed life ring in the bottom left of the photograph makes visible the name of the ship, while one box in the center is tilted on its side, revealing the text "R.E. Byrd Expedition." Such commercially oriented images are typical from this period—similar shots feature food and beverages, such as Horlicks Malted Malt—and these were carefully framed to create a visual link between sponsors and the explorer. This photograph featuring soaps is not only a self-contained advertisement for the products included in the frame, but it also offers the starting point to explore connections between Antarctica and notions of cleanliness, themes that are explored further on several more pages of the 1935 advertising booklet produced by Byrd and Thomas Poulter, *The Romance of Antarctic Adventure*.

An advertisement for Oakite cleaning products on page 26 of *The Romance of Antarctic Adventure* uses elaborate drawings to create a narrative link between the product and the Antarctic. The main heading proudly proclaims the brand name Oakite. It is accompanied by illustrations of an airplane (Byrd was best known by the public as an aviator), a ship, and a man with a dog sled. In the top right-hand corner, a facsimile of a telegraph from Byrd sings the praises of the Oakite product: "Oakite used on both ships and at Little America with excellent results." Two photographs dominate the middle third of the advertisement—the first shows three men "Digging Oakite out of Snow Tunnel" and places the product in the Antarctic, complete with visual evidence of snowy surroundings; while the second is an indoor portrait of the "Kitchen crew at Little America who used Oakite for washing dishes, pots and pans, etc." Together, the images are designed to illustrate the "stark drama of the frozen Antarctic," setting the scene for the product's claim that "All big exploring expeditions use Oakite, because a little does a lot of cleaning." This advertisement functions in a similar way to Heroic Era endorsements, by establishing a link with a well-known polar explorer and expedition and using this as leverage, urging those back home in the United States to "let this sudsless cleaner do the work for you the same as it did for both Byrd Expeditions." Antarctica therefore functions as a testing ground for these commercial products: if they can work in this tough environment, then they can work just as well anywhere in the domestic environments of the U.S. Where it differs from advertisements for clothing and machinery is the way these advertisements place the domestic setting at the center of both the advertisement and the Antarctic environment. Men are presented as domestic pioneers in Antarctica.

A collage of domestic images some ten pages later in *The Romance of Antarctic Adventure*—positioned opposite the dockside crates of Lux and Rinso—goes some way toward explaining this focus. The top half of the page is dominated by a photograph of supply officer Steve Corey, and biologist Paul Siple taking their turn washing dishes with a box of Rinso just visible beside the sink. The headline, "Another Record at Little America," refers to the number of dishes the men had washed in ten minutes with the help of Rinso. The caption also draws out the product name, urging the viewer to "Note how they love this task—so dreaded by some housewives!" In the domestic U.S. context, household tasks were still highly gendered; housewives were the audience for this advertisement, and it was at them that the rhetorical question of the next line was aimed: "Is it because they use Rinso's rich, gentle, yet quick-working suds?" The only way to find out was for those at home to try the product for themselves.

Another type of soap dominates the bottom half of the page, namely Lux Toilet Soap. A carefully staged photograph shows sailor and diver Bob Young taking a bath at "40° below zero," surrounded by four other expeditioners brandishing brushes and soap. The caption builds upon the visual narrative, explaining "Bob Young really doesn't need help in his bath. Lifebuoy or Lux Toilet Soap give him all the help necessary." His companions are, however, "eager to have their enjoyable 'Saturday nighter'" bath before climbing into their woolens, which were also "kept soft and warm with Lux." Here the Lux product is associated with warmth and softness; the soap is portrayed as having a civilizing influence and being associated with a pleasurable experience. How regular these bathing sessions were in practice is another story—an ambient temperature of 40 degrees below zero may not have presented the ideal conditions under which to take a long relaxing soak in the tub. For viewers of the advertisement, however, the comforting connotations of the brand were clear, and that comfort was transferrable into their own households, thanks to the widespread availability of the product. Such a focus on comfort somewhat unsettles traditional models of polar masculinity that paint Antarctica as wild and rough—but it also creates a bridge for the viewer to identify with aspects of the experience.

Where products that activate the extremity frame tend to focus on male consumers, Antarctic advertisements such as these that draw on ideas of cleanliness and purity have women in mind as the target audience. In several of these Byrd advertisements, the images associated with cleaning products highlight the domestic. These kinds of advertisements were designed to speak to the housewives who took care of the cleaning back home, while capitalizing on the contemporary interest in the Byrd Antarctic expedition. Juxtaposing domestic machinery or cleaning products with the extreme environment of the Antarctic suggests they would be effective at creating a cozy atmosphere anywhere in the world—including in the kitchens and laundries of readers. The fact that cleaning products feature so prominently in the book of advertisements (sanitary items account for six of the twenty-five products) indicates the importance of the domestic market for such products. While it was a novelty for a brand's wares to be taken to Antarctica, it was lucrative only if those back home were aware of the association and sought to replicate it for themselves by also purchasing the product.

DRIVE LAUNDRY POWDER

A more contemporary example of Antarctica being enlisted to sell soap draws on science and Antarctica's appearance as a white continent to give the product credentials. The December 1999 advertisement for Drive Advanced Enzyme laundry powder, which appeared in *Australian Women's Weekly*, is divided into three sections, with text on the top third, an image of an iceberg and its reflection in the middle third, and a small icon displaying Drive laundry powder in the right-hand corner of the bottom third. Under the headline "Ever wondered why Antarctica looks so clean and white?" the advertisement sets forth a narrative of science and nature, explaining how "armed with thermal lab coats we sent our scientists to find out." In fact, Drive laundry powder has no actual link to Antarctica, save the narrative constructed by this advertisement, but that narrative engages several common conceptions of the continent, translating them into value for the product in question.

Science is one of the pillars of the ATS, and the Drive advertisement invokes this association. What is the answer to Antarctica's brilliant whiteness? According to the advertisement, it is "enzymes." Enzymes are proteins that catalyze chemical reactions—they are essential for life, and they are found everywhere on the planet. Unsurprisingly, then, they are also found in Antarctica (although it is not specifically Antarctic enzymes that feature in the product). The advertisement text goes on to explain that as "enzymes are one of mother nature's cleaning products," putting them into the Drive soap powder formula makes the product "bring out the whiteness of clothes," thus "reducing the need for other chemicals that may be more harmful." The advertisement taps into several ideas about Antarctica, including purity and cleanliness, as well as scientific advancement and environmental protection. The suggestion is that this product will leave your whites whiter, while also allowing you to protect the sanctity of the natural environment by having less of an impact than any alternative products. The purity of the Antarctic landscape in the illustration is used to stand in for the purity of the earth as a whole, indirectly calling upon the morality of the viewer as well as their aesthetic sense.

The Drive advertisement employs correlation, not causation; at no point is it stated that the Antarctic link is the reason Drive powder will make clothes white. The advertisement does, however, encourage the reader to make their own links between Antarctic enzymes, the white of the ice, and the purity of a Drive laundry clean. The advertisement concludes, "In fact, you could say we went to the ends of the earth to bring you new Drive." In actual fact this advertisement shows just the opposite. It is not necessary to literally go to the ends of the earth to make use of Antarctica in an advertising campaign; instead, advertisers just need to take people on a journey of the imagination, stopping off at recognizable tropes along the way.

Icy White: Alcohol Advertising

Enlisting Antarctic imagery and the icy connotations of the Far South has been successfully used by alcohol companies to take prospective customers on an imaginative journey. For example, Godet cognac and Süd Polaire gin have used stories of the South to sell their spirits, while Nail Ale's Antarctic beer capitalizes on a physical connection with Antarctica. There are parallels between these alcohol advertisements and those for bottled water, such as Evian and Poland Springs, which often feature wintry alpine scenes devoid of human presence. This snowy imagery calls upon "a geographic image of European purity" in order to make the product more desirable; the same effect can be created using Antarctic purity.[43] Alcohol advertisements are consistently symbolic, in that they concentrate on the product image, and this makes them an ideal case study for examining representations of Antarctica. While some tap into the trope of the Antarctic hero, drawing upon associations of masculinity and toughness (the Glenfiddich advertisement in chapter 2 is a prime example), others create conceptual links between the crisp, clear, or pure nature of their product, and that of the Antarctic ice; like bottled water, they "claim a purity through coldness."[44] As with other products, a material Antarctic link is not a necessity. Although some brewers and distillers have traveled to Antarctica prior to making their products, it is equally effective to simply call upon the associated tropes of purity and freshness, cementing Antarctic links via advertising alone.

A journey to Antarctica in early 2008 inspired cognac maker Jean Jacques Godet to create "the original and very pure, Antarctica, Icy White."[45] Godet, whose family has run their cognac business for five generations, traveled to Antarctica from March 14 to May 1, 2008, on board a small yacht and chronicled his voyage in a blog. The blog is curated so as to narrate the history of the Antarctic cognac. Godet claims, "It was while picking up growlers . . . that the idea of Antarctica was born."[46] The labeling, packaging, and marketing material for Godet Antarctica Icy White all reinforce the associations between the drink and its namesake continent; imagery of ice and penguins feature, and the word "purity" is repeated. (In the French version of the website, the tagline "L'original Antarctica, blanc et tres pure" replaces the English, "The original and very pure, Antarctica, Icy White.") Taking center stage on the website and associated advertising, the bottle (figure 14) is placed among the landscape like something monumental that has sprung out of the ice, echoing Antarctica's icebergs. Here it is not only the name of a continent that is co-opted for commercial use, but the associations that the name "Antarctica" carries. One such association is coldness—the product website explains how "as a tribute to the South Pole, Antarctica, Icy White had to be able to face sub-zero temperatures like no other spirit can." The white nature of the Antarctic landscape comes through in the French version of the tagline, which, when translated, reads "the original Antarctica, white and very pure." Godet's final blog post from May 1, 2010, includes a reflection upon the concept of his new product: "The driving impulse for this new product will highlight Antarctica and its soul: Ice, Purity, and Uniqueness."[47]

At times Antarctica's pristine associations are translated onto other landscapes; the Tasmanian-made Süd Polaire Antarctic Dry Gin is a case in point. An advertisement in the literary magazine *Island* (issue 144, page

FIG 14. Promotional image for Godet Antarctica Icy White, featuring the bottle on an icy landscape, 2008. Courtesy of Godet Frères Cognac.

3) calls upon the links between Tasmania and Antarctica to market the locally made spirit. The body text, located in the top right-hand corner of the page, begins by casting the island of Tasmania as "an archetypal wilderness of mountain, mist and cloud forest at the edge of the world." The island's location on the edge of the Southern Ocean and the Antarctic gateway identity claimed by its capital city of Hobart make conceptual links with Antarctica easy to frame. The advertisement does just this, claiming that the gin is "balanced by pristine Tasmanian rainwater swept across a vast expanse of Southern Ocean over polar ice from Antarctica; the coldest, driest, windiest place on earth." The pristine nature of the product comes from its Antarctic origins, with the journey across the Southern Ocean adding to the narrative of distance and distinction. The textual reference to wilderness creates an imagined link to Antarctica, too, as the continent is often described as a (if not the ultimate) wilderness. While the product name and the presented narrative both carry Antarctic associations, the imagery in the advertisement comes from warmer climes; the page is dominated by the outline of a bottle, which is filled with twisting green tree branches. The dissonance created by

the green foliage beneath the Antarctic title makes the advertisement memorable and suggests that Antarctica is closer than viewers may have thought—indeed, a taste is available in the state's capital city in a bar named for the spirit that overlooks docking icebreakers throughout the summer months.[48]

A much more literal taste of Antarctica comes in the form of a thirty-bottle run of Antarctic Nail Ale. The beer, brewed by the Perth-based Nail Ale Company in 2010, was created using water melted from an Antarctic iceberg and marketed as "possibly the world's oldest and purest beer." Marketing expert Betty J. Parker has written about how the "myth promoted by beer manufacturers that beer is natural, pure, and perhaps even healthy," has been constructed in advertising.[49] In this case, the claims to age and purity come directly from this iceberg link—Antarctic icebergs comprise many layers of compacted ice that have slowly flowed down from the polar plateau into the ocean, where they eventually calve off and float away. This process takes a long time, but the purity claim also relates to the fact that human history in the Antarctic region is recent— the suggestion being that the ice is pure and untouched.

Given that the ice itself was harvested using a helicopter and a ship that traveled into the Southern Ocean, the claim to purity insofar as it relates to the lack of a human footprint is problematic. It was, however, a valuable claim to make; Antarctic Nail Ale made headlines as the most expensive beer when a bottle sold at auction for AU$1,850.[50] Proceeds were donated to the Sea Shepherd Conservation Society, and the bottles themselves featured the Sea Shepherd logo and a "save the whales" seal. Sea Shepherd also tried to activate the hero narrative through their activities, such as obstructing whaling vessels on the high seas, and the organization is itself associated with a certain brand of fierce moral purity. This beer, which had direct links to the Antarctic regions, was therefore used to raise the profile of both the Sea Shepherd Conservation Society and Nail Ale brewery. In a 2010 interview with the *Sydney Morning Herald*, brewer John Stallwood was candid about the publicity value of the Antarctic beer: "Small breweries have little advertising budget—especially me—so we rely on publicity."[51] Creating an Antarctic link for the beer may have been a gimmick, but it was one way of drawing attention to the brand. Purity was an instantly recognizable trope to use when creating a product with Antarctic links, and one that fit well with the image of protecting Antarctica and the Southern Ocean region.

The alcohol advertisements examined here show how Antarctica has been used to evoke ideas of purity and whiteness, to create imagined links from afar, and to lend a product authenticity in its claims to purity and age. In analyzing advertisements for bottled water, environmental communications scholar Andy Opel has demonstrated how purity "becomes a site of cultural struggle, with public and private entities vying for the ability to inscribe water (nature) with their cultural identifications."[52] This is also the case with alcoholic beverages that call upon the purity trope, as they make use of the concept for their own commercial purposes. It is significant that Godet cognac, Süd Polaire gin, and Nail Ale beer are all high-end products. While there are also examples of lower end alcohol advertisements using Antarctic imagery (including a 1994 Smirnoff campaign that featured a penguin wearing a tuxedo, viewed through a vodka bottle) such advertisements also tend to call upon notions of the elite. Antarctica lends itself well to this sort of framing, partly because penguins are often anthropomorphized as tuxedo-wearing creatures but also because the continent itself is the domain of only a select few.

Few people will ever travel there, and the taste of Antarctica is also reserved for the few who can afford it. Branding Antarctica as pure therefore reveals a coterie of themes such as domesticity, gender, and exclusivity—as well as more recent connections to science and sustainability.

Beneath the Surface: Health and Bioprospecting

While some have looked to the idea of purity as a selling point, other have looked to Antarctica's elemental qualities and marketed a product on its physical links to Antarctica. Companies have used material found in Antarctica in a wide range of domestic products, with antifreeze proteins, cosmetics, nutraceuticals, food products, medicines, and—in an example reminiscent of the Drive laundry powder advertisement—washing powder formulas all making it onto consumer shelves.[53] As early as 1998, the European COLDZYME project was asserting, "Enzymes found in Antarctic bacteria can be used both in industrial applications and in domestic products such as washing powder as they active [sic] at low temperatures thus giving huge energy savings."[54] The search for novelty in living organisms that can be used for commercial applications is known as biological prospecting, often shortened to "bioprospecting," and is an important new development in the use of Antarctic resources for commercial purposes.

Described as a "hybrid activity—part science, part industry," bioprospecting involves the search for, and possible extraction of, living organisms with commercial intent.[55] As the process extends "beyond the discovery stage to the commercial application stage," marketing is the final phase of bioprospecting.[56] With over two hundred companies and research institutes involved in bioprospecting, including organizations such as Du Pont, Oxford University, and Unilever, this is a growing field.[57] It is also a contentious one: Yves Frenot, former director of the French Polar Institute, has described the economic activity associated with using genetic resources as "difficult to reconcile with . . . the Antarctic Treaty"— free access to information in the spirit of the treaty can be at odds with sensitive commercial interests.[58] Ethical issues can also arise if there are conflicts of interest between scientific inquiry and income-generating opportunities.[59] The topic has been raised at several Antarctic Treaty Consultative Meetings. Although parties declared in 2013 that "the Antarctic Treaty System is the appropriate framework for managing the collection of biological material in the Antarctic Treaty area and for considering its use," tensions between scientific and commercial interests remain.[60] Much of this tension relates to the ways we conceptualize Antarctica as either a pure and untouched wilderness, or a place ripe for human development and consumption. The purity trope casts it as the former, but Antarctica's long human history of commercialization shows that this is not the only way of thinking about the continent.

As the advertisements in this chapter reveal, the idea of untouched wilderness can be valuable when put to commercial purposes, particularly when combined with an Antarctic link. While fish caught in the Southern Ocean is rarely promoted as coming from Antarctica, there are exceptions—the brand Glacier 51 Toothfish, for instance, features icy imagery on consumer packaging and takes its named from Fiftyone Glacier on the sub-Antarctic Heard Island, where the fish with "snow-white flesh" is found.[61] For krill, the origin of location has long been a draw in advertising campaigns, and images of penguins and pristine icescapes abound. So, too, do notions of purity, freshness, and health. When the environmental NGO World Wildlife Fund (WWF) and the natural health company Blackmores partnered in 2012 on the three-year Sustainable Fish Oils Partnership, health was at the forefront. On the "Partners" section of their website, WWF explains how "well-being for us is linked to well-being for the planet," indicating the importance the organization places on sustainability.[62] Such a focus on the health of the earth as well as the health of customers also offered a positive marketing opportunity for Blackmores—one that came through in a 2012–13 campaign for krill oil. Here the physical association with Antarctica's pristine landscape is used to suggest an environmentally friendly message by evoking ideas of nature as pristine.

BLACKMORES ECO KRILL: PURITY AS THE TIP OF AN ICEBERG

When Blackmores Eco Krill was launched in 2012, it was the only sustainably sourced krill oil to be certified by the Marine Stewardship Council (MSC).[63] This link, and the connotations that such accreditation carries for care of the environment, were at the heart of a Xander Creative advertising campaign for the product. Images were displayed across Australia on a range of platforms, including on bus shelters and in print magazines, and the project was also showcased on the Xander Creative website.[64] All of the advertisements feature an image of a penguin and an image of a floating iceberg; the waterline bisects the page and the underside of the iceberg is shown beneath the water. A quote by Albert Einstein at the bottom of the canvas suggests an ecocentric, rather than anthropocentric, approach: "Our task must be to free ourselves . . . by widening our circle of compassion to embrace all living creatures and the whole of nature and its beauty."[65] Language like "the whole of nature" helps to position the Blackmores Eco Krill brand as existing within a wider ecosystem, mirroring the ecosystem-based approach taken by CCAMLR when setting krill catch limits in the Southern Ocean. Both the text and image in the advertisement combine to create the appearance of an environmentally friendly product.

The Blackmores Eco Krill advertisement tagline differs depending on whether it is presented above the water's surface ("On the surface, all krill oils look the same") or below the surface ("Deep down, Blackmores cares where it's from"). "Deep down" can be read as referring to Antarctica as the Far South, to the location of krill that are (sometimes) found deep in oceans, to heartfelt feelings, or to the depths to which a penguin can dive. Employing wordplay in this way means the environment and morality are conflated, with the perceived purity of the first being superimposed upon the second. The play on ideas of surface and depth in the text is mirrored in the image, where the motif of the iceberg is used to suggest that there is more than meets the eye. In this case the suggestion is that the environmental credentials shown in the advertisement are just the tip of the iceberg when it comes to the company's environmentally friendly behaviors. Purity and protection go hand in hand, and here the Blackmores' link to protection is used to reinforce the perceived purity of its product. Purity has therefore been relentlessly commodified over the decades, albeit for different reasons by different stakeholders.

Antarctica is a difficult location to visit, but advances in technology mean it is not a difficult environment to create or enhance digitally. The availability of stock imagery makes the Antarctic setting—and the associated values and themes it can portray, including freshness, cleanness, and purity—available at the click of a button. It can also lead to idealized depictions of Antarctica, with little regard for accuracy. Imagery in all the Blackmores advertisements creates a fantasy version of the Southern Ocean, where penguins, icebergs, and blue skies exist harmoniously. It shows where krill comes from but pictures the wilderness rather than a commercial operation; the ice is very white, not streaked with pink penguin feces, the inevitable result in any real-life situation where penguins, krill, and icebergs coexist. The scene is clean and fresh, suggesting that these qualities are present in the product being advertised. Xander Creative comments directly on the choice of an Antarctic setting: "Obviously location shoots are, well, tough to say the least, so we compiled a range of images and created our own Antarctic environment from scratch."[66] This creative license also resulted in some rather lost penguins—while some Blackmores posters feature gentoos, which are quite at home on the ice, others show the much more temperate Humboldt variety. Geographic reassignment of the species does not detract from the meaning of the advertisement, so their presence points to the continent regardless of their native habitats. The continent, in turn—which is gestured to by both penguin and ice—carries a range of resonances that are activated by the language used to frame the place.

The idea of purity is also invoked through the rhetoric of protection; what is being protected is valued precisely because it has remained untouched. The Blackmores Eco Krill advertisements promote a product sourced in the Antarctic by both employing pristine imagery and by displaying their MSC credentials as a central feature. The idea is that this environment where krill are found needs to be protected to maintain its "pure" status—which is paradoxical, given that animals must be removed from the "untouched" Southern Ocean to make the product in the first place. Blackmores is careful to frame its use of Southern Ocean resources as being sustainable and environmentally friendly—and under CCAMLR the krill fishery has, historically, been one of the best managed in the world. CCAMLR takes an ecosystem-based approach to the use of marine living resources. In the case of Blackmores advertising, an overt association with the MSC is one way of assuring customers that "krill is sourced in a sustainable way."[67]

Nonetheless, it can be problematic to associate the purity of an environment with a product that is created by taking resources from said environment. Several campaigns that have protested against the krill fishing industry have at their heart a "perceived mismatch between the wilderness value of the Antarctic and the commercial activities that are undertaken in the Southern Ocean."[68] Such petitions are predicated on the assumption that "the Antarctic shouldn't be a place for profit," and have described krill fishing as "the plunder of Antarctica and one of the last unspoiled oceans on the planet."[69] Antarctica *is* a place for profit, however, and has been since the first human interactions with the region. Fishing for krill, toothfish, and icefish is a legitimate (thought ideologically contested) activity.[70] I argue that protests about activities in the Southern Ocean result when two different conceptual versions of Antarctica come head to head: on one side, it is framed as an untouched wilderness that should remain so, and on the other, it is a place that provides resources that need to be managed. How different people view the situation depends on their values and on their Antarctic imaginary, or "the cluster of values, tropes and ideas that they associate with the place."[71] This imagined version of the region is shaped by cultural inputs, so marketing is a very important tool for swaying public opinion in one direction or another. Both cultural inputs and attitudes are malleable and change over time, meaning it is necessary to pay attention to the underlying values and assumptions that inform any actions, or reactions, in the Antarctic region.

Pure and Untouched?

While the purity frame casts Antarctica as a place that is, or should be, untouched by humans, it also enables a different sort of harvesting of Antarctica. Purity carries associations of freshness, unadulterated science, and the halting of time. It has been used to sell a range of products, from soaps and skin creams to alcoholic beverages, and is present whenever the themes of wilderness, freshness, or pure science emerge in advertisements. Many of the advertisements examined in this chapter are aimed at women (Oakite, Rinso, Drive, Antarcticine) or at environmentally conscious consumers (Eco Krill Oil, Nail Ale Beer), marking a point of difference compared to the male-oriented advertisements in the heroism and extremity sections. The purity frame is therefore a way of opening Antarctic advertising to wider audiences, while still building upon existing gender stereotypes. In many cases the rhetoric of protection is linked to sexual politics, with language such as "virgin landscape" bringing purity to the fore. The trope of purity—and the associated fear of contamination—was and is used by advertisers to advance their environmental credentials. This can further be seen when examining the frame of fragility, which is addressed in the next chapter. Paradoxically, it is much more common for products that have a direct Antarctic link to call upon purity more than any other themes, despite the inherent contradictions associated with sourcing such products. While this can be problematic, it does indicate the commercial value that the frame carries, and that the association between Antarctica and purity has wide appeal.

If, as Mary Douglas claims, purity is a matter of being in place rather than out of place, then Antarctica fits the bill—the place has become a commercial or branding shorthand for purity itself.

Fragile Antarctica 5

*Ice-Washing and
Protecting the Penguins*

In early 2002, the Larsen B Ice Shelf on the eastern side of the Antarctic Peninsula collapsed with dramatic speed. The break-up was photographed via NASA's MODIS satellite, resulting in a series of images that have since been combined into a time-lapse series. Widely disseminated, these images provide dramatic visuals for the narrative of climate change that continues to circulate today.[1] Never before had such a large area disintegrated so rapidly, and never before had visual imagery of this sort of event been imbued with such strong cultural meaning.[2] Cultural critic Judith Williamson argues that "imagery circulating in our societies has a profound effect on our ability to grasp the world as it is, and imagine how it might be."[3] In the case of the Larsen B Ice Shelf, the imagery of the collapse (figure 15) was transmitted across the globe, used to illustrate news items, and reproduced in print and digital forms. It came to symbolize a fragile climate system that was already melting, cracking, and disintegrating on a very human timescale.

Ice is understood to be particularly vulnerable to anthropogenic climate change, largely because melting can be seen when observed over a period of time, while many other effects of climate change, such as growing concentrations of CO_2 in the atmosphere, remain invisible.[4] As a result, ice often serves as a visual metaphor for change. The visibility of the Larsen B collapse is just as significant as the short timeframe over which it occurred. Geographer Kathryn Yusoff has written that "one can experience the compression of the reality of time and space" within this series of images, where "the predominant narration becomes about witnessing the spectacle of change."[5] Indeed, the time-lapse series makes visible "the moment when disaster strikes."[6] This visibility means that the

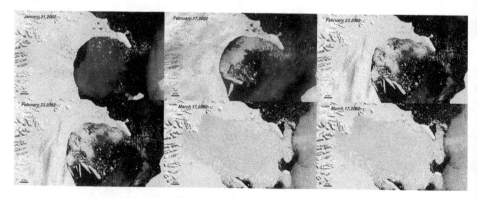

FIG 15. Collapse of the Larsen B Ice Shelf, 2002. NASA/Goddard Space Flight Center, "Collapse of the Larsen B Ice Shelf."

event has had a long afterlife in popular culture. Imagery of the cracking Larsen B Ice Shelf has appeared on film, on T-shirts, and in artwork. It was featured in the opening sequence of the disaster film *The Day After Tomorrow* (2004, directed by Roland Emmerich) while in 2009 online clothing company Zazzle promoted the "Larsen B Ice Shelf Collapse (Picture Earth) Shirt" as a gift "that will surely get others talking about the consequences of global warming. [It is the] Perfect educational science gift for all fans and advocates of the existence of Antarctica, the ice continent!" Multimedia artist Andrea Juan's *Antarctica Project* (2005–2014) includes in-situ Antarctic installations that explore the collapsing ice shelves, while Satoshi Itasaka's resin vase, *Larsen C*, refers to global warming, with the artist stating that his artwork reflects that the disintegration of other ice shelves is simply a matter of time. Although the specific Larsen C collapse was not directly linked to anthropogenic warming, it was presented this way in many media reports.[7] The range of cultural products that reproduce this framing illustrate how melting ice has come to stand for a fragile climate system, with Antarctica standing in for vulnerable ecosystems everywhere.

This framing of Antarctica as fragile is connected to a shift in perception that recognizes Antarctica as playing an important role in global climate systems, rather than existing simply as a far-off continent that few will ever visit. Cold Antarctic bottom water plays a key role in driving global oceanic currents, Antarctica's ice caps hold the vast majority of the world's fresh water, while ice core records from east Antarctica reveal the long history of rainfall and drought across parts of the Australian continent.[8] While oceans and atmosphere connect Antarctica to the rest of the globe, it is ice that is so powerful in capturing imaginations. Comprised of ice and glaciers that are "susceptible to cultural framing as both dangerous and endangered landscapes," Antarctica is seen simultaneously as fragile and treacherous.[9] The continent is cast as a place that both threatens humankind and needs to be protected from the effects of anthropogenic climate change. This dissonance is key to representations that call upon Antarctica to embody environmental ideas.

When it comes to the idea of fragility, the use of the Larsen B imagery to articulate the phenomenon of global change is just the tip of the metaphorical iceberg. The fragile connotations of Antarctic imagery have been employed in advertising material to infer that companies have environmental credentials, resulting in polar ice gaining more visibility—but not necessarily greater protection. This analysis focuses on three international advertising campaigns: ABB's "amazing what you save," Westpac's "Equator Principles," and Diesel's "Global Warming Ready" campaigns.[10] The advertisements for three very different industries are used as a proxy for accessing dominant attitudes toward the Far South and to illustrate a contemporary face of the commercial history of Antarctica. When consumers are environmentally aware and want to protect the planet, enlisting the help of the Far South becomes a useful way to attract business.

Framing Antarctica as Fragile

The framing of Antarctica as a realm of commerce has a long and varied history, encompassing early sealing and whaling, the negotiations throughout the 1980s around the unratified Convention on the Regulation of Antarctic Mineral Resource Activity (CRAMRA), and contemporary fishing and bioprospecting. In recent decades, however, the rhetoric of profit has increasingly given way to that of protection; this is the dominant lens through which the continent is discussed in the Anthropocene. The signing of the Protocol on Environmental Protection to the Antarctic Treaty

(Madrid Protocol) in 1991 marked the culmination of an important shift in how Antarctica was conceptualized at an international level; replacing the earlier CRAMRA negotiations, it brought questions of protection to the fore. Article 2 of the Madrid Protocol designates Antarctica as "a natural reserve, devoted to peace and science."[11] It protects the ecosystems of the Far South, as well as the wilderness and aesthetic values of the region; it also prohibits mining activity. Subsequent annexes on environmental impact assessment (Annex I), waste disposal (Annex III), marine pollution (Annex IV), protected areas (Annex V), and liability arising from environmental emergencies (Annex VI, not in force), all relate to the protection of the Antarctic environment and reflect emerging concerns. Despite the fact that neither the Antarctic Treaty nor the Madrid Protocol has an expiration date, the popular belief that 2048 marks an end date for Antarctic protection continues to circulate. While 2048 marks the opportunity for a review conference of the Madrid Protocol, both this and the Antarctic Treaty have the potential to be modified at any point in time under particular voting conditions, and the prohibition on mining will remain in place unless another instrument (such as the obsolete Convention on the Regulation of Antarctic Mineral Resource Activities [CRAMRA]) is introduced to regulate the activity.[12] That the expiration myth is all-pervasive seems to suggest a will to see Antarctic governance frameworks as more fragile than they are, adding a further dimension to the framing of Antarctica as vulnerable.

Antarctica has been represented as fragile and in need of protection across a range of cultural media and advertising operations. Nongovernmental organizations regularly mobilize this fragile framing when calling for greater protection of Antarctica. For example, the *Last Ocean* film and advocacy campaign that ran in the lead-up to the 2016 adoption by Commission for the Conservation of Marine Living Resources (CCAMLR) of the Ross Sea Marine Protected Area (MPA) used underwater polar imagery to promote preservation of "the most pristine marine ecosystem on earth."[13] Ilija Trojanow presents a portrait of a continent in crisis in his 2011 novel *Lamentations of Zeno*, where the protagonist is plagued by nightmares of melting ice as he mourns both his beloved alpine glacier and the future degradation of Antarctica, lamenting that "no matter how carefully I cradle the ice in my hands it continues to melt."[14] The trope of an impending environmental catastrophe in Antarctica also emerges in popular fiction, such as thrillers, where it is more than just a convenient plot device; Elizabeth Leane suggests that the rhetoric around Antarctica, climate change, and sea-level rise has "generated a kind of real-world thriller narrative in which humans see themselves in a race against time" (with scope aplenty for heroic-savior figures).[15]

The fragility frame is closely linked to the concept of anthropogenic threats and can manifest in contradictory imperatives to either save Antarctica or manage feelings of despair in the face of large-scale and overwhelming environmental challenges. The themes of purity and fragility act as a counterpoint to the tropes of extremity that are present in the framings of Antarctica as a place for heroes or a place of extremes. Rather than depicting Antarctica as a place for humans and machines to tackle the dangers of a hostile landscape, they transfer the vulnerability to the landscape itself. This has implications for branding—rather than a place to claim and master, Antarctica becomes both a place to protect and a place from which humans need protection—it is, therefore, ripe for use in wider environmental messaging and advertising.

The frozen regions of the planet, including glaciers, sea ice, ice sheets, ice shelves, and permafrost, are known collectively as the cryosphere. Where cryosphere denotes the physical properties of an icy place, the term "cryoscape" recognizes that these regions are also home to complex interplays between scientific and cultural knowledges that can be contested and vary in meaning and importance over time.[16] The Far South has stronger associations with purity and fragility than other cryoscapes for a range of reasons. Antarctica's exceptional circumstances—its unowned status, the absence of an Indigenous population, its remoteness and short human history—contribute to its framing as particularly vulnerable. As outlined in chapter 4, these factors mean that Antarctica is more easily understood as "pure wilderness" and more susceptible to human pollution and destruction. Antarctic observations have led to global policy changes in the past. For instance, the ozone hole that was discovered over Antarctica in the 1980s led to the development of the Montreal Protocol, which focused on reducing ozone-depleting gasses being released into the atmosphere. In recent years, this corrupting threat has been from anthropogenic climate change. In March 2015, the monthly global average concentration of CO_2 in the atmosphere surpassed four hundred parts per million, bringing the concentrations into unprecedented territory.[17] The greenhouse effect is becoming ever stronger, leading to increasing temperatures in the atmosphere and the ocean. Climatologist Gavin Schmidt, from NASA's Goddard Institute for Space Studies, warns, "We are a society that has inadvertently chosen the double-black diamond run without having learned to ski first. It will be a bumpy ride."[18]

Physically, politically, and symbolically, then, the Antarctic region has global significance. Climate change has an impact upon ice, ocean, and beyond as the cryosphere acts as "a fundamental control on the physical, biological, and social environment over a large part of the Earth's surface."[19] Changes in the Far South contribute to feedback loops with implications for places much farther afield; sea-level rise and changes in ocean circulation are but two areas "where the processes in Antarctica are fundamentally important globally."[20] Such connections have an impact on how Antarctica is viewed, as the continent transitions from being thought of as somewhere remote and invisible to being understood as part of the global climate system. Indeed, the melting ice makes the effects of climate change tangible. It turns the global and the political into the local and the personal, as Antarctic change is experienced as rising sea levels along faraway coastlines. At the same time, climate change is being "reimagined as an ethical, societal, and cultural problem that poses new questions and reconfigures the geographic imaginaries of the world."[21] Within this reimagining, Antarctica has come to play a dominant role as a symbol for climate change, for fragility, and for the threat of melting ice. This symbol is particularly prominent in media texts and advertisements from the early twenty-first century.

Media and Conservation

The changing attitudes toward Antarctica were also reflected in—and in many respects a product of—changing values within the world environmental context. Environmentalism as a movement had its roots in romantic ideals, with Henry David Thoreau, Thomas Jefferson, and Ralph Waldo Emerson providing the philosophical foundations. During the late 1800s, the conservation movement was led by prominent figures such as John Muir, who founded the Sierra Club, an organization that continues to advocate for protection of the environment with the mission to "explore, enjoy, and protect the wild places of the earth."[22] The Earth Day demonstrations of 1970 that grew after a large oil spill in Santa Barbara, California, in 1969, brought together people who were concerned about oil spills, toxic dumps, pesticides, and the loss of wilderness areas. Providing a focus for their common values, the demonstrations that took place across the United States on April 22, 1970, were seen by some to mark "the birth of the modern environmental movement."[23] This new environmentalism combined the conservation ideas of Thoreau and Muir with lobbying, advertising, and letter-writing campaigns, reaching and mobilizing a wider popular audience than in earlier times. The news media played an important role in communicating information about the demonstrations to a mass audience and in creating public awareness, but not all outlets were sympathetic to the cause. While environmentalism and the media were intertwined much like the media and exploration were at the turn of the century, the relationships took different forms, with critical distance a key factor.

Environmental groups were also becoming more active in other nations: Greenpeace was founded in Canada in 1971, with the aim of bearing witness to the nuclear testing in Amchitka, off the coast of Alaska, while in Australia the United Tasmania Group became the first "green" political party to run for election in 1972.[24] Concern for the environment on a worldwide level led to the United Nations Conference on the Human Environment, June 5–16, 1972, which was an important milestone for environmental politics. Principle 2 of the Declaration of the United Nations Conventions on the Human Environment states: "The natural resources of the earth, including the air, water, land, flora and fauna and especially representative samples of natural ecosystems, must be safeguarded for the benefit of present and future generations through careful planning or management, as appropriate."[25] These conservation ideals were further developed over the coming decades, with the UN Convention on the Law of the Sea (UNCLOS) signed in December 1982; the Montreal Protocol, aimed at phasing out chlorofluorocarbons that were damaging the ozone layer, signed in 1987; and the Intergovernmental Panel on Climate Change (IPCC) formed in 1988. Environmental awareness was developing at a local scale as well, evidenced by the emergence of grassroots groups like the Wilderness Society in Australia in 1976, and Earth First! in the U.S. in 1979.

As environmental consciousness and consumer awareness grew throughout the 1980s so, too, did the potential for capitalizing on this care. The "move to being seen as Green and environmentally friendly" picked up considerable corporate interest during the early years of the twenty-first century, and green alternatives became ever more lucrative as a marketing strategy.[26] As a result, these changing environmental values were also reflected in advertising campaigns—including in those pertaining to Antarctica.

Frozen Imagery and "Ice-Wash"

For most people, access to Antarctica is primarily through the mediation of news images, documentaries, social media, and advertising. When the dominant imagery consists of calving glaciers and melting ice, this helps to frame Antarctica as a fragile place, vulnerable to change. In this way, it shares similarities with the Arctic, where icy imagery has been used discursively to stand for the same environmental issues, although the relationship between forms of media and the politics of Arctic climate change are far better documented.[27] In the South Pole context, penguins and icebergs are often used to suggest that a company has strong environmental credentials. Such promises are not always fulfilled. In *Green Wash*, environmental commentator Guy Pearse highlights the "gulf between the green revolution being advertised and the progress actually occurring."[28] "Ice-washing" is the polar equivalent to Pearse's green wash, with the environmental message conveyed or suggested via images of glaciers and the cryosphere at large.[29]

Several issues are associated with employing polar imagery for commercial purposes. First, the aim of most advertising is to promote consumption. Consumerism and increased consumption, however, are some of the major factors behind environmental problems such as climate change.[30] Advertisements that exhort consumers to buy a particular product to save the environment are rarely self-reflexive about their own role in environmental damage. Environmentally conscious consumers are not immune to these contradictions. Geographer Paul Simpson-Housley has written about how "sometimes the cognitive and affective components (of a perception) clash"—one might be seduced by polar imagery, despite knowing that its visual promise of protection will not be fulfilled, just as one can know that fire pollutes but still enjoy its warm glow.[31] Second, there are particular issues inherent in using snow and ice to represent climate change, particularly changes that manifest as warming. As Judith Williamson has noted, "We see pictures of coldness, not heat, of glaciers, not droughts. Whatever the logical reason for these images, their constant presence, the cultural ubiquity of these frozen landscapes, functions as an imaginative denial of the real nature of climate change, and the situation faced by large parts of humanity today."[32] In this case, the symbolic power of snow and ice in the Antarctic renders invisible contemporary environmental issues in other parts of the globe. Such examples show that employing icy imagery to drive home an environmental message is not straightforward. As the cryosphere has entered more conversations, it has attracted a wider range of symbolic meanings. As geographers Marcus Nüsser and Ravi Baghel put it, "glaciers do not *just* melt; they are imbued with cultural, scientific, political and aesthetic meanings."[33] Ice is not just ice—rather, it carries with it a range of cultural connotations, specific to each time and place in which the imagery appears, leading environmental historian Sverker Sörlin to argue that "we have reached a 'cryo-historical' moment."[34]

The three advertisements examined in this chapter demonstrate how Antarctica has been used as a symbol for both the polar environment and the more-than-human world at large, and how the rhetoric of protection has been deployed in a commercial context. These examples are representative of a much larger body of advertisements that call upon the theme of Antarctic fragility for marketing purposes. Together they signal that, far from being just a marginal mass of ice that is regularly left off the map, Antarctica plays an important role in the cultural imaginary of climate change. In all three cases, large companies capitalize on the symbolic value of the southern continent, transforming the fragility of ice into financial gain.

Saving Ice: The Rhetoric of Protection

In 2002 the global campaign of the robotics and automated technology company ABB featured several dozen Adélie penguins on a large iceberg, accompanied by the question: "Can you stop 50 million tons of CO_2 from happening?"[35] The campaign was repeated in 2005, this time with the Adélies replaced by a close-up row of king penguins on the ice, and updated numbers—68 million tons of CO_2.[36] In 2008 the same king penguins made a reappearance in the MIT European Career Fair booklet, with the number of tons of CO_2 in question boosted to 100 million.[37] The reprise of the campaign suggests a positive reception; zooming in on the penguins in the second and third iterations suggests that these birds are effective at creating meaning in the advertisement. These penguins are not just penguins—rather, they embody an environmental message that has relevance from the poles to the job fairs of Europe. ABB is a Swiss multinational corporation, founded in 1988, with headquarters in Zürich, far from the natural geographical realm of penguins. In this trade context, environmental priorities are presented as a selling point, and they act as a counterpoint against the technological imagery and people used in other advertisements throughout the booklet.

Penguins are often used by advertisers and creators of popular culture to stand in for Antarctica. They are recognizable as a Southern Hemisphere species, associated—thanks to countless photographs, cartoons, emojis, and other appearances in popular culture—with snow and ice. Even though the ABB advertisement features king penguins, which breed on the sub-Antarctic islands rather than the icy continent itself, they serve as a convenient and opportunistic visual shortcut to for Antarctica. A non-Antarctic species is utilized presumably and ironically because it offers a better "Antarctic aesthetic" than the Adélies used in its previous iteration—king penguins are more colourful than the gentoo, Adélie, or chinstrap varieties, and they closely resemble the famous emperor penguins that live on the ice. The ABB penguins act on several levels of their "complex and contradictory symbolic repertoire"—they are used to represent the megafauna of Antarctica, to stand for the environment they live in and around, and to gesture toward the wider issue of climate change.[38] The advertisement assumes that readers are aware of the process by which CO_2 emissions result in the melting of ice, thus endangering wildlife. The presence of penguins is therefore a marker of how far into general society an awareness of anthropogenic climate change has permeated.

ABB's penguin advertisements have been described as part of an "environmentally responsible campaign."[39] They appeared at a time when big business was beginning to see the value in projecting an eco-friendly image. The "amazing what you save" campaign was designed to highlight the company's new automated factory technology—"a variable-speed drive unit"—that allowed factories to slow the emissions put out during quieter production periods, thus "saving energy when the plant was not needed at full capacity production."[40] The monetary savings were a prime selling point of the technology, with the variable-speed drives touted as "major energy savers, environmentally friendly and a wise investment."[41] Environmental issues also translate back into profit when public opinion and the "reflected green glow" of an energy-efficient line are factored in.[42] If a particular product is seen as environmentally friendly, it has implications for the brand as a whole, because "all commercials for a product also advertise the brand."[43] The appearance of a polar landscape in this advertisement, therefore, has wider implications for the company than simply serving to market a single product: it creates an association between the ABB brand and environmental practices and imagery that endures far longer than the ephemeral advertisement itself.

The play on the words "what you save" is pivotal to this ABB advertisement. Taken literally, the term "save" is used in a monetary sense—cutting many millions of tons of CO_2 will reduce energy and business costs. However, thanks to the juxtaposition of text and image, the term "save" can also be understood as referring to the penguins themselves, inviting environmental as well as economic connotations.[44] Penguins have been put to use in advertising imagery in a range of ways over the years but are commonly used to "act as synecdoches for pristine nature."[45] When the penguins are used to stand in for Antarctica as a whole, with Antarctica in turn standing in for the world's environmental systems, the question of what is being saved gains even more significance. As a solution to this problem, consumers are exhorted to buy ABB products, thereby reducing their carbon footprint and saving money, while helping to protect the environment. Antarctica functions as a backdrop to the ABB advertisement, but that backdrop brings salient environmental issues to mind.

As opposed to other advertisements that have traded in fun, the ABB advertisement presents an earnest appeal to consumers that centers on the rhetoric of saving energy, saving money, saving penguins, and saving the polar environment.

Westpac and the Equator Principles

In 2003 the Westpac Banking Corporation linked the equator with the poles, releasing an icy advertisement celebrating its identity as the "first Australian Bank to sign the Equator Principles agreeing not to fund projects that endanger communities or the environment." This initial 2003 advertisement was part of the wider "Building better lives for all Australians" campaign.[46] Created by advertising agency the Campaign Palace—"responsible for much of the advertising that has become part of Australia's popular culture"—the advertisement features a single Adélie penguin atop an iceberg, with explanatory text and the company logo in the bottom right-hand corner.[47] In 2008 the same advertisement was reprised to coincide with the Australian Emissions Trading Scheme and Westpac's Climate Change Position Statement—this time the campaign was rolled out "across a range of media, including television, newspapers and outdoor advertising."[48] The repeated use of such imagery speaks to the success of the earlier campaign, which "capitalized on environmentalism as an opportunity" by "extolling the virtues of the 'Equator Principles'"—a voluntary risk management framework adopted by financial institutions "for determining, assessing and managing environmental and social risk in projects."[49] The advertisement presents Westpac as an environmentally friendly bank with an active interest in reducing pollution. The same Adélie penguin image featured in the Westpac advertisement has made additional appearances in the media, including as the introductory image to a special feature on climate change in the April 9, 2007, issue of *Time* magazine. This context further reinforces the environmental symbolism associated with this stock image animal celebrity. It also adds another layer of transactions to the commercial history of

Antarctica, as the south polar image is a commodity in its own right—like the photographs of the Heroic Era explorers.

The 2008 Westpac advertisement features the tagline, "How many banks does it take to change a globe?" This pun calls upon a history of jokes about changing light bulbs, also known as "globes," but it also carries more serious undertones. In this case, the globe in question is the Earth itself, a message reinforced by the answer provided—"All of them"—and the change referred to is environmental. The fact that only a single penguin is depicted is also significant. Penguins are "often considered the epitome of uniformity" and shown in large groups, preparing to dive into the water one after another.[50] The use of a single penguin in this instance suggests that it takes one—animal or corporation—to dive in first, before others can follow. This idea of leadership is reinforced visually in the advertisement by the use of an iceberg as the second visual element in the scene. Icebergs bring to mind the "tip of the iceberg" analogy, suggesting that only a small part of the company's environmental activities are outlined in the advertisement. As well as referring to the Equator Principles, the secondary advertisement text notes that "Westpac is now also the first Australian bank to sign the UN Global Compact CEO Water Mandate to tackle the emerging global water crisis." Reference to a water crisis makes the background image of an iceberg all the more pertinent: with over two-thirds of the world's fresh water locked up in glaciers and ice caps, the question of water as a resource is closely tied to any changes in that ice, such as melting.[51]

The choice of an image drawn from the cryosphere for the Westpac advertisement is significant because it serves as shorthand for environmental change and signals crossover between different regions. In this case, the allusion is not to the observable melting of Antarctic ice but to halting this process. To understand this message, the audience needs to be familiar with current discourse around climate change. Here, the message created by the advertisement is that Westpac is a responsible corporate citizen; by choosing to bank with them, customers are also choosing to help protect the environment—including the ice at the poles. This message was carefully considered by the advertising company. As Mark Sareff from the Campaign Palace conceded to Westpac stakeholders,

"It's a fine line between building a brand for sustainability—and being accused of greenwash."[52] Antarctic imagery can get caught up in greenwashing when the reality of a company's environmental actions does not match the scope of those promised. The challenge was to present the company as being socially responsible without invoking a cynical response from Westpac's "marketing-savvy consumers."[53] The advertising company's solution was to use inference and association and to employ Antarctic imagery to communicate a message about environmentally friendly behavior.

Penguins serve a similar function in both the ABB and Westpac advertisements: standing on ice, they stand for Antarctica, which in turn stands for the environment as a whole. The birds are remarkably versatile, symbolically speaking. Unlike seals, another common Antarctic animal, the upright status of penguins means they physically resemble people. Literary scholar Elizabeth Leane and curator Stephanie Pfennigwerth have detailed how penguins have been "adopted by environmental groups as poster children for remote wilderness regions" and anthropomorphized to "stand in for humans without the added complication [in 'uninhabited' Antarctica] of actual human presence."[54] There are many other examples of advertisements that employ this technique. A series of advertisements about CFC-free aerosols that appeared in 1988 and 1989 featured a group of Adélie penguins under the heading, "Meeting of leading environmentalists welcomes change in aerosols," to promote the role of new propellant technologies in protecting the ozone layer (figure 16). The advertisements, designed by Sydney-based agency Curtis Jones and Brown Advertising Pty. Ltd., originally appeared in the pages of women's magazines *Cleo, Cosmopolitan, Australian Women's Weekly,* and *Reader's Digest,* between November 1988 and February 1989. In this instance the use of penguins was particularly apposite, as the ozone "hole," which appears annually above the Antarctic, was first discovered by scientists making measurements at the British Faraday and Halley Stations on the Antarctic Peninsula.[55] The penguins are depicted as the ultimate environmentalists, as they live in the polar environment—a message that also comes through in the ABB and Westpac advertisements, where the birds are framed as having the most to gain from any change. Thanks to their upright bodies, tuxedo feather patterns, and comical

FIG 16. Penguin advertisement relating to CFC-free aerosols, 1988–89. The Aerosol Information Service, "Happy 50th Anniversary."

waddle, penguins can also be used to suggest a human presence when there is none, giving the audience more reason to identify with the message. These examples illustrate the ways in which animals can become "symbolic pawns in human debates"—including debates about climate, fragility, and Antarctica.[56]

Penguins aside, both the ABB and Westpac campaigns illustrate how, in light of the "increasing global segment that values environmentalism," "greening" a business is a lucrative proposition.[57] Penguins, like other iconic species in more tropical locations, can help with this. In each of the cases examined here, the advertisement is earnest, suggesting that the consumers of ABB and Westpac products both care about environmental issues and can make sense of Antarctic imagery as a symbol for environmental issues at large.

Antarctica is represented as the ultimate environment to protect, and this framing of the continent continues to be employed in advertising campaigns. Casting Antarctica as a fragile environmental treasure does not always lead to such solemn presentations. Indeed, the same imagery that is used to signal environmental themes has also been used to subvert the very commercial narrative it has helped to build.

Melting Ice: Double Takes and Double Meanings

Having gained sufficient traction as a vehicle for conveying climate narratives in the cultural sphere, the same imagery of ice and penguins became ripe for satire that consciously subverted the protection narrative. In early 2007 Italian clothing company Diesel launched a multi-platform advertising campaign entitled "Global Warming Ready." Designed by the Paris arm of agency Marcel, the campaign rolled out newspaper, magazine, transit, and billboard advertisements across the world. Striking imagery "depicting ordinary scenes in a surreal, post-Global Warming world" was at the heart of the advertisements.[58] Models were portrayed lounging in front of a range of well-known global landmarks, such as the Eiffel Tower in Paris, St Mark's Square in Venice, and Mount Rushmore in South Dakota, but the scenes had been altered to suggest a much warmer climate: jungle in Paris, tropical birds in Venice, sandy beaches around Mount Rushmore—and penguins atop rocky outcrops rather than ice. Each image featured the same minimal text—a red Diesel logo in the bottom-right corner and a stamp in the top-right corner, proclaiming the models "Global Warming Ready." A press release from Diesel described the campaign as "a thought-provocative, international advertising concept designed to ignite debate while raising awareness of the issues surrounding climate change."[59] Debate certainly ensued, with the relationship between climate change and consumption the focus of environmental criticism of the advertisements.[60]

While Diesel claimed the campaign was an ironic way of provoking discussion at a time when, in the words of spokesperson Joelle Berdugo-Adler, "Global warming was a tremendously hot button issue," the company was accused of being "far less concerned with fomenting political activism and lifestyle change than they are with selling their brand."[61] Commentator Guy Pearse pointed out that "Diesel hasn't mentioned the [climate change] issue since the campaign and doesn't publish information on its own carbon footprint," suggesting that the Global Warming Ready campaign was little more than a lucrative way of capitalizing on buzzwords.[62] Nevertheless, the campaign was a success in terms of scale and critical acclaim—Global Warming Ready went on to win a Silver Lion for Print at the 2007 Cannes Lions International Festival of Creativity.[63]

While the power of advertising lies in its ability to persuade consumers to buy a product, the precise meaning of the Global Warming Ready tagline remains ambiguous. Is it the scantily clad models themselves—and therefore the company that makes their scanty clothes—who are ready for a warmer climate? Or is the advertisement meant to suggest that the Diesel brand itself is "going green" by taking an active stance in trying to combat climate change? Should the advertisements be read as a swipe at the concerns of environmentalists, a critique of commercial markets, a call to action, or a playful amalgamation of all three? Supporting promotional materials—including the Diesel website, a documentary-style filmed advertisement, and the booklet *World's Coolest Hotspots Guide* presenting maps of various regions of the world affected by sea-level rise, including a green-colored Antarctica—add little clarity. A short online film, in a serious BBC style, outlined why global warming was "bad," before announcing that "Global warming cannot stop our lives!"[64] Images of the glamorous young people featured in the advertising campaign partying in exotic locations prompted Pearse to claim, "When it comes to the fashion industry and climate change, it *is* mostly about *looking* hot."[65] Taking a stance on global warming is typical behavior for a brand that is trying to promote its environmental consciousness, but such a straightforward reading of the environmental message is denied by the presentation of self-centred people who appear quite content in their post-global-warming lives.

Accompanying links and details on Diesel's campaign webpage are equally contradictory. At first glance, web materials appear to be irreverent: in order to save the planet, visitors to Diesel's website were exhorted to "save the planet by having sex (quietly) to cut down on heating . . . insulating homes with recycled denim, never taking a shower . . . giving fashion magazines to grannies . . . and getting rid of the fridge at home."[66] At the same time, the site promotes Al Gore's famous 2006 climate change film, *An Inconvenient Truth*, and provides a link to Diesel's partner organization, the online grassroots movement StopGlobalWarming.org. Diesel's statement on the movement's website suggested a modicum of self-reflection, with the acknowledgment: "We are only a fashion company and do not think that—with just one campaign—we can save the world."[67] This statement could, however, be read as marketing spin that aims to preempt any critical media reaction to their campaign. It is not uncommon for advertising agencies to use dissonance and subversion to attract attention to brands and products marketed to young people; the shock factor and the pushing of boundaries are part of the attraction.[68] The Global Warming Ready campaign may be designed to shock rather than promote environmental values, but Diesel goes on to suggest that an advertising campaign can nonetheless have an impact: "If our unconventional tone of voice and the reputation of our brand can grab and hold people's attention a little longer than a news feature can, make them think twice about the consequence of all our actions and realize our individual responsibility, then something at least will have been accomplished."[69] The inclusion of such material in the campaign indicates an awareness of the scrutiny the campaign would, and did, provoke. Marketing scholars Micael Dahlen, Fredrik Lange, and Terry Smith asked in 2010 whether Diesel's announcement that its products were "Global Warming Ready" was "a strategic shift to eco-fashion" or "a short-term 'green wash' use of tactical positioning to gain attention."[70] A third possibility exists—that the Global Warming Ready campaign was a play on both and designed to highlight the issues around using buzzwords in advertising, while at the same time doing just that, by using the term "global warming" in order to play to the consumer market. Diesel's clientele are mostly young and have been exposed to the climate change message for much of their lives. Here, Diesel relies on that audience experiencing climate change exhaustion and enjoying the naughtiness of reveling, however briefly, in the prospect of a warmer world. The campaign's intentional ambiguities and the assumed sophistication of the target audience provide important contexts for reading the Antarctic advertisement from the Global Warming Ready series.

In the Diesel advertisement, then, existing visual language is employed to communicate ambivalent and subversive environmental values. The fact that an Antarctic setting—signaled only by penguins—was included in this series of Global Warming Ready advertisements confirms that the continent has come to be understood as the locus of disastrous environmental change. In this Diesel campaign, the melting of Antarctic ice is taken to its extreme conclusion, where there is no longer any ice left to melt. Despite calling upon the rhetoric of melt and change, the advertisement does not carry a sincere message in reference to Antarctica. At first glance, the advertisement seems to assume that for its target audience a balmy climate where one can wear a bikini is preferable to an icescape and that the loss of the cryosphere is no great problem. Alternatively, the advertisement can be read as a reaction to the oversaturation of the media by narratives of climate change in which Antarctic imagery is subverted in order to play into the tongue-in-cheek nature of the overall campaign, thus gaining publicity for the brand at large. Whether one reads it as an ironic comment on how slogans can be used to sell or as a denial of a bleaker future, the advertisement appeals to different values around Antarctica from those of the earlier ABB and Westpac examples. Antarctica is used as a tool through which environmental messages are propagated, represented, contested, and recast for a range of different purposes.

Reflections on a Fragile Continent

When it comes to representations of Antarctica, the frame of fragility is recurrent and manifests itself in different ways. These advertisements are all anthropocentric, presenting humans as the active agents—even when penguins are used as stand-ins for humans, as demonstrated in Westpac's Equator Principles campaign. As such, they do not tell us about Antarctica as a place so much as what Antarctica is used for—the continent becomes a symbol for environmental change. In general, the geographical qualities of Antarctica matter less in these advertisements than the ways Antarctic ice and animals can be drawn upon as a proxy to show or allude to melt and climate change—the mobilization of the fragility theme therefore overlaps with the use of icy imagery from the Arctic in northern campaigns. Imagery ranging from glaciers to penguins to the continent itself has been used to promote "green" products, with a variety of companies capitalizing on the idea that Antarctica needs to be protected. Growing consumer awareness of environmental issues from the 1980s onward meant green initiatives became more valuable. So, too, did icy imagery. The rhetoric of climate change, often symbolized by Antarctica, saturated the media, including appearing in advertise-ments for companies that wanted to push their own green credentials. Penguins and icebergs were employed to stand in for an environment that each company in turn could claim to be protecting, and the idea of Antarctica as a fragile place that is under threat entered into popular consciousness. Once polar imagery gained sufficient cultural traction to be easily understood as a symbol for climate change and the environ-ment, the same imagery could be employed in subversive ways, as seen in the Diesel example.

In its fragility, Antarctica also makes humans fragile and vulnerable to the impacts of anthropogenic climate change—some more so than others. To take one dominant and very visual example: if Antarctica is at risk of melting, coastlines the world over are also at risk of flooding due to sea-level rise, with low-lying countries and small-island developing states at the greatest risk. This kind of bad-news story is not employed in our advertising examples, however; their purpose is to sell products or services to people, not to preach dystopian futures. This drive to sell lies behind the rhetoric of protection that urges consumers to buy this product and protect that ice. Such a message brings security and a feeling of agency to the consumers who make market choices based on their own environmental values, and it brings profits to the companies that employ environmental rhetoric in their advertising campaigns. For Antarctica itself, such shifts in framing might ultimately make little difference. Back home, however, they reveal dominant values and showcase what is valued. No matter the tone or intended message, in the advertisements considered, Antarctica is there for the melting.

Destination Antarctica 6

Tourism and the
Polar Product

In June of 2014, John Oliver aired an anti-tourism campaign on his show, *Last Week Tonight*.[1] The clip, which runs for just over a minute, features a range of familiar images that signify "Antarctica"—including penguins, seals, and ice. It begins with panoramic views of icebergs and wildlife, accompanied by a voiceover: "Antarctica. The majestic seventh continent. An unspoiled land of incredible ice formations that you simply have to see." The imagery and language initially mirror those used in regular tourism campaigns, but the message soon shifts, with the narrator quipping: "Seeing as how you're looking at them right now, you've technically seen them." The spoof advertisement addresses the motivations people may have for visiting—that it is exotic or that wildlife can be seen up close—then offers alternatives: go to Belgium instead—"Have your friends been to Belgium? No? Then it's exotic to them"—or watch the video of a seal with 3D glasses—"it's like you're actually here." And if you really must have ice, the clip suggests a visit to Alaska instead—when you show people your photos, "they won't know the difference." This satirical treatment of the branding of Antarctic tourism shines a light on the industry in an irreverent way, while touching on several concerning elements of the practice. While Oliver's punchline is "Stop Coming Here!," the reality is that thousands of people *do* go to Antarctica every year, and high-definition film footage is considered a poor substitute for the real thing. Thanks to tourism, Antarctica is now being marketed as a commodity in its own right.

Antarctic tourism poses a perceived threat to the branding image of a pristine and untouched continent as it draws attention to the human presence. Oliver's anti-tourism segment was aired shortly after a report highlighting the need for better protection of Antarctica was released.[2]

Findings from the research paper were widely reported in the Australian media, with the message, "Antarctica needs to be better protected from human visitors, including tourists and researchers."[3] This in turn was picked up by Oliver, who pointed out the disconnect between a TV segment that talks about the vulnerability of Antarctica to melt, while showing the host eating a chunk of Antarctic ice.[4] Such satirical treatment of the topic of Antarctic tourism indicates that the presence of people in Antarctica has come to the attention of the general public as a mainstream issue. Like all good satire, the "Don't Visit Antarctica" clip elicits a laugh but also touches a nerve.

The tourism context foregrounds Antarctica as a material presence as opposed to a proxy or metaphor; it is a place visited by tourists and workers alike. These days it is no longer harvestable seals, whales, and minerals that are of interest commercially but rather the commercially exploitable sense of "wilderness" of the continent, and the "cool" and profitable use of the materiality of ice. Thanks to a range of tourism providers, that ice is no longer entirely out of physical reach—instead, embodied experiences of interactions with Antarctica are for sale. These interactions are often intertwined with familiar themes related to Antarctica—heroism, extremity, fragility, and purity. All have been reprised in the context of Antarctica as a destination, with different framings appealing to different markets. The tourism model of engagement allows far more women and people of color to travel to Antarctica compared to the explorer-science model of engagement, presenting opportunities for personal development, but also for the continent to transform into a place of meaning for a much wider range of people.

In asking what promises have been made to prospective consumers of the Antarctic landscape, this chapter also explores the concept that travel to Antarctica is a life-changing experience. As an extension of tourism and Antarctic voyages being sold as transformational experiences, the very *idea* of Antarctica as a place for transformation has also been mobilized in commercial situations—including those far from the ice itself. As the advertisements and branding examples in this chapter show, Antarctica is more than just a travel destination—it is a carefully curated polar product that reflects back the interests and desires of tourists and armchair travelers alike.

Transformational Antarctica: A Life-Changing Branding

A 2017 video from Intrepid Travel outlines "5 Life-Changing Experiences in Antarctica," including "kayaking to icebergs" and "experiencing the elusive 7th continent."[5] This video articulates a concept that is common in representations of Antarctica across a range of media: Antarctica is a place of transformation, where life-changing experiences take place.[6] Literary scholar Elizabeth Leane has detailed this phenomenon at length in *Antarctica in Fiction*; in a chapter entitled "The Transforming Nature of Antarctic Travel" she claims, "the 'Antarctica of the mind'—the continent as a place of soul-searching and personal transformation—has come into its own as a theme within Antarctic fiction during the late twentieth century."[7] This "Antarctica of the mind" also presents a branding opportunity for self-improvement. For those seeking a change in their everyday lives, the inhospitable and wild nature of Antarctica provides an ideal backdrop against which to examine priorities—it is therefore an ideal, if very exclusive, location to run programs on leadership.[8] When it comes to the Far South, media scholar Arthur Asa Berger posits that "there may be a mythic impetus, of which we are unaware, behind our desire to see Antarctica or land on the continent"—such an impetus can make south polar branding all the more alluring.[9] The trope of transformation in the Antarctic parallels the structure of familiar fairy tales that feature metamorphosis as a central element: hero sets out on a journey, faces adversity, overcomes challenges, gains new insights, and returns home (an arc familiar from the analysis of heroes in chapter 1). In the case of Antarctica, tourists must first set sail into stormy seas and brave the Southern Ocean to enjoy the wonders of the frozen continent.

Physical travel to Antarctica is often mirrored by internal feelings, as transformation is about going forth into the unknown, and the unknown provokes anxieties and provides opportunities. The journey to Antarctica can therefore act as a metaphor for an internal journey of discovery—as is also the case in other extreme environments. Polar and high mountain areas have employed similar branding strategies, using extremity as a draw. Adventure historian Jeff Maynard sees both the North Pole and Mount Everest as similar goals: people "feel they have 'conquered' it, while in truth they have really conquered fears, shortcomings, and limits of physical endurance within themselves."[10] In the Antarctic context, the notion of personal growth leading to a changed outlook is central to the concept of the "Antarctic ambassador." This idea holds that travel to Antarctica is one way of creating advocates for the frozen continent who will take action for the protection of the region and educate others about environmental protection.[11] While studies have shown little change to behaviors back home following an Antarctic voyage, the idea of the ambassador endures and is often figured as a rallying point around which tourists can share images and reflect on their own personal experiences.[12] Human geographer Karen Alexander and her coauthors propose defining an Antarctic ambassador as "someone [i.e., individual or group] who has a connection to, knowledge of and passion for the Antarctic (as a space, place or idea), who represents and champions Antarctica and its values, and who supports Antarctica through communication and behaviour"—they note that visiting Antarctica is not a requirement for becoming an ambassador for the place, opening the door to discussions about virtual travel as well as embodied journeys.[13] A voyage south can thus be conceptualized in several ways—a physical journey, an exploration of imagined landscapes as they are replaced by experience, and shifting attitudes and transformations within oneself. All these versions have been seized upon by advertisers, brand managers, and industry and subsequently emerge in advertisements for the Antarctic tourism product.

Antarctic Tourism: Setting the Scene

While Antarctica may be sliced off the bottom of most Mercator maps, it is nevertheless home to a thriving tourism industry, with over seventy-four thousand people heading south for leisure in the pre-COVID-19 summer season of 2019–20.[14] Definitions of Antarctic tourism range from encompassing "all human activities either mainly pursuing recreational and/ or educational purposes" on the continent, to specific descriptions of "the commercial (for profit) transport (including accommodation and catering) of non-government travelers to and from Antarctica for the purpose of pleasure."[15] Accordingly, it could be argued that the wealthy New Zealand farmer George Buckley fitted the "tourist" bill back in 1907.[16] Having donated to Shackleton's 1907 *Nimrod* expedition, he was permitted to accompany the ship to the edge of the ice and back for recreational reasons.[17] Other scholars have suggested that Lawrence Oates and Apsley Cherry-Garrard—both of whom received a place on Scott's 1911 *Terra Nova* expedition in exchange for donations—could be described as tourist-like as a result of the financial exchanges that took place.[18] By this logic, Antarctic tourism is over a century old.

Antarctic tourism on a commercial scale, however, did not begin until the late 1950s. In 1956 an Argentinian Douglas DC-6B aircraft offered a four-hour scenic flight for sixty-six passengers over the peninsula region, while the Argentine ship *Les Eclaireurs* headed for the South Shetland Islands in 1958.[19] Swedish entrepreneur Lars-Eric Lindblad, who is often hailed as the father of polar expedition cruise tourism, began offering regular voyages to the Antarctic Peninsula for fare-paying passengers in the late 1960s, and this set the precedent for modern-day tourism—tourist expeditions have headed to Antarctica every year since 1966. Lindblad was responsible for building the *Lindblad Explorer*, the world's first ship designed for Antarctic tourism, and his model of small expedition-style vessels continues to be used today.[20] Over forty Category 1 (13–200 passengers) and Category 2 (201–500 passengers) vessels regularly head south, and these ships carry the bulk of tourists who visit Antarctica every season.[21] Following the introduction of the Polar Code in January 2017, which provided certainty regarding operating in polar waters, many companies commissioned new vessels, expanding the fleet. A handful of companies also offer small-group expeditions to the continent's interior. These tourists go South to voyage in the footsteps of Heroic Era explorers; to participate in extreme sports events, including marathons; to view emperor penguin colonies; or to scale peaks.[22] Overflights continue to be offered from Australia, but the 1979 Erebus disaster in which 257 people were killed when an Air New Zealand plane crashed into the side of Mount Erebus put an end to flight departures from New Zealand and highlights the dangers that can be associated with travel to remote areas. As of 2022 most tourists travel to the edges of the continent, which are comparatively easier to access, and they do so more often by sea than by air. The Antarctic Peninsula is therefore the region the majority of people encounter when they go to Antarctica.

FIG 17. *National Geographic Explorer* in fast ice near the Antarctic coast, 2008. Photo by Jason Auch, via Wikimedia Commons.

ANTARCTIC CITIES

Tourists embarking on an Antarctic voyage usually leave from one of five so-called Antarctic gateway cities: Ushuaia in Argentina and Punta Arenas in Chile are busy tourist hubs, while Cape Town, South Africa, and Hobart, Australia, and Christchurch, New Zealand, play significant roles for National Antarctic Programs. The much smaller centers of Bluff, in southern New Zealand, Stanley, in the Falkland Islands/Islas Malvinas, and Puerto Williams in Chilean Patagonia are sometimes cited as Antarctic gateways and promote themselves as such, but they play a smaller role. Antarctic gateway cities claim various connections to the Antarctic, including political, cultural, historical, and commercial links. Social scientist Gabriela Roldán writes how "positioning a city with the highly sought-after brand Antarctica" has been valuable in recent years, as Antarctic gateway cities have promoted their south polar identities.[23] Links to the Antarctic past are showcased in waterfront displays and signage—prominent examples include a replica of Douglas Mawson's huts on the Hobart waterfront, busts of key figures from Antarctic history along Ushuaia's waterfront, and "Antarctic Gateway" signage at the port in Punta Arenas, while promotional material also highlights local associations with the Antarctic. Tourism scholar C. Michael Hall notes that "Antarctic travel and tourism are unusual in that the economic impact does not primarily occur at the destination."[24] While passage on a vessel represents a significant initial outlay, there are not many places for tourists to spend their money once in the Antarctic region. Instead, it is the geographical gateways to Antarctica that stand to gain the most financially from Antarctic tourism (and indeed science) as visitors transit through the hubs.

The value of Antarctic branding is acknowledged by these gateway cities. Each October the city of Hobart hangs banners featuring icebergs and the tagline "Gateway to Antarctica" to coincide with the annual Conservation of Antarctic Marine Living Resources (CCAMLR) meeting—which draws delegates from around the world to discuss conservation and rational use of the Southern Ocean—ensuring this aspect of its identity is visible (figure 18). The Antarctic sector is worth $160 million annually to the local economy, and the brand aspect is explicitly identified in the 2022 Tasmanian Antarctic Gateway Strategy, where a goal is to "Build Antarctic community awareness, brand and workforce."[25] Variations on the term "Antarctic gateway" also appear in branding material produced by other local or state governments, often in conjunction with past and present polar connections that are highlighted as a draw for tourists visiting their towns and cities. Ushuaia, Hobart and Christchurch have offered "Antarctic experience" tourist attractions for those visiting the cities, delivered via a virtual reality ride, a museum, and the International Antarctic Centre's interactive museum campus, respectively. Punta Arenas is currently planning its own Antarctic tourism facility. Such attractions suggest there is potential for the Antarctic gateway cities to further develop their identities both as logistically and culturally important Antarctic places. Further examples of Antarctic-specific local tourism experiences are the *Polar Pathways* booklet that highlights historical sites of polar importance in Hobart and a *Traces of Antarctica* booklet that emphasizes connections between Punta Arenas and Heroic Era figures such as Ernest Shackleton—

FIG 18. The city of Hobart advertises itself as the "Gateway to Antarctica," 2020. Photo by Hanne Nielsen.

both showcase the wealth of significant Antarctic sites within the cities. While some attractions are targeted at tourists en route to Antarctica, many appeal to a much wider audience. Antarctic-specific festivals, such as IceFest in Christchurch and the Australian Antarctic Festival in Hobart, are opportunities for these places to promote Antarctic connections to a local audience. While southern connections occur on a range of scales, local governments in gateway cities are increasingly invested in Antarctic place branding.

The concept of Brand Antarctica is therefore valuable to a range of invested stakeholders at these jumping-off points for tourists and expeditioners, as well as when examining the Antarctic continent itself.

The Antarctic tourism product follows a similar format across opera-tors. With the majority of tourism concentrated around the Antarctic Peninsula, vessels leave from Ushuaia or Punta Arenas and spend two days crossing the Drake Passage before arriving at the South Shetland Islands. During this time, guests are entertained with on-board lectures, bird-watching from the decks, and social events such as quizzes. Those traveling with an IAATO operator also attend a mandatory briefing, which outlines acceptable behaviors in the Antarctic, before scrubbing outer layers of clothing and boots in preparation for their first landing. Once in the Antarctic Peninsula region, a typical day for an average vessel (200–500 passengers) includes a landing, a Zodiac cruise, and short edu-cational lectures in the evening to recap the day's events—these aspects are showcased in a Chimu Adventures brochure about the region (figure 19). The Expedition team mediate the Antarctic experience—they ferry guests to shore, act as guides at the landing sites, provide commentary on Zodiac cruises, and ensure everyone respects minimum distances from wildlife. Highlights of a typical trip could include a continental landing at Brown Bluff or Neko Harbor, a visit to a historically significant site like Whaler's Bay or Port Lockroy, encounters with glaciers and icebergs, and seeing wildlife, such as penguins, seals, and whales.

With the growth in the Antarctic tourism market, Brand Antarctica is becoming more diverse, with various market segments targeted in different ways as companies seek to differentiate their polar product from others on the market. In some cases, operators promote their green credentials, such as new hybrid vessels or B Corp certification, to appeal to environmentally conscious travelers. In others, the standard peninsula experience is augmented by adventure activities that include opportuni-ties to camp on the ice, go kayaking or paddle boarding, and even view the underwater environment in a submarine. These activities are presented as unique additions to the polar product package—as the Far South becomes more accessible thanks to a growing number of vessels operating in the area, the place itself is no longer enough of a selling point. Instead, the focus shifts to "what I did" rather than simply "where I went," centering tourists within the environment, with Antarctica as a backdrop.

Chimu

PRISTINE ANTARCTICA
ABOARD THE MV HONDIUS
Live for today...

Explore Antarctica early in the season. This magical time allows to admire vast swathes of sea ice, a large quantity of expanded icebergs and an abundance of wildlife such as penguins, seals and albatrosses.

DEPARTS: 22 NOV 2019   DURATION: 11 DAYS

Highlights and inclusions:

- Sail aboard the MV Hondius for an expedition cruise in Antarctic waters. This new brand vessel is available for the first time from 2019 and is one of the strongest ice-strenghtened vessels in the Polar regions.
- Explore deep into the White Continent and encounter an incredible variety of wildlife.
- Wander on the spectacular shores of the Antarctic Peninsula, completely blanketed in pure white snow.
- Take advantage of the early season and admire large quantities of extensive icebergs, glaciated mountains and volcanoes.
- Enjoy regular zodiac excursions and on-shore landings.
- Benefit from a variety of on-board activities including educational lectures on the history, geology and ecology by the expedition team.
- Enjoy the amenities on board including expedition lounge, restaurant, bar, pool, jacuzzi, library, gym and sauna.
- Your cruise is full-board including all breakfast, lunch, dinner and snacks.
- Take advantage of optional activities during the voyage such as kayaking, camping and snowshoeing.

FIG 19. Chimu Adventures advertisement featuring "pristine" branding of Antarctica, as featured on websites, partner collateral, and trade shows, 2019. Courtesy of Chimu Adventures.

Antarctic tourism is currently managed by the International Association of Antarctica Tour Operators (IAATO). The association was founded by industry players in 1991 to "advocate, promote and practice safe and environmentally responsible private sector tourism to the Antarctic."[26] Since then the Antarctic tourism sector has continued to grow, and IAATO has been at the forefront of management and regulation, creating guidelines for operators and attending the Antarctic Treaty Consultative Meeting (ATCM) as an invited expert. IAATO presents information at each ATCM, outlining the tourist activities of the previous season and providing a detailed breakdown of the activities that have taken place at each site, from camping and Zodiac cruising to scuba diving and endurance races. As an industry body conscious of the connections between the image of tourism and the social license to operate, IAATO also hosts social media accounts on Facebook (8,700 followers) and Instagram (8,000 followers) for the "Antarctic Ambassadors" brand. People who have traveled to Antarctica are encouraged to share experiences and images, which often echo marketing photos from promotional brochures, and promote the protection of the continent. These accounts highlight the importance of the tourism sector in mediating human experiences of the Far South both in situ and online and reinforce the leading role IAATO plays as an industry body in both branding the practice of Antarctic tourism and facilitating wider discussions about Antarctica.

The effective management of Antarctic tourism is an ongoing challenge, particularly in light of COVID-19. The global pandemic threw the expedition industry into turmoil, with border closures and the fast spread of the virus leading to the cancellation of the 2020–21 polar tourism seasons. The fact that operators shifted bookings to the 2021–22 season and picked up with similar marketing material in pre-pandemic times suggests that the continent continues to hold allure for would-be tourists. Although the last virus-free place on earth is once again open for business, the pandemic has had both operational and branding implications for the industry. In addition to these lost seasons, the expedition cruise industry had to grapple with reputational damage in relation to the pandemic, with cruise ships regularly described in the media as "petri dishes," and the Antarctic cruise vessel *Greg Mortimer* becoming an example of how a virus can spread on the confines of a ship. As a result, the hygiene procedures and amenities on board vessels featured more explicitly in collateral in the following seasons, adding a further health-focused layer to the existing purity rituals associated with biosecurity.

Criticisms have also been leveled at the current model of Antarctic tourism management due to the central role the tourist industry plays. With a growing number of operators entering the Antarctic market, there have been periodic calls for greater oversight of Antarctic tourism through the ATS. The pandemic-induced pause in operations led zoologist and expedition leader Peter Carey to argue that 2020 marked the ideal time to transition from "managing" Antarctic tourism in a reactive way to proactively "regulating" the practice.[27] Carey suggests that this regulation could be linked to the existing framework for Antarctic Specially Protected Areas (ASPAS), or addressed via a specific tourism annex. Any changes to the management of Antarctic tourism would come with their own challenges. Decisions can take much longer within the consensus-based ATS than they do within the dynamic industry-based body of IAATO. For example, IAATO created guidelines for the use of drones in the Antarctic several years before this was recognized as an issue on the ATCM stage. In announcing a new policy on fuel consumption data in 2022, Amanda Lynnes of IAATO noted "one of IAATO's strengths is the ability of its diverse membership to take collective action, often over and above what is required by global regulators."[28] Being visibly proactive in the environmental protection space is important to IAATO for both operational reasons and in terms of social license—protection of the Antarctic is central to the polar tourism product and also IAATO's own organizational brand. The IAATO brand is particularly visible on board member vessels, with posters, briefing slideshows, and in some cases even guide and tourist clothing featuring the logo – the brand has been so successful it has led some within the industry to associate IAATO, rather than the ATS, with all Antarctic tourism governance responsibility.[29]

Something for Everyone: Types of Tourism

Tourism in Antarctica takes many forms, with trips to the South exhibiting hallmarks of adventure tourism, extreme tourism, ecotourism, and last chance tourism, among others. These aspects are foregrounded to different degrees by various operators, with Antarctica described as "so extreme and remote that it barely feels like it's part of Earth at all" and a "fragile Antarctic ecosystem" to which humans have responsibilities.[30] Expeditions present a range of experiences, drawing upon historical links, unique encounters, and natural features, depending on location, season timing, and nearby points of interest. Prospective tourists can browse marketing collateral to find an Antarctic offering that aligns best with their interests and values—this material therefore deserves attention.

As the final continent to be explored by humans, Antarctica has long been cast as a "last frontier" by a range of interested parties, including governments, media, the tourism industry, and gateway cities. For seasoned travelers, it is often understood to be continent number seven, so a trip south completes the set; classic ten-day voyages to the Antarctic Peninsula have been labeled "Discovering the 7th Continent" for this reason.[31] This kind of marketing has parallels to examples of extreme advertising discussed in chapter 3, including those relating the band Metallica's concert tour to all seven continents. While increased ship traffic has raised questions about the appropriateness of marketing Antarctic voyages as "expeditions," rather than the less daring sounding term "cruises," the term continues to be used within the industry.[32] This language choice has direct branding implications, drawing a link between modern activities and Heroic Era expeditions. "Expeditioner" is also a term used by National Antarctic Programs and can be seen to confer more legitimacy upon the experience than the term "tourist."

Antarctica's natural environment is a key drawcard for tourists who head south. Images of penguins and pristine scenery are common in advertising materials, and tourists are often eager to recreate these images themselves. In their analysis of a series of tourist surveys, tourism researchers Machiel Lamers, Eke Eijgelaar, and Bas Amelung concluded that the elements of "wildlife, scenery, adventure and remoteness" were "the most important motives for travelling to Antarctica."[33] Many operators also promote their on-board enrichment and lecture programs, designed to provide further context for guests. This has led some scholars to characterize Antarctic tourism as ecotourism.[34] According to tourism scholar Elspeth Frew, ecotourism should include a nature-based element, an element of education, and should be sustainable, both environmentally and socio-culturally.[35] Given the debates over the sustainability of an industry that relies heavily on fossil fuels, not all Antarctic tours fit the bill. The term "ecotourism" has itself come under fire, with some seeing the concept of ecotourism as "little more than a marketing concept attached to almost any tourist product to attract those sympathetic to environmental causes."[36] Nevertheless, an interest in the natural environment (and at times its preservation) remains a strong motivating factor for many Antarctic tourists.

Both wilderness and fragility framings of Antarctica can provide motivations for a tourist to visit, by activating anxieties associated with last chance tourism. Last chance tourism, which has been defined as "a niche tourism market where tourists explicitly seek vanishing landscapes or seascapes, and/or disappearing natural and/or social heritage," offers a different sort of framing.[37] In the case of Antarctica, Lamers, Eijgelaar, and Amelung explain how this "last chance" discourse is "centered around the disappearance of ecosystems (visit before their grandeur is gone) and congestion (visit before it is too crowded)."[38] While this offers a particular way of looking at Antarctica, the concept of last chance tourism is not often popular among tour operators; although "last chance" might be the tourist's motivation, the operator cannot be seen to pander to this because it makes the tourist sound selfish and undermines their own focus in helping to protect Antarctica. IAATO explicitly requests members to avoid using language such as "see it before it is gone," noting that it instead seeks to work together "with the Antarctic community to protect the continent for future generations."[39] As a result, the fragility framing appears far less in tourism advertising material than in other framings of Antarctica. This is not unexpected; in her study of World Heritage Sites, Frew found that "only a small number of tour operators capitalized on aspects of global warming to promote their tours."[40] Instead, the focus is on what remains, and images promise snow and ice.

ADVERTISING, PHOTOGRAPHY, AND SYMBOLIC CONSUMPTION

The images that a tourist is exposed to prior to an Antarctic voyage play an important role in shaping their own response to the Antarctic environment. Given communications scholar Keyan Tomaselli's assertion that "tourists as consumers tend to demand an idealized experience promised by the glossy catalogue," those images matter.[41] A far more diverse visual economy is at play today compared to thirty years ago, and advertising photography has been given increasing attention by operators in recent years. The 2020 IAATO Annual Marketing and PR Self-Audit reminds members of the power that images have in establishing and tempering guest expectations. For example, operators were asked to consider whether the images they used reflected the ATS's adopted guidelines and recommendations, with a checklist item on small boat depictions accompanied by the note, "If lens foreshortening makes the boat appear closer, use supporting text to explain that the vessel is a safe distance from the glacier."[42] This is particularly important due to both safety concerns when operating around ice and reputational concerns should the image be "taken out of context by the public, media, and Antarctic Treaty nations who authorize tourism activities."[43] Images of particular tourism activities could have a direct impact on permitting and the ability of companies to continue their operations into the future. The IAATO guide also reminds operators to take care with wildlife depictions and to avoid showing seals with open mouths (as this implies the animal is in distress) or featuring emperor penguins unless the itinerary specifically focuses on this species. This demonstrates an awareness that the images selected for advertising material in fact serve many purposes, including setting guest expectations and depicting best practices in safety and wildlife interactions. Advertisements for Antarctic tourism not only make promises to consumers but also represent the public face of the broader industry.

Antarctic tour operators market the opportunity to take the same photographs that abound in brochures, tour guides, and on social media. Elements such as icebergs and penguins are often used to stand in for the continent, creating a vocabulary of ice and charismatic megafauna that comes to be inextricably linked to the destination itself. As photographer Anne Noble puts it, the Antarctic Peninsula is "the perfect place to take people to recapture that photograph, that image of Antarctica they already have."[44] Companies offer specific "Antarctic Photography Safari" packages, advertise free polar photography handbooks, and often have an on-board photographer to create an official record of the voyage and to help guests with their own camera equipment.[45] The desire to take photographs is identified as a key motivator in several advertising brochures for Antarctic tours, which feature stunning scenes of penguins, whales, and icebergs in brilliant sunshine. These act as a suggestion of what a prospective guest can expect to encounter through their lens; Chimu Adventures even titled a ten-day Antarctic Peninsula voyage "Images of Antarctica." Photography is not just a means to produce images but also a process that contributes to a tourist's overall experience of any given destination. For those in Antarctica, the practice of photography helps to frame the tourist experience. Tourism and visual technologies scholar Caroline Scarles explains how "photography and the visual have long been understood as fundamental to tourism"—they are important because "photographs and photography facilitate the enlivening and creation of place and experience."[46] A tourist may take a photograph of a whale's fluke that is identical to those of dozens of other people on the same ship, but the process of taking the image helps to create the overall encounter, and the resulting image helps link the Antarctic to the tourist's own personal experience.

What is promised and what is delivered in terms of branding and advertising come together with the click of each camera shutter.

Reprising Frames: Familiar Themes in Inhospitable Terrain

Tourism and advertising go hand in hand: both have a commercial focus, and both offer the promise of a different way of being. Tourism scholar Charlotte Echtner has argued that tourism can be seen as "a form of symbolic consumption whereby tourists display their identity and social roles through the destinations they choose."[47] For tourists, the choices they make about travel destinations are informed by preexisting ideas and myths. As sociologist Mark Paterson explains, these "myths pervade tourist brochures and websites, helping to confirm existing beliefs about places, cultures and nature."[48] These narratives continue to be perpetuated throughout the experience of travel itself. Aware of the existing tropes and myths about the destination, actors such as tour operators and guides actively construct experiences that will meet with expectations and allow tourists to use their chosen destination as a badge of identity. In the case of advertisements for Antarctica, the symbolism and discourse associated with the continent—including transformation, sublimity, and exclusivity—is just as important as the actual destination itself.

Antarctic tourism marketing material primes tourists for their impending south polar encounter. As tourism scholars Nigel Morgan and Annette Pritchard put it, "leisure and tourism experiences are literally constructed in our imagination through advertising and the media," so the process of imagining a destination is a more influential process than any subsequent travel.[49] In the case of Antarctic cruise tourism, common myths, messages, and themes are also apparent in onboard materials, including the IAATO *Going Ashore* briefing video. The short clip, which outlines the rules and regulations associated with an Antarctic visit, evokes ideas of extremity by explaining how "the Antarctic environment is inhospitable, unpredictable and potentially very dangerous, with hidden crevasses and frequent blizzards." It also uses the theme of purity when urging for ongoing protection: "Largely untouched and undisturbed, special guidelines exist to ensure it continues to be a constant source of wonder and inspiration." Finally, the IAATO briefing video encourages visitors to become ambassadors for Antarctica, and to think about the future of the continent while visiting and once they return home because "respecting and appreciating your surroundings is the easiest way to ensure this experience lasts for all those who come after you."[50] The use of the terms like "beautiful," "unique," and "untouched" reinforces existing tropes about the continent and mirrors the terms used in various cruise brochures in order to build on tourists' existing Antarctic imaginary with a further layer, namely a message of protection.

The following examples—representing only a small selection of all existing advertisements—show how marketing material for Antarctica as a destination has reprised the themes from earlier chapters. All those who travel south carry an imagined continent with them already, and subsequent on-ice experiences are then viewed through these lenses.

ECHOES OF HEROISM IN MODERN-DAY ANTARCTICA

The centenary of Heroic Era voyages in recent years has been a selling point for many Antarctic tour operators. Key dates included 2011–14 for the Scott-Amundsen South Pole centenary events, and 2014–17 for those relating to Shackleton's *Endurance* expedition. Operators marketed the opportunity to travel in the footsteps of Heroic Era explorers or offered special centenary cruises where a particular expedition was the focus of history lectures—most Antarctic tour operators offered a footsteps-style expedition during the centenary of Scott's *Terra Nova* (1911–14) or Shackleton's *Endurance* (1914–17) expeditions, and some have continued these sailings; examples include Heritage Expeditions' 2023–24 In the Wake of Scott & Shackleton: Ross Sea Antarctica; Chimu Adventures' 2017 In the Wake of Mawson; and Aurora Expeditions' 2016 In Shackleton's Footsteps sailings. This follows a general trend seen in tourism advertising, where "aspects of the past are increasingly used in the construction of tourism products."[51] Tourism and empire have close historical associations, not least because "the end of empire coincided with the development of mass tourism and the commodification of leisure."[52] In the Antarctic context, narratives of empire have remained dominant, even as understandings of adventure and heroism have shifted with time. The cover of Lindblad Expeditions/National Geographic's 2015–16 cruise brochure sums up this idea: the title reads "Antarctica. Once in a Lifetime. Once in a Century. Celebrating the Centennial of the Imperial Trans-Antarctic Expedition." A trip to Antarctica is often described as a "once in a lifetime" event—largely owing to the huge financial costs involved—and here the viewer is encouraged to have that one trip coincide with centenary celebrations. The accompanying imagery suggests the sights to be seen on this kind of voyage—Adélie penguins but also icebergs, depicted as a reflection in the subject's sunglasses. This layout invites the viewer to place themselves in the shoes of the person depicted and to look back on history as they look out at the frozen icescape.

The mention of Shackleton's Imperial Trans-Antarctic Expedition is also an invitation. Renewed public interest in Shackleton's story since the late 1990s has been fueled further by tour operators wishing to attract aficionados; Aurora Expeditions promised guests "we'll even have the chance to re-enact the final leg of Shackleton's epic trek from Fortuna Bay to Stromness whaling station, then toast 'The Boss' and Frank Wild beside their graves in Grytviken cemetery."[53] Lindblad Expeditions/National Geographic advertised their centennial voyages by claiming that "Shackleton has been our inspiration, the 'patron saint' of our expeditions, since Lars-Eric Lindblad took the first citizen explorers to Antarctica in 1966."[54] The company also offered a limited-edition parka to celebrate the Shackleton centenary: "Designed specifically for the Centennial, this distinctive patch on your parka indicates that you were there during a special moment in Antarctica's history, and marks you as a polar explorer."[55] Tourists, therefore, have the opportunity to follow in the footsteps of Heroic Era figures both literally and metaphorically, adding further layers to the history of heroism in the Antarctic in the process.

The sites frequented by tourists are also revealing of the extent to which the dominant Heroic Era narratives still linger about the continent. For those who travel into the Ross Sea region, the historic huts of explorers Scott and Shackleton are draws.[56] These huts are maintained by the New Zealand Antarctic Heritage Trust (NZAHT), which has the mission "to conserve, share and encourage the spirit of exploration."[57] Every year a team of conservators travel south to dig out the winter's accumulation of ice and snow from the huts' interiors and to undertake maintenance and repair in order to ensure "the expedition bases and thousands of artifacts left behind survive and are preserved for the benefit of current and future generations" (the case of Shackleton's whisky discovered in 2007 was once such artifact).[58] The small number of tourists who have the privilege of visiting the huts are often motivated in part to visit Antarctica by the opportunity to encounter tangible reminders of Antarctica's Heroic Era history. Klaus Dodds and Kathryn Yusoff explain how the tourism industry plays an important role in maintaining "a view of the Antarctic as a space of heroic endeavor, or adventure tourism."[59] Antarctica is far more accessible than ever before, but this does not mean that past conceptions of the continent as a place for heroes have faded. Instead, past notions of Empire that have been overwritten elsewhere throughout the twentieth century remain alluringly acceptable in the Far South, as evidenced by expeditions with names such as Footsteps of Mawson. As cultural studies scholar Elena Glasberg observes, "if everyone now travels to the poles, everyone can be a hero, too."[60] Heroic Era narratives motivate the tourists to visit, and they in turn keep the stories in circulation. Heritage and modern-day leisure expeditions are therefore not mutually exclusive but rather they work together to both foment and promulgate a potent brand mythology about Antarctica, heroism, and exploration.

Quark Expeditions' 2024 Antarctic brochure and associated campaign featured the bold tagline "Explorers Wanted." Potential tourists are invited to become explorers by going outside their comfort zones and traveling "off the beaten path."[61] While present in advertisements for cruising, this distinction between hero, adventurer, and tourist is particularly pertinent when examining small, deep-field expeditions that follow in the footsteps of Heroic Era explorers such as Robert Falcon Scott, Roald Amundsen, and Ernest Shackleton. Well-known examples in include Ranulph Fiennes's In the Footsteps of Scott expedition (1984–86) and, more recently, Henry Worsley's 2008, 2011, and 2015 expeditions. Rebecca Farley argues that those seeking to undertake a reenactment "'follow in Shackleton's wake' from the moment they conceive their expeditions and begin seeking sponsorship," and it is precisely this practice "that marks their activities as 'exploration' rather than 'tourism.'"[62] In actual fact, the line is not so easy to draw; almost all Antarctic "expeditions" are supported by a company such as Adventure Network International (ANI) and so can be read as "tourism" in that sense, even if they are not guided. Elizabeth Leane goes so far as to argue that "in a continent where no one lives permanently, and no one can last without outside support, everyone is, potentially, a tourist."[63] The desire to make a distinction between tourism and other modes of travel is nothing new, nor is it exclusive to Antarctica. Geographer Tim Edensor claims that "in their quest for distinction backpackers are often concerned to distinguish themselves from others— from package tourists, who they often regard as unindividualistic," while Kate Jackson notes that during the late 1800s the media baron George Newnes, financer of the first land-based Antarctic expedition, "made a conscious effort to distinguish his perspective as a 'traveler' from that of the mere 'tourist.'"[64] In Antarctica, intrepid expeditioners continue to invoke frames of heroism and extremity in order to legitimize and gain media coverage for their undertakings, while tour companies employ terms such as "expedition" rather than "cruise" in order to align their brands with a history of heroes.

At the same time they represent themselves as unique expeditioners, many Antarctic explorers seek to travel not into new terrain, but where their role models have gone before. "In the footsteps of" expeditions do all they can to replicate earlier journeys, setting off at the same time of day, aiming to make particular milestones at the same time. For Henry Worsley, who led the 2008 In Shackleton's Footsteps expedition to the South Pole (following Shackleton's *Nimrod* route), such replication "was what this expedition was all about—to stand where Shackleton, Wild, Marshall and Adams had stood and to honour their astonishing achievement."[65] A family connection to Frank Worsley was also a selling point. Here nostalgia replaces precedence as the key thread of the expedition.[66] In many instances, recalling a famous narrative from an earlier era was also a way of gaining attention—and therefore sponsorship for the expedition, including reprisals from companies who were supporters during the Heroic Era. Heroic associations are therefore useful for modern-day explorers as they seek funding. As the centenary examples examined above have shown, those associations also carry powerful symbolic weight. Tourism operators continue to draw upon the discourse of the heroic explorer, even as they deliver fully catered packaged holidays, while centenary celebrations have seen an upsurge of interest in historic Antarctic narratives. The figures of the Heroic Era may be depicted in sepia-toned images, but their exploits are alive and well in the public imagination and therefore continue to be valuable today.

MARKETING THE EXTREME EXPERIENCE

In promotional materials for Antarctica, the ideas of adventure and extremity often go hand in hand. Adventure tourism is all about the creation of new experiences that involve a controlled risk and personal challenge in a natural environment.[67] Antarctica's remote location and chilly temperatures heighten the element of danger—not only is the landscape hostile but help is far from hand. Extreme tourism in Antarctica is a part of a wider selling of risk. Sociologist Catherine Palmer has analyzed the "corporate colonization of Everest," where money is seen to mitigate the risks of summiting the mountain.[68] Focusing on the 1996 Everest disaster, when eight people on commercial climbing expeditions were killed in a storm, Palmer argues that "the subjective experience of the risk and dangers involved in climbing the world's most feared and most famous mountain has been diluted, or stripped from the activity itself, through its construction and presentation in a range of commercial avenues."[69] Antarctica, too, has been presented as a commercial destination and carries many parallels to the Third Pole of Everest; the Antarctic is an extreme environment, safety is not guaranteed, and access is expensive. Nevertheless, tourists pay to "ski the last degree" to the South Pole, or to climb Vinson Massif, the tallest mountain on the continent. Paradoxically, the very activities that provide the risk experience act to decrease the perception of risk, as it is precisely the elements of both exclusivity and risk that make such propositions attractive.

Antarctica is hard to get to, with notoriously rough sea passages, and the choice of destination therefore marks a tourist as unique, daring, and adventurous. The extremity frame also comes through in advertisements for unusual Antarctic tourism activities like marathons. What could be more extreme than taking part in extreme sports in Antarctica's extreme environment? Several operators now offer this experience (317 runners took part in the 2019–20 season), while other companies have used the event to leverage attention for their brands. A June 2004 advertisement for Adidas Supernova Cushion shoes showcases not only the footwear but also the Antarctic Marathon itself. A map of Antarctica, photographs of a cruise ship (runners were transported on board the *Lyubov Orlova*), the runner and motivational speaker Kitty Cole, and a pair of running shoes hanging by their laces are the visual elements used to create a story about adversity and triumph. The information about the shoes themselves is the smallest text in the advertisement and relegated to the bottom left-hand corner. The advertisement's title text reads "26.2 miles by land; 422 laps around the 6th deck if you can't make it ashore," while the body copy goes on to describe the "gale force winds, snow squalls and subzero temperatures" that relegated the runners to the ship's deck.[70] In the case of this particular race (February 6, 2001), the text asks "Less than ideal? Maybe. Impossible? Never," linking the situation to the Adidas slogan "Impossible Is Nothing."

Running a marathon in Antarctica—or on an Antarctic cruise vessel—may be unexpected and challenging but does not pose an insurmountable obstacle. Adidas made use of an Antarctic link in this instance to suggest that their footwear possesses the same qualities: they can deal with unexpected terrain and extreme conditions and adapt for purposes as needed. The advertisement therefore carries echoes of Heroic Era endorsements for items such as Burberry clothing. The layout of the advertisement is unexpected, with a chaise lounge juxtaposed with paraphernalia—photos and a map—from the Antarctic marathon itself. The scrapbook quality of the imagery is low-key and suggests that the viewer could attempt (and conquer) a similar challenge at home. This message is reinforced by Kitty Cole's appearance in the advertisement—she started running as a forty-five-year-old after her brother collapsed and died on a marathon course. She has since run marathons on all seven continents.[71]

The notion of Antarctica standing as a metaphor for a personal challenge is explored more below, but this is not the only way the continent functions in this context. Here the idea of collecting the seventh continent is also associated with entry into another more exclusive club—those who have taken part in an extreme race while visiting, thus marking themselves out as more daring and adventurous than anyone else. The Adidas brand also makes use of this association, suggesting that their tough product is ideal for fearless people who enjoy living life to the extreme and attempting the impossible. The implied message, familiar from chapter 4's analysis of extremity, is that the shoes survived the blizzards of the Far South and will therefore perform admirably anywhere else on the planet. While the marathoners braved the cold, for those back home, Antarctica acts as a proxy environment. This advertisement also functioned to promote the Antarctic Marathon event by virtue of the heading and associated text and imagery. The event regularly sells out, so it requires little additional marketing beyond circles of endurance athletes—after all, who wouldn't want to enjoy "ice views" after undertaking such a grueling race?

PURITY AS COMMODITY

The "Pristine Antarctica" experience is sold using blue skies, white ice, and calm oceans, with humans on the margins of the image, if not cropped out altogether. In some cases, purity manifests through imagery of pristine icescapes, while in others, such as Fathom Expeditions or Chimu Adventures that separately set sail under the same title Pure Antarctica, it is more explicit.[72] The implied message across the board is that Antarctica is untouched, pristine, and just waiting to be discovered by the viewer. This imagery carries echoes of the ice-washing discussed in chapter 5, because travel to Antarctica does come with an environmental price tag: ironically, the per passenger CO_2 emissions on Antarctic cruise vessels exceeds that of an average international trip.[73] Unsurprisingly, the environmental impacts of polar cruise travel are rarely mentioned in promotional material—the aim of which is to attract more guests onto the itinerary. As media scholar Peter Krapp explains in his analysis of polar media, "the idea of an untouched, unexposed purity must be preserved and protected from expeditions motivated by it."[74] Whenever Antarctica is cast as a pristine destination, visible exhaust from the vessels will be tactfully cropped out of the image.

A desire to encounter nature in a place devoid of humans can provide a strong motivating factor for prospective Antarctic tourists. In reflecting on his own voyage to Antarctica, South African communications scholar Keyan Tomaselli was struck by a fellow passenger's negative reaction to a visit to Port Lockroy, which is run by the UK Antarctic Heritage Trust (UKAHT) and hosts a museum and gift shop: "She wanted ONLY nature, nature, nature (i.e., ice, penguins, birds and sea creatures)."[75] Penguins, sea creatures, and landscapes form an important part of the Antarctic imagery that is in common circulation; tins of food, magazines, and scientific equipment dating to the 1950s do not. Tourists often exhibit similar reactions when visiting Antarctic stations and encountering piles of rubbish close to the landing sites where it is waiting to be shipped out; the everyday, human imagery is not congruent with their imagined version of Antarctica and therefore not understood to be part of the "real" Antarctic experience. This visible human presence also led to criticisms of Antarctic science operations in the 1980s and 1990s. Tomaselli goes on to provide further explanation for his fellow tourist's reaction: "Nature was seen as a return to values, the healing of the body and mind. . . . It was a quest for a return to innocence in an attempt to regain physical and spiritual healing."[76] Themes of purity, wilderness, and transformation come through in these desires—whether it is possible to encounter such innocence is another question.

Despite the contradiction that visiting "untouched" places will ultimately remove their untouched nature, these parts of the world hold strong branding allure. In marketing the Pristine Antarctica experience, Chimu Adventures described a place "completely blanketed in pure white snow," while a 2017 Hurtigruten banner advertisement for Antarctica cast the place as "isolated and untouched," calling upon the same purity trope.[77] The desire to visit these untouched locations is shared by both Antarctic tourists and expeditioners: when traveling overland to the South Pole in 2008, Worsley was annoyed by signs of human presence in the Antarctic, such as skidoos and planes flying overhead.[78] The implication that wilderness should be devoid of people, save the one experiencing it, raises questions of accessibility, elitism, and environmental impacts. It is, however, a strong selling point: remote icescapes available only to those who book a tour. The preservation of—a perception of—wilderness is also a principle recognized by tour operators: IAATO's "wilderness etiquette" (since superseded by IAATO's vessel code of conduct) stated that "IAATO Member vessels are to be kept out of sight from each other as far as is practicable and work co-operatively to ensure that they give a 'buffer' time (of a recommended 30 to 60 minutes) between visits at landing sites."[79] Buffers ensure environmental guidelines are adhered to, but can also benefit guests. Having been fed a diet of imagery featuring glaciers, icebergs, penguins, and snowy panoramic vistas, with not another ship in sight, tourists bring a strong expectation that their Antarctic experience will reinforce the remote, wild, and pure aspects of the continent.

MELTING ICE: "GO BEFORE IT'S TOO LATE"

Presenting Antarctica as a fragile place can be fraught for the tour operators who visit—yet it also presents opportunities to showcase green credentials. An April 2021 *National Geographic* article by Emma Gregg headlined "Leave No Trace: Exploring the Fragile Frontiers of Antarctica and South Georgia" highlights the "eco-friendly" aspects of expedition cruising, including hybrid engines in newly built vessels, thorough biosecurity checks, and an in-depth educational program. Brochures from individual operators point to newly built vessels that feature streamlined hulls to enhance efficiency and use battery power to reduce fuel consumption. Such reassurances to potential guests are necessary in an age where the direct human impacts on Antarctica are gaining greater attention—a 2022 paper showing higher black carbon concentrations in snow around stations and popular tourist sites sparked discussions with echoes of John Oliver's "Don't Go" punchline.[80]

Operators are preempting criticisms by taking actions on a range of levels. At IAATO's annual meeting in 2022, operators pledged to create a climate strategy—this included "calculating and reducing industry emissions and setting meaningful and inclusive science-based targets."[81] In some cases, entire voyages are devoted to the topic of climate change— Aurora Expeditions' February 2023 Antarctic Climate Expedition is a key example. This sailing, hosted by well-known ocean advocate Dr. Sylvia Earle, included a climate summit (held against the backdrop of Antarctica) focused on developing creative ways to reduce carbon emissions— participants were invited to help "formulate 23 resolutions to inspire transformative changes for global net-zero emissions by 2035."[82] This is an example of tourism and environmental advocacy having explicit overlap and of the fragility framing of Antarctica being monetized to sell a trip. Celebrity also plays a role, with Dr. Earle's presence on board the vessel a draw for potential guests. This product is the perfect fit for those who care about Antarctica but are conscious of their footprint, as care for the fragile Antarctic environment is central to the (high-end) tourism product on offer.

Although the environmental credentials of new vessels are highlighted in select recent marketing materials, the majority of tourism advertisements have been largely uncritical of the environmental effects of actually traveling to Antarctica. These contradictions are highlighted in a sculptural April 2006 advertisement for student travel agency KILROY. Advertising agency Saatchi & Saatchi (Copenhagen) explain: "To highlight the more off-beat destinations KILROY has to offer we placed an iceberg on the grounds of a University Campus in Copenhagen. This allowed our primary target (KILROY are the student travel experts) to witness the melting of 'Antarctica' proving the tagline for KILROY Travels: 'Go before it's too late.'"[83] While the advertisement is unlikely to make the student audience rush to book a trip to Antarctica, the installation is eye-catching and raises brand awareness for the travel agency. KILROY had previously used the tagline "Go before it's too late" across a range of advertisements with no link to the Antarctic. Another 2006 example included an iceberg overlaid with graffiti, while in other examples the tagline related to ideas of authenticity in places such as the African savannah and British industrial heritage.[84] In this particular example, Antarctica was employed because of its association with melting ice. The melting ice, in turn, acted as a good metaphor for the "too late" message—in this visual version, being too late means the ice is no more and there's nothing to see. The KILROY advertisement is environmentally problematic—it carries an anthropocentric message, urging the audience not to miss out, rather than avoid going at all. It also highlights one of the prime issues with representing climate change in a visual medium: communications scholar Anabela Carvalho notes that "climate change is particularly 'invisible,' given the nature of the problem and the temporal and spatial scales that characterize it," and the KILROY advertisement addresses these in a novel way.[85] The original advertisement took the form of a sculpture, meaning that the temporal aspect of climate change could be accounted for—the ice melted over a period of time. Subsequent visual representations of the original installation include several panels, with images taken at intervals to show change. This allows the advertisement to do what single static images cannot; it represents change and a dynamic environment. By using the temporal element of melting to mimic processes underway in Antarctica, this KILROY advertisement both echoes the series of Larsen B ice shelf collapse images and neatly illustrates the trope of fragility. Here, that trope is harnessed to market a range of unrelated travel destinations, placing Antarctica as central part of a global climate system. Symbolically, this is last chance tourism at its finest. For Antarctica itself, the puddle left in the final panel predicts bad news.

From heroism to extremity, and purity to fragility, the themes addressed in the previous chapters have also been deployed in advertising material designed to attract tourists to the continent itself. That they are not used in equal proportions reveals the sway that the heroism frame and the associated idea of extremity continues to hold over the public imagination of Antarctica. Imagery that evokes notions of purity and wilderness is also favored, and this acts as a promise to those who purchase voyages, standing in for the photographs they themselves could take. The fragility frame is often avoided, largely because of problematic associations between global tourism and its environmental impacts—instead, this aspect of environmental protection is alluded to through references to environmental certification and new ship specifications. Advertisements for Antarctic tourism experiences, therefore, can and often do activate more than one framing of the place.

Metaphors and Challenge: What's "Your Antarctic"?

Much as melting ice can be used to stand in for climate change, the idea of Antarctica can also be used to stand in for a challenge, a state of mind, or a personal goal. The use of the continent in such a metaphorical way became particularly evident in the late twentieth and early twenty-first centuries and is often linked with the narrative and burgeoning reputation of Shackleton. His supposed quote, "Everyone has an Antarctic," is called upon to market personal development products, management books, and leadership courses.[86] The quote, like his famed "Men Wanted" job advertisement, seems to be apocryphal. Perhaps the closest source is a character in Thomas Pynchon's novel *V*, who declares, "You wait. Everyone has an Antarctic" with connotations of foreboding rather than challenge.[87] Despite these confused origins, the idea that everyone has an Antarctic, or a challenge to overcome, carries powerful cultural currency. Casting Antarctica as a metaphor, thus allowing the wider public imaginative access to the continent, has also been a lucrative proposition for a number of companies and organizations.

Antarctica as a metaphor for challenge is central to the ethos of the Shackleton Foundation. Founded in 2007 by descendants of those involved in Shackleton's *Nimrod* expedition (1907–9), the foundation has the mission "to support social entrepreneurs who exemplify the spirit of Shackleton." The foundation website explains the parallels between Shackleton helping his crew to overcome doubts and fears in the face of adversity and modern-day leaders who demonstrate similar resilience and big-picture thinking: "We are looking for individuals who display those same characteristics of courage and resilience, who have a big idea to help others (we call it your 'Antarctic') and are prepared to take the risk to turn it into reality."[88] Another way of defining this "Antarctic" is as something that "scares you, but a challenge you would also secretly love to conquer"—for instance, former All Blacks rugby captain Anton Oliver, who had no musical background, took on the challenge of performing *Peter and the Wolf* with the New Zealand Symphony Orchestra.[89] The question "What's your Antarctic?" allows any difficulty to be translated into an icescape that is ready to be conquered. It therefore harkens back to much earlier ways of seeing Antarctica, conjuring up the narrative of blank space waiting to be trodden and claimed by hardy explorers.

Grape-Nuts cereal ran a similar advertisement series based on the idea of Antarctica and challenge in 2014. The wider "What's Your Mountain?" campaign, launched in 2013 to mark the sixtieth anniversary of the first summiting of Everest, ran across TV, a mobile app, social media, and at events and resulted in more than 295 million earned media impressions.[90] As part of this campaign the company sponsored an Antarctic expedition in which cancer survivor Sean Swarner and film director Dave Ohlson hiked to the South Pole. The South Pole was intended to stand in for other challenges faced by those back home; Ohlson explained, "I hope our journey inspires others to conquer their own personal mountains and strive to meet their goals."[91] As was the case with the earlier Antarctic expeditions of the Heroic Era, media played an important role in the trek, only this time the delay in relaying information was much less. The men provided images and short videos for use on social media platforms, and the "Antarctic Challenge" was also advertised via the Grape-Nuts Facebook page. The company drew upon its earlier Antarctic links in the associated marketing material, with a short promotional video opening with the line "80 years ago, Grape-Nuts helped Admiral Richard Byrd reach the South Pole. This year, we sent one man back."[92] A copy of the General Foods map created for Byrd's second Antarctic expedition— originally available to those who mailed in Grape-Nuts cereal tokens during the 1930s—was also offered as a "random giveaway" prize to a member of the public. Grape-Nuts marketing director Mangala D'Sa also called upon historic links, asserting that "Grape-Nuts has been a part of some of the greatest expeditions of the past hundred years, and the latest Grape-Nuts Antarctica trip will surely be another historic moment for the brand."[93] Customers were encouraged to consider what their own mountain or challenge might be throughout the entire What's Your Mountain? campaign, and advertising material suggested that no matter what form the challenge took, Grape-Nuts would help consumers to succeed. After all, as one of the Antarctic recordings put it, "If Grape-Nuts can take someone to the end of the earth, where will it take you?"[94] Grape

Nuts has continued this Antarctic connection, sponsoring ten women adventurers bound for Everest or the South Pole in 2022–23—in doing so, the company reprised connections with the cryosphere while addressing historical gender imbalances in sponsorship. This in turn helps the product appeal to wider audiences at home (those with their own 'Antarctic'). Both the Shackleton Foundation and Grape-Nuts cereal examples show Antarctica being used as a metaphor, to stand in for other challenges in peoples' lives. Antarctica is not limited by its icy edges but rather extends much farther north through imagination, metaphor, and the concept of overcoming adversity.

The idea of transformation through tourism can also take a philanthropic angle, where travel to Antarctica is used to support another cause. Chimu Adventures and the McGrath Foundation teamed up in 2015 with "PinKtarctica" (figure 20). A half-page version of the advertisement appeared in the Royal Automobile Club of Tasmania magazine beneath an advertorial about Antarctica as a destination and was used to promote a fundraising voyage for the McGrath Foundation, which raises funds to support those affected by breast cancer.[95] Pink is the color associated with breast cancer awareness, hence the name of the voyage. The top left-hand corner of the page is dominated by an icy image of a Zodiac cruising in front of a glacier, beneath the headline, "A Life-Changing Antarctic Adventure." The choice of language immediately suggests transformation, and this theme is continued in the body text of the advertorial: "Due to the life-changing nature of Antarctic journeys, Chimu Adventures saw it as the perfect location for their next exclusive 'departure with a cause.'" The text goes on to explain how "Everyone who travels to Antarctica returns with a greater respect for the environment—and travelers with Chimu are also helping families in need during difficult times in their lives." This mention of assistance—in both environmental and human terms—speaks directly to the viewer's intrinsic values, such as benevolence and universalism.[96] This voyage included special guests Tracy Bevan from the McGrath Foundation and Ken Done, a well-known artist—inviting high profile personalities on board is an additional technique for attracting guests to this specific voyage and one that carries echoes of the celebrity product endorsements of earlier eras. The advertisement in the bottom half of the page also features icy imagery and is dominated by an iceberg

FIG 20. PinKtarctica Voyage advertisement, 2015. Courtesy of Chimu Adventures.

bathed in the pink light of a setting sun, reinforcing the visual connection with the pink color of the breast cancer charity. The message is simple: "Join this extraordinary journey supporting the McGrath Foundation," and change both your life, and those of others, because "together we can make a difference."

WORKING AT THE EDGE OF THE WORLD

Another, more extreme, way to change your life is to spend a prolonged period in Antarctica in a professional capacity. Shackleton's apocryphal Antarctic advertisement famously sought men "for hazardous journey, small wages, bitter cold, long months of complete darkness, constant danger, safe return doubtful." While health and safety requirements mean that working at an Antarctic station is in many ways less risky than a century ago, the challenges of cold and darkness remain for the thousands of people who head south for work each year. Antarctica is often thought of as a wilderness, without any humans; in fact, it is home to between a thousand people in the winter and five thousand in the summer, who are based at a range of stations run by National Antarctic Programs. Contrary to popular belief, those who head south are not only scientists but support staff, including chefs, engineers, carpenters, communications operators, and guides who are also vital to the operations. In order to be appointed to these positions, people respond to recruitment advertisements. These advertisements commonly make use of the dominant heroic-masculinist narratives about Antarctica and feed into the existing Antarctic imaginary. They cannot be "just a promotional piece for the Antarctic," however—instead, the advertisements need to clearly communicate that there is serious job to do.[97]

This makes the aspects that are foregrounded all the more important—while images of penguins and icebergs or human figures in a blizzard have been used to attract attention, recent examples consciously feature real people in real workplaces. Being aware of the image that is projected through recruitment material may help to attract the best candidates for Antarctic positions—those who are able to function well in a confined space with little variety—rather than adventure-seekers who are disappointed to encounter the mundane realities of everyday life on a station.[98] However, the teamwork aspect is also vital. Antarctica New Zealand's "Apprent-ICE" program (2014, 2016) to send an apprentice to work in Antarctica was designed to raise the public profile of trade jobs in Antarctica. As Antarctica New Zealand CEO Peter Beggs put it, "The Apprent-ICE is designed to enhance the awareness of the building industry about Antarctica and the interdependent relationships required to work in one of the harshest environments on the planet."[99] Advertisements set the tone for the culture and expectations associated with the job, which in remote environments is also a lifestyle. That same imagery also offers one way to address historical power imbalances in the Antarctic sphere—picturing diverse cohorts of workers can be the first step toward recruiting a more diverse national Antarctic program workforce. Those same recruitment advertisements also function to raise awareness of Antarctica among the wider public. Representations of Antarctica in advertising are therefore useful not only for selling holidays but also for recruitment purposes and for shaping the ideas about the place in circulation at any given moment.

Traveling and Transforming Brand Antarctica

This book began with an overview of Antarctica's commercial past, including sealing and whaling. We come full circle, with a return to Antarctica as a tangible and valuable continent. This time the desire is not for resources so much as for the continent itself—both the experience of ice and the abstracted idea of Antarctica. Antarctica is a commodity to be visited, photographed, worked on, and figured as a metaphor for change, while wilderness and aesthetic values are marketed as experiences, accessible via a trip south. This Antarctica is very much a part of the global branding-commercial system, connected not only in terms of the environment but also—as the job advertisements highlight—of commerce. Tourism, a commercial activity, is now the main vehicle through which humans encounter Antarctica. This makes the branding for such encounters all the more significant in the contemporary context.

The Antarctic continent has been painted, performed, photographed, filmed, and marketed as a place for heroes, a place of extremity, a place of purity, a place in need of protection, and as a place of transformation. That transformation can be physical, as in the melting and shifting of the ice, or metaphorical, understood as a challenge or a change in mindset, either back home or instigated by a "life-changing" journey south. Representations of Antarctica in tourism advertising material play a key role in shaping how the continent is imagined as a destination. From blue skies to charismatic wildlife to Heroic Era stories, the preconceptions and expectations of tourists weigh as heavily upon the mind as do their suitcases upon the docks. Celebrity guests provide endorsements for particular voyages and are an attraction in their own right.

Advertisements for these experiences sell Antarctica, but they also have a wider influence. For the hundred thousand tourists who visit Antarctica in any given season, there are millions back home who encounter Antarctica vicariously through marketing materials. Examining the branding of Antarctic gateways reveals there are opportunities to rethink our relationship with Antarctica on a larger scale—rather than "Don't Come Here," the branding could pivot to "Let Us Bring Antarctica to You"—in a brochure, at a gateway, in the imagination. At a time when visiting the ends of the earth is no longer out of the question, Antarctica holds more allure and branding opportunities than ever before.

Conclusion

Brand Antarctica Past, Present, and Future

Ever since the adoption of the Antarctic Treaty in 1959, commercialization has been seen as anathema to Antarctic values. This attitude is central to ongoing debates about resources and tourism, where Antarctica is commonly framed as a fragile place to protect—and yet the continent continues to be valuable, both in its materiality and symbolism.[1] This book has provided the historical, social, cultural, and geographic context for understanding the ways the South has been used to sell products, as well as stories, experiences and ideas. In doing so, it has revealed how the idea of a place immune to the interests of the markets has, in fact, been put to work culturally for commercial purposes ever since the first interactions with the continent.

Those who have headed to the Far South over the past few centuries have been whalers, sealers, explorers, scientists, station support personnel, sailors, and wealthy tourists. Historically they have largely been male and white, and it is their gaze that has determined the images of the region that circulate in the public domain. By contextualizing and analyzing a series of case-study advertisements that exemplify a range of common themes, this book has demonstrated how questions of power and commerce help define the cultural context within which Antarctic images and advertisements are created and circulated. That context includes other forms of cultural production, like books, films, and photographs, in which Antarctica is represented; national, social, and political circumstances; Antarctic-specific developments, such as the addition of instruments to the Antarctic Treaty System; and ideological assumptions around race and gender. Advertisements, as an ephemeral text form designed specifically to sell, offer a window into past views of the Far South. They are therefore an ideal medium through which to study the ways various framings of Antarctica have been prioritized over time.

The close relationship of media and Antarctic exploration during the early twentieth century provides useful background to discussions about Antarctica's commercial links. Heroic Era explorers had lucrative deals with newspapers, and stories were a valuable asset. By the 1930s, Adm. Richard Byrd's mastery of the "hero business" and his savvy dealings with sponsors and media outlets had come to epitomize the commercial nature of early explorers' relationships with the world of business. Explorers' stories also shaped the perceptions of those back home; Antarctica entered into the cultural imagination via both verbal and visual representations in newspapers and magazines. As explorers discovered Antarctica step by step, media consumers also made discoveries, page by page. Understanding the emergence of the modern media landscape, therefore, helps us to understand the ways we view Antarctica, by providing the commercial background to early narratives of south polar exploration.

The dominant ways of framing Antarctica identified in this book—as a place for heroes and transformation, a place of extremity, purity, and fragility—continue to influence the ways we view Antarctica today. Ever since the Heroic Era of Antarctic exploration, the continent has been depicted as a place for masculine figures to battle the elements. While the sepia-toned days when heroes made quests for geographic firsts may be long gone, the specter of the hero continues to loom large over the Antarctic ice, as the trope is recycled in new guises. Product rereleases and new iterations of the hero themes—particularly in conjunction with centenary events in the early twenty-first century—demonstrate that the hero narrative is still valuable in the commercial context. Heroism is closely linked to the idea of extremity, which casts the southern continent as a place for superlatives and superior performance. This framing is often called upon when marketing machinery; it feeds into the myth of Antarctic exceptionalism by arguing that any products that have been used in the Far South must be exceptionally tough. The frames of heroism and extremity cast Antarctica as a place to be challenged and overcome by humans, bringing an anthropocentric approach to the fore. Just as early whalers and sealers saw Antarctica as a far-off place where resources were ripe for the taking, the heroism and extremity themes emphasize the otherness of the Far South, celebrating feats of human domination.

The purity framing works against notions of heroism and extremity, presenting Antarctica as a place that should remain untouched by humans and machines. Antarctica's literal whiteness and its young human history mean the continent has been used to illustrate the idea of purity itself. While Antarctica carries traces of human impacts in each layer of ice and is therefore not as pure and untouched as has been suggested, the purity framing is a myth that captures imaginations; it is deeply entangled with value systems back home, as notions of gender, race, and environmental protection are projected onto the ice. Paradoxically, the products marketed using this frame have often been sourced from the Far South; the tension between the notion of purity and the practices involved in sourcing "pure" Antarctic products creates ground for fertile analysis. More recently the fragility frame demonstrates how the continent has been used as a symbol for environmental vulnerability, especially to climate change. Rather than a place untouched by humans, fragility sees Antarctica as actively threatened by anthropogenic climate change. This framing has not been as dominant in advertising campaigns, which tend to focus on positive associations. Despite this, a close examination of advertisements has demonstrated that in the age of the Anthropocene, ice is not just ice but rather a symbol for Antarctica and for the global environment at large. With fragility Antarctica shifts from being seen as a place to conquer to a place of interconnection and of global importance; a distant place that becomes tangible because of the ways it can impact lives back home in profound and uncomfortable ways.

In recent years Antarctica has been valued both physically, as a commodity for tourists to visit and photograph, and symbolically, as a metaphor for a range of challenges experienced back home. The final section of this book returned to Antarctica, using the twin lenses of travel and transformation to explore the ways the themes from previous chapters have been manifested in encounters with the Far South. In bringing notions of challenge, transformation, and life-changing experiences to the fore, it demonstrated how the continent has become personally relevant to those in faraway places, thanks to the way personal challenges have been addressed via the question "What's your Antarctic?" In examining the phenomenon of Antarctic tourism, this book has argued that the Antarctica that is experienced by tourists is by no means unmediated nor is it "natural." Tour companies are active agents that work hard to create an Antarctic experience that includes all the expected highlights, such as whales, seals, icebergs, a continental landing, and, invariably, penguins. Tourists travel south with a shopping list of expectations, informed by the images that feature in the glossy advertising brochures for the continent, and "become players in the game of directed viewing," with guides and tour brochures alike suggesting particular framings for each site encountered.[2] Historic links to Heroic Era figures, allusion to the untouched nature of the continent, and the chance to step onto the seventh continent are all par for the course. When it comes to advertisements for Antarctic tourism and, to a certain degree, for Antarctic jobs, what is being sold is the *promise* of Antarctica, a mythical combination of images and language that construct an anticipatory story of a faraway place.

Taken together, the advertisements examined in this study help to reveal the most prominent positive framings of Antarctica. These frames are not exclusive, nor are they strictly linear in their development. Although a frame such as heroism dates to the turn of the last century, its prominence has waxed and waned over the intervening years, and in response to events such as the Heroic Era centenary celebrations. Other ways of seeing the continent have been layered over the top, leading to a richer thematic vocabulary of the Antarctic. Multiple frames are often in operation simultaneously; they can reinforce one another, as is the case with heroism and extremity, but they can also directly contradict each other. The purity frame, for instance, sits in opposition to the idea of Antarctica as a place to conquer. Being aware of these framings allows one to be alert to what discourses are drawn upon in particular texts. Using advertisements and related commercial products as a proxy, this book has tracked how values and attitudes toward the Far South have changed over time. However, the findings are applicable more broadly, as the dominant framings of Antarctica identified here can be used as a lens to critically analyze any new text related to Antarctica.

Future Directions: Language, Geography, and Place

Although its conclusions rest upon a large collection of primary sources, this analysis does not claim to be exhaustive or to present all the possible frames through which Antarctica has been viewed. Due to the nature of the material considered, the framings that have emerged in this project are positively skewed; advertisements are designed to sell things, and therefore negative narratives of Antarctica are not prominent. As a result, this project does not address the gothic tradition that has long been associated with Antarctica or depictions of the place that show a dystopian or apocalyptic future. The trope of the alien that is present in other types of cultural texts (John Carpenter's 1982 film *The Thing* is a prime example) is also absent. Antarctica can function as a place upon which humans project their fears or as the epitome of the sublime, but such framings do not emerge in advertising, being better suited to different kinds of texts such as thrillers or popular films.[3] Future projects could build upon the findings of this work by taking the identified frames as a starting point and expanding the scope of the texts studied to address film and radio or to cover texts outside of the English-speaking world. Given differences in national and cultural value and communication systems, a study of similar texts that have appeared in other languages, such as Chinese or Spanish, would present a useful comparison. Further studies that examine Antarctic advertisements and commercial materials produced in places other than the Western world would add nuance and allow for analysis of the similarities and differences in how Antarctica has been framed in different places at various points in time.

Another point of comparison is with the Arctic and cryoscapes more generally. A transpolar analysis would be valuable for identifying parallel representations, particularly around the fragility theme. Despite aesthetic similarities, the Arctic and Antarctic are culturally very different places. Most obviously, the Arctic has a long human history and is home to many different Indigenous groups that have deep relationships with the many specific places that can be glossed over by the wider term "Arctic." The 2016 furor over Alaska Airlines' use of the phrase "Meet Our Eskimo" in advertising material illustrates the additional dimensions at play when it comes to advertisements of the Far North. Indigenous groups objected to the use of the possessive "our," as it "implied that the airline owned an eskimo," and others highlighted the use of the term "eskimo" as a racial slur; the campaign missed its mark.[4] While a future project that tracked the emergence of Arctic framings in advertising would provide a fascinating counterpoint to this current book, there are many local Arctics to consider. The north and south polar regions differ historically, linguistically, socially, and culturally and therefore also deserve to be investigated independently.

This book's findings contribute to wider discussions about the relationship between Antarctica and "place." Whether the continent is conceived of as a single place or a series of discrete places has an impact upon framings and understandings of the continent. When writing on Antarctic thrillers, Elizabeth Leane observes that "the place identity these texts draw from and contribute to is that of the whole Antarctic region," and the same is true of advertising texts.[5] As of 2022, the advertisements that have featured Antarctica have used the continent as a single, homogenous place in order to evoke ideas such as heroism, extremity, and purity. Although "a synoptic and general view of Antarctica predominates" in common discourse about the continent, new ways of thinking about place have also been applied to the Far South.[6] The recognition within both the scientific and political realms of discrete biogeographic zones in Antarctica signals an important shift in the way the continent is conceptualized.[7] Environmental historian Alessandro Antonello suggests that "engaging with places rather than the whole might inject a new dynamic into Antarctic Treaty politics and diplomacy"—and that such a paradigm shift may also have the potential to "more thoroughly entrench a consciousness of maintaining the Antarctic environment well into the future."[8] Work such as Antonello's that is attentive to the theorization of place in relation to Antarctica (and vice versa) could shift the way this project is viewed in future; whether the public at large will ever think of Antarctica as a range of specific locations rather than a single icy continent at the bottom of the world—and therefore whether this perspective will filter through to mainstream advertising material—remains to be seen.

Naming and Framing: An Iceberg called #ExxonKnew

In mid-2017 a specific Antarctic place was thrust into the spotlight as a 5,800km² iceberg calved away from the Larsen C Ice Shelf. Described by *Rolling Stone* magazine as a "made-for-media crack-up, one that has played out in a visible, dramatic way," the crack that preceded the calving event was "easy to photograph, easy to understand, easy to worry about."[9] The resulting iceberg was assigned a standard identifier, and officially termed A68 (so-called because it originated in the "A" Sector [between 0–90w] and was the 68th iceberg to be named), yet that is not the way it was referred to by all. How a particular mountain, bay, or iceberg is known is part of a complex process of meaning-making (as is the question of whether it is named at all), and activists were well aware of the powerful framing work a name can perform. In the lead-up to the calving, the climate-focused NGO 350.org ran a petition urging the United States National Ice Center to name the Larsen C iceberg after Exxon, and "put the #ExxonKnew Iceberg on the map."[10] They argued that climate change is linked to the burning of fossil fuels, and therefore Exxon, as a fuel company, should take responsibility for the melting Antarctic ice and the freshly calved iceberg (although whether this particular berg calved as a direct result of anthropogenic climate change remains unclear).[11] An historical commercial was central to the argument; in promoting the campaign, climate activist Aaron Packard called upon both a 1968 report, prepared by the Stanford Research Institute for the American Petroleum Institute, and a 1962 Humble advertisement, featuring a glacier front and the tagline "each day Humble supplies enough energy to melt 7 million tons of glacier!" to further his case that "Exxon knew about climate change half a century ago."[12]

This example stands in contrast to the geographical feature Mobiloil Bay, with which this book began. Where that bay was named in celebration of the sponsors of Hubert Wilkins's 1928 expedition, here third-party NGOs attributed a naming interest to Exxon in an attempt to publicly shame the company. With the naming campaign, 350.org drew a direct link between the burning of fossil fuels in faraway places, growing levels of CO_2 in the atmosphere, and the melting of Antarctic ice and inscribed this upon a temporary Antarctic entity. The ephemeral quality of the ice speaks to the fragility frame, while the proposed name neatly encapsulates environmental concerns. That the iceberg became a flashpoint for debate around climate change culpability indicates that Antarctica is very much connected to the wider world of both politics and commerce.

It invokes the anti-exceptionalist argument by positioning Antarctica as part of a global system; actions in other parts of the world affect physical processes in the Far South, just as the idea of the continent lingers far from the ice, in imaginations across the globe.

As the calving of A68 and the media attention it garnered make clear, Antarctica is not static; rather, it is being constantly reimagined and reframed. This makes Antarctic humanities scholarship all the more important. As historians Peder Roberts, Lize-Marié van der Watt, and Adrian Howkins argue, the field articulates an "understanding that the Antarctic is a series of representations that are always selected, distilled, and packaged by humans."[13] This book contributes to the wider cultural understanding of Antarctica by analyzing a selection of advertising texts and revealing how the Far South has long been embroiled in the world of commerce and the ways this intersects with imagination. Those connections are both influenced by and have an impact upon common framings of the continent. Given that "perceptions of novel environments are always framed by personal experience, in terms of culture and politics, in addition to specialized scientific knowledge," acknowledging the contextual experiences, assumptions, and everyday cultural input of the viewer is particularly important when dealing with a part of the world where very few people will ever go.[14]

Antarctica holds many resonances and can be framed in multiple ways for a variety of ends. It is a powerful cultural symbol that can and has been put to use for a wide range of commercial purposes over the course of its human history. Just what Brand Antarctica will look like in ten, fifty, or one hundred years remains to be seen, but commercial links—and the specters of past framings—will not be far away.

Notes

Introduction

1. Fox and Bazeley, "Naming the Unnamed."
2. Wells, *Land Matters*, 3.
3. Roberts, "Antarctica—Anything is Possible."
4. Neufeld et al., "Valuing Antarctica," 249.
5. Walton, "Discovering the Unknown Continent," 25.
6. Clancy, Manning, and Brolsma, *Mapping Antarctica*, 61.
7. Riffenburgh, *The Myth of the Explorer*, 3.
8. Williamson, "Unfreezing the Truth."
9. Glasberg, "The Last Place on Earth," 65.
10. Chapple "Harvest of Souls."
11. Branston and Stafford, *The Media Student Book*, 365.
12. McClintock, "Soft-Soaping Empire," 758.
13. Leiss et al., "Social Communication in Advertising," 168.
14. Leiss et al., "Social Communication in Advertising," 199.
15. Leiss et al., "Social Communication in Advertising," 190.
16. *Oxford English Dictionary*, s.v. "advertisement," accessed December 15, 2021, https://www.oed.com/view/Entry/2978?redirectedFrom=advertisement #eid.
17. "Coca-Cola/Coke—Polar Bears/Penguins (2005) 0:30 (USA)," Adland, accessed August 19, 2017, http://www.adland.tv/commercials/coca-cola -coke-polar-bears-penguins-2005-030-usa.
18. Dali, "Advertising as a Semiotic System of Space," 339, 340.
19. Wehi et al., "A Short Scan of Māori Journeys to Antarctica."
20. Baughmann, *Before the Heroes Came*, 7.
21. Baughmann, *Before the Heroes Came*, 7.
22. Pearce, "Boiled-to-Death Penguins Are Back from the Brink."

23. Clark and Lamberson, "An Economic History and Analysis of Pelagic Whaling," 104.
24. Hince, *The Antarctic Dictionary*, 312; Dibbern, "Fur Seals, Whales and Tourists," 212.
25. Maizonave et al., "Integrated System for Intelligent Street Lighting," 721.
26. Orheim, "Managing the Frozen Commons," 274.
27. "About CCAMLR," Commission for the Conservation of Antarctic Marine Living Resources, accessed March 1, 2017, http://www.ccamlr.org/en/organisation.
28. Antonello, *The Greening of Antarctica*.
29. Jackson. *Who Saved Antarctica?*, 275.
30. Hult and Ostrander, *Antarctic Icebergs*; "UAE Firm Plans to Haul Iceberg from Antarctica to Solve Water Problem," *Indian Express*, May 7, 2017, http://www.indianexpress.com/article/world/to-tackle-water-scarcity-uae-firm-plans-to-haul-icebergs-from-antarctica-report-4644350.
31. Matuozzi, "Richard Byrd, Polar Exploration, and the Media," 210.
32. Ryan, *Photography and Exploration*, 8.
33. Wilson, *The Lost Photographs of Captain Scott*, 19.
34. Conboy, *The Press and Popular Culture*, 107.
35. Anderson, *Imagined Communities*, 39.
36. Conboy, *The Press and Popular Culture*, 49.
37. Conboy, *The Language of Newspapers*, 112.
38. Ryan, *Photography and Exploration*, 8.
39. Riffenburgh, *The Myth of the Explorer*, 106.
40. Leane and Nicol, "Filming the Frozen South," 129.
41. Roberts, "The Politics of Early Exploration," 321.
42. Nielsen, "Selling the South," 189.
43. Riffenburgh, *The Myth of the Explorer*, 164.
44. Letter from William Heinemann letter to Fridtjof Nansen, March 18, 1912. Universitätsbibliothek Oslo, MS Fol 1924. 5:3, Amundsens Hjemkomst fra Sydpolen.
45. Mayer, *Shackleton*, 97.
46. Craciun, "Oceanic Voyages, Maritime Books, and Eccentric Inscriptions," 181.
47. Riffenburgh, *The Myth of the Explorer*, 3.
48. Leane, "Introduction," 150.
49. Roberts, "The White (Supremacist) Continent," 121.

50. van der Watt and Swart, "The Whiteness of Antarctica," 136.

51. "Shackleton Returns: Hyundai Santa Fe Conquers the Antarctic Driven by Great Grandson of Sir Ernest Shackleton," Hyundai, April 20, 2017, https://www.hyundai.com/au/en/news/vehicles/shackleton-returns-hyundai-santa-fe-conquers-the-antarctic-drive.

52. Gilchrist, "Gender and British Climbing Histories," 224.

53. Williamson, "Unfreezing the Truth."

54. Judith Williamson, interview by Kathryn Ryan, *Nine to Noon*, Radio New Zealand, May 25, 2010, http://www.radionz.co.nz/national/programmes/ninetonoon/audio/2303801/feature-guest-judith-williamson.

55. Tungate, *Adland*, 252.

1. Heroic Antarctica

1. Elmore, *Quit You Like Men*, 53.

2. Elliot, "In Detroit."

3. Leane, *Antarctica in Fiction*, 85.

4. Hince, *The Antarctic Dictionary*, 167.

5. Berger, *Media Analysis Techniques*, 10.

6. Jones et al., "Decolonising Imperial Heroes," 789.

7. Jones et al., "Decolonising Imperial Heroes," 795.

8. Leane, *South Pole*, 54.

9. Riffenburgh, *The Myth of the Explorer*, 5.

10. Jones, *The Last Great Quest*, 98; McEwen, "The National Press during the First World War," 466.

11. Huxley, *Scott's Last Expedition*, 545.

12. Huntford, *The Last Place on Earth*, 481.

13. Bown, *The Last Viking*, 88.

14. Bown, *The Last Viking*, 177.

15. Nasht, *The Last Great Explorer*, 177.

16. Nasht, *The Last Great Explorer*, 222.

17. Norman, "What Is the 'Holy Grail of Climate Science'?"

18. Matuozzi, "Richard Byrd, Polar Exploration, and the Media," 210.

19. Advertisement in *The Strand* 46, no. 275 (November 1913).

20. Ryan, *Photography and Exploration*, 27.

21. Blum, *The News at the Ends of the Earth*, xiii.

22. Leane, "The Polar Press," 33.

23. Leane, "The Polar Press," 33.

24. Byrd, "This Hero Business," in *Skyward*, 211.
25. Grow, "Stories of Community," 165; "Home," GoPro, accessed December 14, 2021, https://gopro.com/en/us/; "World Blood Donor Day: 'Every Blood Donor Is a Hero.' 14 June 2012," Pan American Health Organization, accessed August 22, 2017, https://www.who.int/news-room/events/detail/2012/06/14/default-calendar/world-blood-donor-day-2012.
26. Jones et al., "Decolonising Imperial Heroes," 790.
27. Cox, "Charles Lindberg and Mobiloil," 98.
28. Lucas et al., "A Flight of the Imagination," 71.
29. Shackleton's slogan was used in Bovril advertising materials throughout World War I, with the addition of the tagline "British to the Backbone." Hadley, *The History of BOVRIL Advertising*, 19.
30. Hadley, *The History of BOVRIL Advertising*, 7; "How Lord Roberts Spells Bovril."
31. McClintock, "Soft-Soaping Empire," 758.
32. Bush, *Imperialism and Postcolonialism*, 149.
33. Hadley, *The History of BOVRIL Advertising*, 3.
34. Thompson, *Handbook of Patent Law of All Countries*, 42.
35. Guly, "Medical Comforts during the Heroic Age of Antarctic Exploration," 110.
36. Hadley, *The History of BOVRIL Advertising*, 13.
37. Hadley, *The History of BOVRIL Advertising*, 62.
38. Hadley, *The History of BOVRIL Advertising*, 105.
39. Huntley & Palmers Polar Biscuits advertisement, 1912, from *Pictures of 1912*, 140.
40. Huntley & Palmers Polar Biscuits advertisement, 1912, from *Pictures of 1912*, 140.
41. Griffiths, *Slicing the Silence*, 347.
42. Griffiths, *Slicing the Silence*, 347.
43. McClintock, "Soft-Soaping Empire," 755.
44. Robert F. Scott, "Letter from Captain Scott to Huntley & Palmers 20 October 1911," HP134, The Huntley & Palmers collection at the University of Reading, Accessed 14 December 2021, http://www.reading.ac.uk/web/files/special-collections/huntleypalmer.pdf (page discontinued).
45. Griffiths, *Slicing the Silence*, 349.
46. Moss, *Scott's Last Biscuit*, ix.
47. Fiennes, *Race to the Pole*, 352.
48. Griffiths, *Slicing the Silence*, 348.

49. "British Antarctic Expedition, 1911," The Huntley & Palmers Collection, Reading Biscuit Town, accessed November 11, 2015, http://www.huntleyand palmers.org.uk.

50. Trove, The National Library of Australia, "The Intrepid Explorer," *BANZARE— Sea Shanties—RRS Discovery I or SY Discovery*, Eric Douglas Antarctic Collection, December 3, 2011, http://trove.nla.gov.au/list?id=17915.

51. "Southward Ho with Yalumba," Glug: Wine Makers and Wine Merchants of the Barossa Valley, accessed June 11, 2016, http://www.glug.com.au (page discontinued).

52. Australian Associated Press, "Historic Mawson Bottle Could Fetch $15,000," *The Age*, November 30, 2011, http://www.theage.com.au/victoria/historic -mawson-bottle-could-fetch-15000-20111129-1o4x6.html.

53. "Report of the AAP Mawson's Huts Foundation Expedition 2000–01," Department of Agriculture, Water and the Environment, the Australian Government, March 2001, https://mawsonshuts.antarctica.gov.au/site/assets/files /1567/expeditionreportmawsonshuts2000-01easther.pdf.

54. "Yalumba," Halliday Wine Companion, accessed 5 May 2017, http://www .winecompanion.com.au.

55. "Shackleton's Whisky," Antarctic Heritage Trust, January 31, 2010, https:// nzaht.org/shackletons-whisky/.

56. "Our Whisky Discovered under Ice," The Shackleton Whisky, accessed November 18, 2022, https://www.theshackletonwhisky.com/discover-shackleton -whisky/.

57. Pryde et al., "Sensory and Chemical Analysis of 'Shackleton's' Mackinlay Scotch Whisky," 156.

58. "The Great Whisky Crate Thaw," Canterbury Museum, May 10, 2011, accessed September 5, 2011, http://whiskythaw.canterburymuseum.com/ (site discontinued).

59. O'Shaughnessy and Stadler, *Media and Society*, 99.

2. In the Footsteps of Heroes

1. "Geico: Dora the Explorer at South Pole," April 24, 2015, 0:00:30, https:// www.youtube.com/watch?v=2D3zu6R6_Vk.

2. "Geico: Dora the Explorer at South Pole."

3. Nash et al., "'Antarctica Just Has This Hero Factor.'"

4. Barczewski, *Antarctic Destinies*, xv.

5. Jones et al., "Decolonising Imperial Heroes," 804.

6. Barczewski, *Antarctic Destinies*, xii.

7. Farley, "'By Endurance We Conquer,'" 231.

8. Farley, "'By Endurance We Conquer,'" 246.

9. Worsley, *In Shackleton's Footsteps*, 247.

10. Richard Morrison, "Pray for a Shackleton," *The Times*, October 2, 2001, 2.

11. Roberts, "The White (Supremacist) Continent," 117.

12. van der Watt and Swart, "The Whiteness of Antarctica," 44.

13. Maddison, *Class and Colonialism in Antarctic Exploration*, 159.

14. van der Watt and Swart, "The Whiteness of Antarctica," 146.

15. Maynard, *Wings of Ice*, 3.

16. Rodgers, "Richard E. Byrd's First Antarctic Expedition," 158; Maynard, *Wings of Ice*, 201.

17. Byrd, *Alone*, 8.

18. Matuozzi, "Richard Byrd, Polar Exploration, and the Media," 234.

19. "Mawson's Huts Replica Museum," Mawson's Huts Foundation, accessed March 22, 2017, https://www.mawsons-huts.org.au/mawsons-men/.

20. Aidan Dooley, "Tom Crean: Antarctic Explorer," accessed August 22, 2017, http://www.tomcreanshow.com/about; "Tom Crean Trail," Dingle Peninsula Tourism Alliance, accessed December 14, 2021, https://dingle-peninsula .ie/30-attractions-on-the-dingle-peninsula/walking-hiking-on-the-dingle -peninsula/161-tom-crean-trail.html.

21. "Tom Crean Explores New Heights on Norwegian Air Tailfin," *Irish Times*, July 16, 2017, https://www.irishtimes.com/business/transport-and-tourism /tom-crean-explores-new-heights-on-norwegian-air-tailfin-1.3156966.

22. Farley, "'By Endurance We Conquer,'" 233.

23. Farley, "'By Endurance We Conquer,'" 245.

24. Spears, Royne, and van Steenburg, "Are Celebrity-Heroes Effective Endorsers?," 28.

25. Sullivan, "In Which Robert Falcon Scott's Jacket Is Resurrected."

26. Worsley, *In Shackleton's Footsteps*, 36.

27. Worsley, *In Shackleton's Footsteps*, 247.

28. Endeavour Fund, accessed March 14, 2017, http://www.endeavourfund .co.uk (site discontinued). The Endeavour Fun is now part of the Invictus Games Foundation, see "Endeavour Fund Transferred to the Invictus Games Foundation," Invictus Games Foundation, June 1, 2020, https:// invictusgamesfoundation.org/endeavour-fund-transferred-to-the-invictus -games-foundation/.

29. "William and Harry's Sadness Over Antarctic Adventurer Henry Worsley's Death," *Daily Mail*, updated January 25, 2016, http://www.dailymail.co.uk /wires/pa/article-3415429/Antarctic-explorer-Henry-Worsley-dies-failed -challenge.html.

30. "Explorer Henry Worsley Dies Attempting Antarctic Crossing," BBC *News*, January 25, 2016, http://www.bbc.com/news/uk-35398552; Richard Pendlebury, "The Smiling Selfies That Turned to Despair: How Swashbuckling Adventurer Who Saw It as His Duty to Live Like a Hero from a Bygone Age Met a Tragic End Trying to Trek across Antarctic Alone," *Daily Mail*, January 26, 2016, http://www.dailymail.co.uk/news/article-3416547/The-smiling -selfies-turned-despair-Tragic-end-adventurer-saw-duty-live-like-hero-form -age.html#ixzz4qyrtSy3o.

31. "Explorer Henry Worsley Dies," BBC *News*.

32. Tom Rowley, "Explorer Henry Worsley's Widow Plans Antarctic Voyage to Say a 'Final Goodbye,'" *The Telegraph*, January 7, 2017, http://www.telegraph .co.uk/news/2017/01/07/explorer-henry-worsleys-widow-plans-antarctic -voyage-say-final.

33. Harpreet Chandi, "Polar Preet: Breaking Boundaries," accessed November 18, 2022, https://polarpreet.com/.

34. Harry Adams, "Watch: Polar Preet Gets Hero's Welcome after Record-Breaking Antarctic Challenge," *Forces Net*, January 14, 2022, https://www .forces.net/news/polar-preet-given-heros-welcome-after-record-breaking -antarctic.

35. Henry Evans, "International Scott Centenary Expedition: A Scientific Legacy to Celebrate," *The Telegraph*, June 22, 2012, http://www.telegraph.co.uk /news/worldnews/antarctica/robert-falcon-scott/9349109/International -Scott-Centenary-Expedition-a-scientific-legacy-to-celebrate.html.

36. "To Strive, To Seek, To Find and Not to Yield," British Services Antarctic Expedition, accessed November 24, 2015, http://www.bsae2012.co.uk.

37. "Open Letter from the Chairman of Trustees," Help For Heroes, accessed November 24, 2015, https://www.helpforheroes.org.uk/resources/news /open-letter-from-the-chairmen-of-trustees/.

38. "To Strive, To Seek, To Find and Not to Yield," British Services Antarctic Expedition.

39. "Home," Walking with the Wounded, accessed August 22, 2017, http://www .walkingwiththewounded.org.uk/who-we-are/the-expeditions.

40. "About," Walking with the Wounded, accessed August 22, 2017, http://www .walkingwiththewounded.org.uk/Home/About/62.

41. "Team Glenfiddich," Captive Minds, November 4, 2013, accessed August 22, 2017, https://captiveminds.com/brands/team-glenfiddich/.

42. Chris Harding, "Glenfiddich Champions Walking with the Wounded Race to the South Pole," *Campaign*, October 31, 2013, http://www.campaignlive .co.uk/article/glenfiddich-champions-walking-wounded-race-south-pole /1218990.

43. "Team Glenfiddich," Captive Minds.

44. Quoted in Alex Brownsell, "Prince Harry Pays Tribute to Charity Sponsors Virgin Money and Glenfiddich," *Campaign*, January 21, 2014, https://www .campaignlive.com/article/prince-harry-pays-tribute-charity-sponsors-virgin -money-glenfiddich/1228090.

45. Peat, *Shackleton's Whisky*, 10.

46. Emma Barnett, "Why Is Whisky Still a 'Man's Drink'?" *The Telegraph*, October 11, 2013, http://www.telegraph.co.uk/women/womens-life/10372412/Why -is-whisky-still-a-mans-drink.html.

47. Julie Bindel, "Whisky: The Drink That Sorts the Women from the Girls," *The Spectator*, February 8, 2017, accessed March 22, 2017, http://www.life .spectator.co.uk/2017/02/whisky-drink-sorts-women-girls (page discontinued); Barnett, "Why Is Whisky Still a 'Man's Drink'?"

48. "Team Glenfiddich," Captive Minds.

49. "Glenfiddich Spirit of a Nation," Captive Minds, December 10, 2013, https:// captiveminds.com/brands/glenfiddich-spirit-of-a-nation/.

50. Farley, "'By Endurance We Conquer,'" 247.

51. Perkins et al., *Leading at the Edge*.

52. Farley, "'By Endurance We Conquer,'" 240.

53. Worsley, *In Shackleton's Footsteps*, 135.

54. Farley, "'By Endurance We Conquer,'" 247.

55. Farley, "'By Endurance We Conquer,'" 247.

56. Maddison, *Class and Colonialism in Antarctic Exploration*, 194.

57. "Shackleton Beers Now in Jarrod's Store," The Great British Banjo Company, June 17, 2014, accessed March 22, 2017, http://www.thegreatbritishbanjoblog .com/2014/06/shackleton-beers-now-jarrolds-store.html (site discontinued).

58. "The Shackleton Story," The Shackleton Company, accessed April 11, 2023, https://shackleton.com/en-au/pages/about-shackleton.

59. "The Shackleton Story," The Shackleton Company.

60. "Shackleton x Leica: Frank Hurley Photographer's Jacket," Shackleton, accessed May 14, 2021, https://shackleton.com/en-us/blogs/articles/shackleton-x-leica?_.
61. "Endurance Is Found," Endurance22, March 9, 2022, https://endurance22.org/endurance-is-found.
62. Spears, Royne, and van Steenburg, "Are Celebrity-Heroes Effective Endorsers?," 20.
63. Wheeler, *Terra Incognita*, 1.

3. Cold Weather Branding

1. "Deep Freeze—International Antarctic Centre," Resene, accessed November 10, 2022, https://www.resene.co.nz/archspec/products/antarctic.htm.
2. Jamie Morton, "Keep It Green: Scott Base to Stay Its Signature Colour," *New Zealand Herald* June 15, 2022, https://www.nzherald.co.nz/nz/keep-it-green-scott-base-to-stay-its-signature-colour/AVM75TFUVQJRQ4SIG4PPH2YASU/.
3. "Deep Freeze—International Antarctic Centre," Resene.
4. Palmer, "Shit Happens," 325.
5. Miller, "Wired," 481.
6. "8 of the Deepest Places Earth Can Offer," Red Bull, accessed May 2, 2017, http://www.redbull.com/au-en/8-of-the-deepest-places-the-earth-can-offer; "World Record Jump," Red Bull, accessed May 2, 2017, http://www.redbullstratos.com/the-mission/world-record-jump.
7. "Red Bull Surfing Antarctica," Red Bull, accessed October 10, 2022, https://www.redbull.com/us-en/videos/red-bull-surfing-antarctica.
8. Amanda Davis, "This IEEE Fellow Blazed a Trail for Female Scientists in Antarctica," *The Institute: The IEEE News Source*, April 14, 2016, accessed May 2, 2017, http://www.theinstitute.ieee.org/tech-history/technology-history/this-ieee-fellow-blazed-a-trail-for-female-scientists-in-antarctica (site discontinued).
9. "Shackleton Returns: Hyundai Santa Fe Conquers the Antarctic Driven by Great Grandson of Sir Ernest Shackleton," Hyundai, April 20, 2017, https://www.hyundai.com/au/en/news/vehicles/shackleton-returns-hyundai-santa-fe-conquers-the-antarctic-drive.
10. Le Blond, *True Tales of Mountain Adventure*, ix.
11. Gilchrist, "Gender and British Climbing Histories," 224.
12. Belanger, *Deepfreeze*, 131.

13. Dodds, "The Great Trek," 109.
14. Day, *Antarctica*, 478.
15. Talbot, "A Study of the Techniques Used by the Ross Sea Committee to Raise Funds," 12.
16. Dodds, "The Great Trek," 100.
17. "Gateway to Antarctica," Christchurch Antarctic Office, accessed November 1, 2022. https://www.christchurchnz.com/christchurch-antarctic-office.
18. "Expedition South—Conserving Sir Edmund Hillary's Antarctic Hut," Massey Ferguson, August 19, 2016, http://www.masseyferguson.com.au /expeditionsouth.aspx.
19. "The International Geophysical Year," The National Academies: Sciences, Engineering, Medicine, accessed July 14, 2017, http://www.nas.edu/history /igy (page discontinued).
20. Nielsen, "From Shelter to Showpiece," 3.
21. Tungate, *Adland*, 38.
22. Fox, *The Mirror Makers*, 187.
23. As quoted in Fox, *The Mirror Makers*, 179.
24. Leiss et al., *Social Communication in Advertising*, 211.
25. Samuel, "Thinking Smaller."
26. Samuel, "Thinking Smaller"; Hallberg, *All Consumers Are Not Created Equal*, 133.
27. Long and Matthews, *Knowing Australian Volkswagens*, 68.
28. Long and Matthews, *Knowing Australian Volkswagens*, 71.
29. Matthews, "Antarctica 1—Volkswagens in Antarctica."
30. "Advertising Campaign," 7.
31. "Advertising Campaign," 7.
32. Branston and Stafford, *The Media Student Book*, 381.
33. Glasberg, *Antarctica as Cultural Critique*, 87.
34. Russell Hotten, "Volkswagen: The Scandal Explained," *BBC News*, December 10, 2015, http://www.bbc.com/news/business-34324772.
35. Gunster, "'You Belong Outside,'" 4.
36. Volkswagen Advertisement, "The First Car at the Bottom of the World," that appeared in *Life Magazine*, January 15, 1965.
37. Phil Matthews (editor at the Volkswagen Club in Sydney), pers. comm, July 29, 2015.
38. Long and Matthews, *Knowing Australian Volkswagens*, 77.
39. "The Singer in the Antarctic" *The Strand* 46, no. 275 (November 1913).
40. Griffiths, *Slicing the Silence*, 18.

41. "Aurora Basin: Drilling Ice Cores in the Heart of Antarctica," Australian Antarctic Program, accessed September 16, 2016, http://www.antarctica.gov.au/science/climate-processes-and-change/antarctic-palaeoclimate/aurora-basin.
42. Tsujimoto, Imura, and Kanda, "Recovery and Reproduction of an Antarctic Tardigrade," 78.
43. Leane, "The Land That Time Forgot," 199.
44. Steel, "Extreme and Unusual," 368.
45. "Temperatures," British Antarctic Survey, accessed April 27, 2017, http://www.bas.ac.uk/about/antarctica/geography/weather/temperatures.
46. "About Homasote and Homasote Company," Homasote, accessed April 26, 2017, http://www.homasote.com/about.
47. "Polar Clothing Contract Goes to New Zealand Company," Antarctica New Zealand, February 27, 2009, accessed April 13, 2015, http://www.antarcticanz.govt.nz/images/pdfs/2009_press/pr_clothing27feb09.pdf (site discontinued); Tina Law, "Unexpected Windfall from Antarctic Contract," *Stuff*, April 17, 2009, https://www.stuff.co.nz/business/industries/2297431/Unexpected-windfall-from-Antarctic-contract.
48. Lai, *Pentothal Postcards*, 8.
49. Lai, *Pentothal Postcards*, 6.
50. "IAATO Overview of Antarctic Tourism: A Historical Review of Growth, the 2020–21 Season, and Preliminary Estimates for 2021–22," International Association of Antarctica Tour Operators, ATCM XLII 2021, IP110.
51. Coke Zero also donated new laboratory equipment to Carlini Base, "which focuses on scientific investigations and international cooperation." "Cool Concert: Coke Zero Presents Metallica's First-Ever Show in Antarctica," Coca-Cola, December 13, 2013, accessed 10 April 2017, http://www.coc-colacompany.com/coca-cola-music/coll-concert-coke-zero-presents-metallicas-first-ever-show-in-antarctica (site discontinued).
52. "Metallica—Freeze 'Em All: Live in Antarctica (FULL CONCERT) [HD]," Metallica TV, December 23, 2013, video, 1:12:20, http://www.youtube.com/watch?v=2hi2u98vkxc (page discontinued).
53. "Journey to the Bottom of the Earth," Metallica, October 24, 2013, accessed November 18, 2022, https://www.metallica.com/news/345705.html.
54. "Editorial Press Release: Oceanwide Expeditions Heads South with Metallica," Oceanwide Expeditions, October 30, 2013, http://www.oceanwide-expeditions.com/blog/editorial-press-release-oceanwide-expeditions-heads-south-with-metallica.

55. Powell, Kellert, and Ham, "Antarctic Tourists," 239.

56. "Our Mission," International Association of Antarctica Tour Operators, accessed November 30, 2022, https://iaato.org/about-iaato/our-mission/.

57. "Pan Am Posters," Everything Pan Am, accessed December 14, 2021, http://www.everythingpanam.com/Promo_Buttons.html.

58. Ryan Air, Twitter Post, November 4, 2020, 3:15 a.m., https://twitter.com/Ryanair/status/1323660203783606273?ref_src=twsrc%5etfw%7ctwcamp%5etweetembed%7ctwterm%5e1323660203783606273%7ctwgr%5e%7ctwcon%5es1_&ref_url=https%3a%2f%2fonemileatatime.com%2fryanair-trolls-presidential-election-twitter%2f.

59. U.S. Antarctic Program, "Time Line: U.S. Antarctic Moments from Deep Freeze to the Present," *Antarctic Sun*, December 25, 2005, accessed July 14, 2017, http://www.antarcticsun.usap.gov/pastIssues/2005-2006/2005_12_25.pdf (site discontinued).

60. "Pan-Am Way Down South," Pan Am Historical Foundation, accessed August 8, 2016, http://www.panam.org/images/Stories/Pan-Am-Way-Down-South.pdf.

61. "Air Hostesses To Judge Polar Beards," *Lodi (CA) News Sentinel*, October 14, 1957.

62. David Boyer, quoted in Belanger, *Deepfreeze*, 131.

63. Lewander, "Women and Civilisation on Ice," 89.

64. Benjamin Wright, "British Adventurer Maria Laijerstam Achieved World First by Cycling to the South Pole," *The Independent*, December 27, 2013, http://www.independent.co.uk/news/uk/home-news/british-adventurer-maria-leijerstam-achieves-world-first-by-cycling-to-south-pole-9026928.html.

65. Palmer, "Shit Happens," 333.

66. "Ray-Ban 12k GF Deep Freeze Double Gradient Mirror Sunglasses," Vintage Sunglasses Shop, accessed July 13, 2017, http://www.vintagesunglassesshop.com/item_vs351.html.

67. Admiral Reedy (1968) quoted in Chipman, *Women on the Ice*, 87.

68. Leiss et al., *Social Communication in Advertising*, 163.

69. Blum, *The News at the Ends of the Earth*, 2.

4. Purifying Antarctica

1. Leane, "The Land that Time Forgot," 199.

2. "Skin Doctors Antarcticine," Salonlines Hair and Beauty, accessed July 18, 2017, http://www.salonlines.co.uk/skin-doctors-antarctilyne-plump.php.

3. Leane, "Freezing Time in Far Southern Narratives," 200.

4. "Discover the New Ultra Hydrating Hydra Antarctica Serum by Pure Altitude," Be Well in Beirut, Health Essentials, February 19, 2017, http://bewellinbeirut .healthessentials-sal.com/pure-altitude-hydra-antarctica/.

5. *Oxford English Dictionary Online*, "pure," accessed December 14, 2021, https:// www.oed.com/search?searchType=dictionary&q=pure&_searchBtn= Search.

6. Dillard, *Teaching a Stone to Talk*, 59.

7. Colin Cosier, "Antarctic Rubbish Tip Will Cost Millions to Clean Up" *Sydney Morning Herald* February 17, 2014, https://www.smh.com.au/environment /antarctic-rubbish-tip-will-cost-millions-to-clean-up-20140216-32tr1.html.

8. Joyner, "The Evolving Minerals Regime for Antarctica," 131.

9. Convention on the Regulation of Antarctic Mineral Resource Activities (CRAMRA), "Preamble."

10. Orheim, "Managing the Frozen Commons," 287.

11. Messner, *Antarctica*, 35.

12. Day, *Antarctica*, 518.

13. Day, *Antarctica*, 517.

14. Gilbert, "A Continent for Peace and Science," 348.

15. Jackson, *Who Saved Antarctica?*, 366.

16. Tin, Summerson, and Yang, "Wilderness or Pure Land," 314.

17. Cronin, "The Trouble with Wilderness," 79.

18. Roberts, "Antarctica—Anything Is Possible."

19. Leane, "Antarctic Travel Writing and the Problematics of the Pristine," 1; *Oxford English Dictionary Online*, "pristine," accessed December 14, 2021, https://www.oed.com/view/Entry/151585?redirectedFrom=pristine#eid.

20. Manhire, *The Wide White Page*, 21.

21. van der Watt and Swart, "The Whiteness of Antarctica," 126.

22. van der Watt and Swart, "The Whiteness of Antarctica," 126.

23. Roberts, "The White (Supremacist) Continent," 108.

24. Robin McKie, "Antarctica Is Earth's One Virus-Free Continent: Science Fights to Keep It That Way," *The Guardian*, November 1, 2020, https://www .theguardian.com/world/2020/nov/01/next-stop-antarctica-british-team -covid-free-coronavirus.

25. "COVID-19 Outbreak Prevention, Mitigation & Management Response," Council of Managers of National Antarctic Programs, accessed November 10, 2021, https://www.comnap.aq/projects.

26. Hughes and Convey, "Implications of the COVID-19 pandemic for Antarctica," 430.

27. Barbosa et al., "Risk Assessment of SARS-COV-2 in Antarctic Wildlife," 1.

28. Lukin and Vasiliev, "Technological Aspects of the Final Phase of Drilling," 85, 87.

29. Gramling, "Mysterious Antarctic Lake Will Remain Out of Reach," 494.

30. Fricker et al., "An Active Subglacial Water System," 1544.

31. See Madrid Protocol, Annex V. Antarctic Treaty Secretariat, "The Protocol on Environmental Protection to the Antarctic Treaty," accessed April 10, 2023, https://www.ats.aq/e/protocol.html.

32. Ruddiman, "The Anthropocene," 45.

33. Lubick, "DDT Levels in Antarctic Penguins," 3909; Delmas et al., "Bomb-test 36Cl Measurements in Vostok Snow," 494.

34. Hodgson-Johnston et al., "Cleaning Up after Human Activity in Antarctica," 135.

35. Cherry-Garrard, *The Worst Journey in the World*, vii.

36. "Visitor Guidelines," International Association of Antarctica Tour Operators, accessed November 20, 2022, http://www.iaato.org/visitor-guidelines.

37. Douglas, *Purity and Danger*, 21.

38. Dodds and Yusoff, "Settlement and Unsettlement," 149.

39. "About COMNAP," Council of Managers of National Antarctic Programs, accessed December 11, 2021, http://www.comnap.aq/Members/SitePages /Home.aspx; "An Inclusive Network of Racial & Ethnic Minorities and Allies in the Polar Research Community," Polar Impact Network, accessed November 10, 2021, https://www.polarimpactnetwork.org/.

40. McClintock, "Soft-Soaping Empire," 752.

41. McClintock, "Soft-Soaping Empire," 753.

42. Byrd and Poulter, *The Romance of Antarctic Adventure*, 36.

43. Opel, "Constructing Purity," 73.

44. Opel, "Constructing Purity," 73.

45. "Antarctica," Godet, accessed May 12, 2017, http://www.antarcticagodet .com (site discontinued).

46. "Antarctica," Godet.

47. "Antarctica," Godet.

48. "Süd Polaire Antarctic Dry Spirit," Süd Polaire, accessed December 14, 2021, https://www.sudpolaire.com/products/sud-polaire-antarctic-dry-gin.

49. Parker, "Exploring Life Themes and Myths in Alcohol Advertisements," 105.

50. Yenne, *Beer*, 200.

51. David Wilson, "Pricey Pint: How I Developed the World's Most Expensive Ale," *Sydney Morning Herald*, November 30, 2010, http://www.smh.com

.au/small-business/entrepreneur/pricey-pint-how-i-developed-the-worlds
-most-expensive-ale-20101130-18ers.html.

52. Opel, "Constructing Purity," 75.

53. "Enzymes from Antarctica Have Industrial Use," Agencia Iberoamericana
para la Difusión de la Ciencia y la Tecnología, October 28, 2014, http://www
.dicyt.com/news/enzymes-from-antarctica-have-industrial-use.

54. "Molecular Characterization of Cold-Active Enzymes from Psychrophilic
Microorganisms as the Basis for Novel Biotechnology," Cordis, European
Union, September 8, 1998, http://www.cordis.europa.eu/result/rcn/21104
_en.html.

55. Hemmings, "'Environmental Management' as Diplomatic Methoda," 82;
Nielsen, "Selling the South," 186.

56. New Zealand and Sweden, Resolution 6 (2013). ATCM 36–CEP 16, Brussels,
"Biological Prospecting in Antarctica," Paragraph 327, accessed August 28,
2017, http://www.ats.aq.

57. Dodds, *The Antarctic*, 125.

58. Quoted in Alister Doyle, "Antarctic Patents Strain Goals of Shared Science,"
Reuters, February 6, 2009, http://www.reuters.com/article/us-antarctica
-companies-idustre51503220090206.

59. Hughes and Bridge, "Potential Impacts of Antarctic Bioprospecting," 14.

60. Resolution 6 (2013). ATCM 36–CEP 16, https://www.ats.aq/devAS/Meetings
/Measure/559.

61. "Glacier 51 Toothfish," Austral Fisheries, accessed November 18, 2022, https://
www.australfisheries.com.au/our-brands/glacier-51-toothfish.

62. "Blackmores," World Wildlife Foundation, accessed July 17, 2017, http://
www.wwf.org.au/about-us/partners/blackmores.

63. "Blackmores and WWF Announce Sustainable Fish Oils Partnership," Blackmores, October 4, 2012, accessed July 17, 2017, http://www.blackmores.com
.au/about-us/media-centre-old/media-releases/blackmores-and-wwf
-announce-sustainable-fish-oils-partnership (page discontinued).

64. "Blackmores Krill Oil," Xander Creative, accessed October 18, 2016, http://
www.xandercreative.com.au/.

65. "Blackmores Krill Oil."

66. "Blackmores Krill Oil."

67. "Blackmores Responds to Sea Shepherd," Blackmores, July 6, 2015, accessed
July 19, 2017, http://www.blackmores.com.au/blackmores-responds-to-sea
-shepherd (page discontinued).

68. Nielsen, "Selling the South," 185.

tes to Pages 126–130   211

69. "Petition to Stop Blackmores Sale of Krill Products," Sea Shepherd, accessed July 19, 2017, http://www.seashepherd.org.au/blackmorespetition (page discontinued); "cvs: Vacuuming Antarctica for Krill," Sum of Us, accessed July 19, 2017, http://www.actions.sumofus.org/a/cvs-antarctic-krill (site discontinued).

70. Brooks, "Competing Values on the Antarctic High Seas," 280.

71. Nielsen, "Selling the South," 183.

5. Fragile Antarctica

1. Jeremy Plester, "Continuing Collapse of Antarctic Ice Shelves Will Affect Us All," *Guardian Online*, May 16, 2016, https://www.theguardian.com /news/2016/may/15/weatherwatch-antarctic-ice-shelf-collapse-global -implications.

2. Rebecca Lindsey, "Collapse of the Larsen-B Ice Shelf." NASA Earth Observatory, January 31, 2002, www.earthobservatory.nasa.gov/Features /WorldOfChange/larsenb.php.

3. Williamson, "Unfreezing the Truth."

4. Carvalho, "Reporting the Climate Change Crisis," 498.

5. Yusoff, "Visualizing Antarctica as a Place in Time," 387.

6. Yusoff, "Visualizing Antarctica as a Place in Time," 387.

7. Adrian Luckman, "I've Studied Larsen C and Its Giant Iceberg for Years and It's Not a Simple Story of Climate Change," *The Conversation*, July 12, 2017, https://theconversation.com/ive-studied-larsen-c-and-its-giant-iceberg-for -years-its-not-a-simple-story-of-climate-change-80529.

8. Kiem et al., "Learning from the Past."

9. Nüsser and Baghel, "The Emergence of the Cryoscape," 138.

10. "Cut 68 million tons of CO_2 and its [sic] amazing what you save," ABB advertisement, *Animals in advertising—Penguins*, 2005, accessed February 8, 2019, http://www.elve.net/panim/ill400/im411.jpg; "Cut 100 million tons of CO_2 and its [sic] amazing what you save," ABB advertisement, *European Career Fair, MIT European Club*, 2008, accessed August 22, 2017, http://documents .mx/documents/2008-ecf-booklet-55a236eed0863.html; "PACT: Sustainability and Community News, no. 5," Westpac Banking Corporation, 2008, accessed December 20, 2018, https://www.westpac.com.au/docs/pdf/aw /pactv5.pdf (page discontinued); Adnews, "Diesel Breaks Global Warming Ready Campaign," February 1, 2007, https://www.adnews.com/23110.

11. Protocol on Environmental Protection to the Antarctic Treaty, October 4, 1991, 30 ILM 1455 (1991); Antarctic Treaty Secretariat, "The Protocol on

Environmental Protection to the Antarctic Treaty" accessed April 10, 2023, https://www.ats.aq/e/protocol.html.

12. Gilbert and Hemmings, "Antarctic Mythbusting," 29.

13. "Home: The Last Ocean Charitable Trust website," The Last Ocean Charitable Trust, accessed December 14, 2021, http://www.lastocean.org/.

14. Trojanow, *Lamentations of Zeno*, 37.

15. Leane and McGee, *Anthropocene Antarctica*, 97.

16. Nüsser and Baghel, "The Emergence of the Cryoscape," 150.

17. "Greenhouse Gas Benchmark Reached," NOAA *Research News*, May 6, 2015, https://research.noaa.gov/article/Artmid/587/Articleid/780/Greenhouse-gas-benchmark-reached-.

18. "NASA Scientists React to 400 ppm Carbon Milestone," NASA *Global Climate Change: Vital Signs of the Planet*, 2013, accessed August 22, 2017, https://climate.nasa.gov/400ppmquotes/.

19. Vaughan et al., "Observations: Cryosphere," 319.

20. Rodger, "Antarctica," 324.

21. Yusoff and Gabrys, "Climate Change and the Imagination," 517.

22. "About the Sierra Club," Sierra Club, accessed April 2, 2023, https://www.sierraclub.org/about-sierra-club.

23. "The History of Earth Day," Earth Day Network, accessed August 22, 2017, https://www.earthday.org/history/.

24. "About," Greenpeace, accessed December 14, 2021, https://www.greenpeace.org.au/about/; "The Story of the Australian Greens," Australian Greens, accessed August 22, 2017, https://greens.org.au/about/our-story.

25. Stockholm Declaration on the Human Environment, in Report of the United Nations Conference on the Human Environment, UN Doc. A/CONF. 48/14, at 2 and Corr. 1 (1972).

26. West, Ford, and Ibrahim, *Strategic Marketing*, 450.

27. Christensen, Nilsson, and Wormbs, *Media and the Politics of Arctic Climate Change*.

28. Pearse, *Green Wash*, 246.

29. Williamson, "Unfreezing the Truth."

30. Hillary Mayell, "As Consumerism Spreads, Earth Suffers, Study Says," *National Geographic News*, January 12, 2004, https://www.nationalgeographic.com/environment/article/consumerism-earth-suffers.

31. Simpson-Housley, *Antarctica*, xv.

32. Williamson, "Unfreezing the Truth."

33. Nüsser and Baghel, "The Emergence of the Cryoscape," 150.

34. Sörlin, "Cryo-History," 327.

35. Hicks, "Sustainability: Can Advertising Save the World?"

36. "Cut 68 million tons of CO_2 and its [sic] amazing what you save"; West, Ford, and Ibrahim, *Strategic Marketing*, 450.

37. "Cut 100 million tons of CO_2 and its [sic] amazing what you save."

38. Leane and Pfennigwerth, "Marching on Thin Ice," 40.

39. West, Ford, and Ibrahim, *Strategic Marketing*, 450.

40. West, Ford, and Ibrahim, *Strategic Marketing*, 450.

41. Savolainen, "Driving Towards a Better Future," 34.

42. Pearse, *Green Wash*, 18.

43. Pearse, *Green Wash*, 37.

44. Savolainen, "Driving Towards a Better Future," 34.

45. Leane and Pfennigwerth, "Marching on Thin Ice," 30.

46. Sareff, "Campaign for Change," 26.

47. McDonough and Egolf, *The Advertising Age Encyclopedia of Advertising*, 252.

48. Leslie Nielson, "Emissions—Who Is Trading What?" *Parliament of Australia*, August 15, 2008, accessed August 24, 2017, http://www.aph.gov.au/About_Parliament/Parliamentary_Departments/Parliamentary_Library/pubs/bn/0809/Emissions (page discontinued); "Westpac Climate Change Position Statement: Financing the Transition to a Low Carbon Economy," Westpac Banking Corporation, 2010, accessed December 20, 2018. https://www.westpac.com.au/docs/pdf/aw/Transit_to_low_carbon_econo1.pdf (page discontinued); "PACT: Sustainability and Community News, no. 5," Westpac Banking Corporation, 2008, accessed December 20, 2018, https://www.westpac.com.au/docs/pdf/aw/pactv5.pdf (page discontinued).

49. Fletcher and Crawford, *International Marketing*, 208; "About the Equator Principles," Equator Principles Association, accessed December 18, 2018, https://equator-principles.com/about/.

50. Leane and Pfennigwerth, "Marching on Thin Ice," 37.

51. "Ice, Snow, and Glaciers and the Water Cycle," United States Geological Survey, June 7, 20019, https://www.usgs.gov/special-topics/water-science-school/science/ice-snow-and-glaciers-and-water-cycle.

52. Sareff, "Campaign for Change," 25.

53. Sareff, "Campaign for Change," 25.

54. Leane and Pfennigwerth, "Marching on Thin Ice," 30, 32.

55. "The Ozone Hole," British Antarctic Survey, June 30, 2022, http://www.bas.ac.uk/data/our-data/publication/the-ozone-layer.

56. Leane and Pfennigwerth, "Marching on Thin Ice," 36.

57. Fletcher and Crawford, *International Marketing*, 208.

58. "Diesel Launches Global Warming Ready Campaign," *Newswire* (Canada) press release, 2007, accessed August 22, 2017, https://www.newswire .ca/news-releases/diesel-launches-global-warming-ready-campaign -533357341.html (page discontinued).

59. "Diesel Launches Global Warming Ready Campaign."

60. Paul Harrison, "Diesel Ads Hardly 'Global Warming Ready,'" *The Varsity*, February 27, 2007, http://www.thevarsity.ca/2007/02/27/diesel-ads-hardly -global-warming-ready.

61. Quoted in Dahlen, Lange, and Smith, *Marketing Communications*, 157; Harrison, "Diesel Ads Hardly 'Global Warming Ready.'"

62. Pearse, *Green Wash*, 78.

63. "Diesel: Global Warming North Pole," Ads of the World, 2012, accessed December 18, 2018, https://www.adsoftheworld.com/cannes_lions_2007 _winners_press_silver (page discontinued).

64. "Global Warming Ready," *YouTube*, 2007, accessed May 10, 2016, http://www .youtube.com/watch?v=v5op3gmwwnY (page discontinued).

65. Pearse, *Green Wash*, 86.

66. "Featured partners: Diesel," StopGlobalWarming.org, 2007, accessed July 21, 2015, http://www.stopglobalwarming.org. Historic version via https:// web.archive.org/web/20080621121507/http://www.stopglobalwarming .org/sgw_partner.asp?668919.

67. "Featured partners: Diesel."

68. Andersson et al., "Violent Advertising in Fashion Marketing," 96.

69. Cited in "Featured partners: Diesel."

70. Dahlen, Lange, and Smith, *Marketing Communications*, 157.

6. Destination Antarctica

1. John Oliver, "Don't Visit Antarctica." *Last Week Tonight with John Oliver*, accessed February 9, 2017, http://www.youtube.com/watch?v= dH573B1bkHI.

2. Shaw et al., "Antarctica's Protected Areas Are Inadequate."

3. Hunt and Ikin, "Antarctica Under Threat from Human Visitors."

4. Oliver, "Don't Visit Antarctica," 0:1:15.

5. "5 Life-Changing Experiences in Antarctica," Intrepid Travel, October 5, 2017, https://www.facebook.com/intrepidtravel/videos/10159477610585644/.

6. "Antarctica: A How-To Guide to a Safe and Rewarding Antarctica Experience," Lindblad Expeditions, accessed February 14, 2017, https://au.expeditions

.com/brochures/antarctica-a-how-to-guide-to-a-safe-and-rewarding
-antarctica-experience.

7. Leane, *Antarctica in Fiction*, 133.
8. "About," Homeward Bound, accessed August 12, 2017, https://homeward boundprojects.com.au/.
9. Berger, "Antarctica," 103.
10. Maynard, *Wings of Ice*, 15.
11. "Welcome to Antarctic Ambassadors," International Association of Antarctica Tourism Operators, accessed November 29, 2022, https://iaato.org/antarctic -ambassadors/antarctic-ambassadors/.
12. Powell, Kellert, and Ham, "Antarctic Tourists"; Lamers, Eijgelaar, and Amelung, "Last Chance Tourism in Antarctica."
13. Alexander et al., "What and Who Is an Antarctic Ambassador?," 502.
14. "Tourism Overview," International Association of Antarctica Tourism Operators, accessed October 22, 2022, http://www.iaato.org/tourism-overview.
15. Haase, "Tourism in the Antarctic," 48; Bauer, *Tourism in the Antarctic*, 15.
16. Nielsen, "Selling the South," 187.
17. "The Antarctic Expedition," *Otago Daily Times*, January 3, 1908, https:// paperspast.natlib.govt.nz/newspapers/ODT19080103.2.69?query=Buckley %20Antarctica.
18. Leane, *South Pole*, 175.
19. Headland, "Historical Development of Antarctic Tourism," 275.
20. "Tourism Overview," International Association of Antarctica Tourism Operators.
21. "Tourism Overview," International Association of Antarctica Tourism Operators.
22. "South Pole & Emperors" White Desert Antarctica, accessed April 10, 2023, https://white-desert.com/adventures/south-pole-emperors.
23. Roldán, "A Door to the Ice," 57.
24. Hall, "The Tourist and Economic Significance of Antarctic Travel," 157.
25. "Tasmanian Antarctic Gateway Strategy 2022–2027," Tasmanian Government Department of State Growth, accessed November 10, 2022, https://www .antarctic.tas.gov.au/__data/assets/pdf_file/0008/404684/FINAL_TAG _Strategy_2022_-_27.pdf.
26. "What is IAATO?," International Association of Antarctica Tourism Operators, accessed February 20, 2022, http://www.iaato.org/what-is-iaato.
27. Carey, "Is It Time for a Paradigm Shift?," 11.

28. "Antarctic Tour Operators' Fuel Consumption to Be Analysed as They Embark on Climate Strategy," International Association of Antarctica Tour Operators, October 6, 2022, https://iaato.org/antarctic-tour-operators-fuel -consumption-to-be-analysed-as-they-embark-on-climate-strategy/.

29. Nielsen and Roldan, "Polar Policy in Practice."

30. "Antarctica Tours," G Adventures, accessed November 18, 2022, https:// www.gadventures.com/destinations/polar/antarctica/; "Responsible Travel in Antarctica," Intrepid Travel, accessed November 18, 2022. https://www .intrepidtravel.com/au/antarctica/responsible-travel-in-antarctica.

31. "Antarctic Explorer: Discovering the 7th Continent," Quark Expeditions, accessed February 6, 2017, http://www.quarkexpeditions.com/au/antarctic /expeditions/antarctic-explorer-discovering-the-7th-continent.

32. Lamers, Eijgelaar, and Amelung, "Last Chance Tourism in Antarctica," 29.

33. Lamers, Eijgelaar, and Amelung, "Last Chance Tourism in Antarctica," 32.

34. Stonehouse, "Ecotourism in Antarctica"; Thomas, "Ecotourism in Antarctica."

35. Frew, "Advertising World Heritage Sites," 118.

36. Wall, "Ecotourism," 165.

37. Lemelin et al., "Last-Chance Tourism," 478.

38. Lamers, Eijgelaar, and Amelung, "Last Chance Tourism in Antarctica," 36.

39. "Marketing Antarctica: An Advisory from IAATO for IAATO Member Staff and Agents Engaged in Marketing/Public Relations," International Association of Antarctica Tourism Operators, accessed December 10, 2021, https://iaato .org/wp-content/uploads/2020/04/IAATO_Internal-Marketing-Antarctica .compressed.pdf.

40. Frew, "Advertising World Heritage Sites," 129.

41. Tomaselli, "Consuming Nature," 339.

42. "IAATO Annual Marketing & PR Self-Audit," International Association of Antarctica Tourism Operators, accessed December 10, 2021, https://iaato .org/wp-content/uploads/2020/04/Agenda-Item-11b.-IAATO-Marketing -PR-self-Audit.pdf.

43. "Marketing Antarctica," International Association of Antarctica Tourism Operators.

44. Noble, "Antarctica Nullius."

45. "Ultimate Antarctica Photography Safari." Natural World Safaris, September 30, 2016, https://issuu.com/naturalworldsafaris/docs/ultimate_antarctica _photography_saf; "Photography Antarctica, the Arctic and Beyond," Aurora

Expeditions, accessed November 18, 2022, https://aurora.uberflip.com/i
/1476509-mini-photography-brochure/.

46. Scarles, "Becoming Tourist," 465, 466.

47. Echtner, "The Semiotic Paradigm," 52.

48. Paterson, *Consumption and Everyday Life*, 134.

49. Morgan and Pritchard, *Advertising in Tourism and Leisure*, 10.

50. *Going Ashore in Antarctica—IAATO Briefing Film 2018*, International Association of Antarctica Tourism Operators, accessed 30 November 2022, https://iaato .org/visiting-antarctica/visitor-briefings/.

51. Ashworth, "Historical Tourism," 277.

52. Jones et al., "Decolonising Imperial Heroes," 807.

53. "2016–2018 Antarctica," Aurora Expeditions, accessed February 6, 2017, http://www.aurora.uberflip.com/i/774486-2016-18-antarctica-brochure.

54. "Celebrating the Centennial: A Once-in-a-Lifetime Destination Is Now a Once-in-a-Century Must-Explore," Lindblad Expeditions, accessed April 3, 2016, http://www.expeditions.com/destinations/polar-regions/antarctica /the-experience/celebrating-the-centennial (page discontinued).

55. "Celebrating the Centennial," Lindblad Expeditions.

56. "In the Footsteps of Scott & Shackleton," Heritage Expeditions, February 6, 2010, accessed February 14, 2017, http://www.heritage-expeditions.com /trip/in-the-footsteps-of-scott-and-shackleton-2665-5 (page discontinued).

57. "About Us," New Zealand Antarctic Heritage Trust, accessed November 7, 2016, http://www.nzaht.org/about-aht.

58. "About Us," New Zealand Antarctic Heritage Trust.

59. Dodds and Yusoff, "Settlement and Unsettlement," 151.

60. Glasberg, "'Living Ice,'" 222.

61. "Explorers Wanted," Quark Expeditions, accessed November 18, 2022, https:// explore.quarkexpeditions.com/brochures/antarctic-brochure.

62. Farley, "'By Endurance We Conquer,'" 241.

63. Leane, *South Pole*, 176.

64. Edensor, "Performing Tourism, Staging Tourism," 74; Jackson, *George Newnes and the New Journalism in Britain*, 169.

65. Worsley, *In Shackleton's Footsteps*, 103.

66. Leane, *South Pole*, 178.

67. Morrison and Sung, "Adventure Tourism," 11.

68. Palmer, "Shit Happens," 332.

69. Palmer, "Shit Happens," 330.

70. Chalufour, "Whistling Up the Wind."

71. Jennifer Abplanalp, "Running 26.2 Miles to Nowhere," *Online Clarion*, April 28, 2011, http://www.theonlineclarion.com/sports/2011/04/28/running -26-2-miles-to-nowhere.

72. "Pure Antarctica," Chimu Adventures, accessed February 6, 2017, https:// www.chimuadventures.com/en-au/antarctica. Fathom Expeditions, "Hello explorers! Pure Antarctica cruise in February, 2018. Just one female berth left on the ship. Give us a call and make it yours today!" Facebook, June 1, 2017, https://www.facebook.com/FathomExpeditions/photos/a .372738169416463/1556243217732613.

73. Lamers, Eijgelaar, and Amelung, "Last Chance Tourism in Antarctica," 29.

74. Krapp, "POLAR MEDIA," 832.

75. Tomaselli, "Consuming Nature," 337.

76. Tomaselli, "Consuming Nature," 337.

77. "Pure Antarctica," Chimu Adventure; "Antarctica," Hurtigruten Expeditions, accessed November 18, 2022, https://www.hurtigruten.com/en-us /expeditions/destinations/antarctica-cruises/; Fathom Expeditions, "Hello explorers!"

78. Worsley, *In Shackleton's Footsteps*, 107.

79. "ATCM 33 Appendix A: Environmental Aspects of Antarctic Ship-Borne Tourism," International Association of Antarctica Tourism Operators, 2010, accessed February 14, 2017, http://ats.aq/documents/atcm33/att/atcm33 _att024_e.doc.

80. Cordero et al. "Black Carbon Footprint of Human Presence."

81. "Antarctic Tour Operators' Fuel Consumption to Be Analysed as They Embark on Climate Strategy," International Association of Antarctica Tour Operators, October 6, 2022, https://iaato.org/antarctic-tour-operators-fuel -consumption-to-be-analysed-as-they-embark-on-climate-strategy/.

82. "Antarctic Climate Expedition 2023," Aurora Expeditions, accessed November 18, 2022, https://www.auroraexpeditions.com.au/antarctic-climate -expedition-2023/.

83. Saatchi & Saatchi, Copenhagen, Denmark, (creative director: Simon Wooller; art directors: Cliff Kagawa Holm, Silas Jansson; copywriters: Cliff Kagawa Holm, Silas Jansson). See https://adsspot.me/media/prints/kilroy-travels -antarctica-df9713b438b6 and https://www.adforum.com/creative-work /ad/player/6683435/iceberg/kilroy.

84. Cederholm and Hultman, "Tourists and Global Environmental Change," 298.

85. Carvalho, "Reporting the Climate Change Crisis," 498.

86. Perkins et al., *Leading at the Edge*; Morrell and Capparell, *Shackleton's Way*.

87. Pynchon, *V*, 241; Leane, *Antarctica in Fiction*, 4.

88. "About the Foundation," Shackleton Foundation, accessed July 23, 2014, http://shackletonfoundation.org/?page_id=28.

89. "Anton Oliver's 'My Antarctic' Challenge," Shackleton Foundation, http://shackletonfoundation.org/?p=441.

90. Stuart Elliot, "Grape-Nuts Wants You To Climb Every Mountain," *New York Times*, May 28, 2013, http://www.nytimes.com/2013/05/28/business/media/grape-nuts-wants-you-to-climb-every-mountain.html.

91. "Post Grape-Nuts Brings the 'What's Your Mountain?' Campaign to the South Pole," Post Grape-Nuts, December 20, 2014, http://www.multivu.com/players/English/7395851-post-grape-nuts-bring-what-s-your-moutain-campaign-to-south-pole/.

92. "GrapeNuts Antarctica—Historical Version," Ursus Films, May 16, 2015, http://www.vimeo.com/128032023.

93. "Grape-Nuts Fit Granola Re-Launch: Grape-Nuts Explores Adventurous Heritage on Historic Antarctica Trek," Prepared Foods, December 16, 2014, http://www.preparedfoods.com/articles/114788-grape-nuts-fit-granola.

94. "GrapeNuts Antarctica—Historical Version," Ursus Films.

95. "About the McGrath Foundation," McGrath Foundation, accessed November 9, 2016, http://www.mcgrathfoundation.com.au/AboutUs.aspx.

96. "How Values Work," Common Cause Foundation, accessed November 9, 2016, http://www.valuesandframes.org/handbook/2-how-values-work.

97. "Antarctic Answers," BAS & Co., December 23, 2010, http://www.basfieldassistants.blogspot.com.au.

98. Nielsen and Jaksic. "Extremity and the Mundane."

99. Certified Builders Association press release, "Antarctic Apprent-ICE: An Opportunity of a Lifetime," *Business Scoop*, October 30, 2014, https://business.scoop.co.nz/2014/10/30/antarctic-apprent-ice-an-opportunity-of-a-lifetime.

Conclusion

1. Nielsen, "Selling the South," 193.

2. Scarles, "Becoming Tourist," 478.

3. Leane, "Unstable Places and Generic Spaces."

4. Groden, "Alaskan Airlines Apologizes"; Matt Hunter, "Alaska Airlines' Meet our Eskimo Advertising Campaign Sparks Furious Reaction and Accusations of Racism as Chief Executive is Forced to Apologize," *Daily Mail*, January 30, 2016, http://www.dailymail.co.uk/news/article-3422931/Alaska-Airlines

-Meet-Eskimo-advertising-campaign-sparks-furious-reaction-accusations -racism-chief-executive-forced-apologize.html.

5. Leane, "Unstable Places and Generic Spaces," 32.

6. Antonello, "Finding Place in Antarctica," 182.

7. Terauds and Lee, "Antarctic Biogeography Revisited"; Resolution 6 (2012) ATCM 30–CEP 15, Hobart, "Antarctic Conservation Biogeographic Regions," accessed 15 August 2017, https://www.ats.aq/devAS/Meetings/Measure /520; See also Antarctic Environments Portal, which links Antarctic science and policy, https://environments.aq/.

8. Antonello, "Finding Place in Antarctica," 199.

9. Goodell, "The Larsen C Crack-Up on Antarctica."

10. Aaron Packard, "One Of The World's Largest Icebergs Is About to Break Off Antarctica. Here's What It Should Be Named," *Huffington Post*, updated June 25, 2017, http://www.huffingtonpost.com/entry/the-worlds-largest-iceberg -is-about-to-break-off-antarctica_us_594643e5e4b0940f84fe2f78; Aaron Packard, "Exxon's Denial Created This Iceberg," *350.org*, accessed June 18, 2017, http://www.350.org/exxons-denial-created-this-iceberg.

11. Goodell, "The Larsen C Crack-Up."

12. "The #ExxonKnew Iceberg Has Broken Free," *350.org*, https://act.350.org /letter/exxonknew-iceberg.

13. Roberts, van der Watt, and Howkins, "Antarctica," 14.

14. Roberts, "The White (Supremacist) Continent," 108.

Bibliography

"Advertising Campaign." *vwa Review* (June 1963): 2–7.

Alexander, Karen A., Daniela Liggett, Elizabeth Leane, Hanne E. F. Nielsen, Jennifer L. Bailey, Madeline J. Brasier, and Marcus Haward. "What and Who Is an Antarctic Ambassador?" *Polar Record* 55, no. 6 (2019): 497–506.

Anderson, Benedict. *Imagined Communities: Reflections on the Origin and Spread of Nationalism*. London: Verso, 1983.

Andersson, S., A. Hedelin, A. Nilsson, and C. Welander. "Violent Advertising in Fashion Marketing." *Journal of Fashion Marketing and Management* 8, no. 1 (2004): 96–112.

Antarctic Treaty Secretariat. "Antarctic Treaty (1959)." Accessed August 16, 2017. http://www.ats.aq/documents/ats/treaty_original.pdf.

Antonello, Alessandro. "Finding Place in Antarctica." In *Antarctica and the Humanities*, edited by Peder Roberts, Lize-Marié van der Watt, and Adrian Howkins, 181–204. London: Palgrave Macmillan UK, 2016.

———. *The Greening of Antarctica: Assembling an International Environment*. Oxford: Oxford University Press, 2019.

Ashworth, G. J. "Historical Tourism." In *Encyclopedia of Tourism*, edited by Jafar Jafari and Honggen Xiao, 277. Cham, Switzerland: Springer International, 2010.

Barbosa, Andrés, Arvind Varsani, Virginia Morandini, Wray Grimaldi, Ralph E. T. Vanstreels, Julia I. Diaz, Thierry Boulinier, Meagan Dewar, Daniel González-Acuña, Rachael Gray, Clive R. McMahon, Gary Miller, Michelle Power, Amandine Gamble, and Michelle Wille. "Risk Assessment of SARS-COV-2 in Antarctic Wildlife." *Science of The Total Environment* 755, no. 2 (2021): 1–8.

Barczewski, Stephanie. *Antarctic Destinies: Scott, Shackleton, and the Changing Face of Heroism*. London: Hambledon Continuum, 2007.

Bauer, Thomas. *Tourism in the Antarctic: Opportunities, Constraints, and Future Prospects*. New York: Haworth Hospitality, 2001.

Baughmann, T. H. *Before the Heroes Came: Antarctica in the 1890s*. Lincoln: University of Nebraska Press, 1994.

Belanger, Dian O. *Deep Freeze: The United States, the International Geophysical Year, and the Origins of Antarctica's Age of Science*. Boulder: University Press of Colorado, 2006.

Berger, Arthur A. "Antarctica." In *Theorizing Tourism: Analyzing Iconic Destinations*, edited by Arthur A. Berger, 99–104. Walnut Creek CA: Left Coast, 2013.

———. *Media Analysis Techniques*, 3rd ed. London: Sage, 2005.

Blum, Hester. *The News at the Ends of the Earth: The Print Culture of Polar Exploration*. Durham NC: Duke University Press, 2019.

Bown, Stephen. *The Last Viking: The Life of Roald Amundsen, Conqueror of the South Pole*. London: Aurum, 2012.

Branston, Gill, and Ray Stafford. *The Media Student Book*, 3rd ed. New York: Routledge. 2003.

Brooks, Cassandra. "Competing Values on the Antarctic High Seas: CCAMLR and the Challenge of Marine-Protected Areas." *Polar Journal* 3, no. 2 (2013): 277–300.

Bush, Barbara. *Imperialism and Postcolonialism*. New York: Pearson Longman, 2006.

Byrd, Richard E. *Skyward: Man's Mastery of the Air as Shown by the Brilliant Flights of America's Leading Air Explorer*. New York: G. P. Putnam's Sons, 1928.

———. *Alone: The Classic Polar Adventure*. New York: G. P. Putnam's Sons, 1938.

Byrd, Richard E., and Thomas C. Poulter. *The Romance of Antarctic Adventure*. New York: J. W. Clement, 1935.

Carey, Peter. "Is It Time for a Paradigm Shift in How Antarctic Tourism Is Controlled?" *Polar Perspectives* 1 (2020): 1–14.

Carvalho, Anabela. "Reporting the Climate Change Crisis." In *The Routledge Companion to News and Journalism Studies*, edited by S. Allan, 485–95. Oxford: Routledge, 2010.

Cederholm, E. A., and J. Hultman. "Tourists and Global Environmental Change: A Possible Scenario in Relation to Nature and Authenticity." In *Tourism and Global Environmental Change*, edited by S. Gössling and C. M. Hall, 293–304. New York: Routledge, 2006.

Chalufour, Marc. "Whistling Up the Wind: The Story of the Ill-Fated Antarctica Marathon." *Runner's World*. May 31, 2001. http://www.runnersworld.com/where-to-run/whistling-up-the-wind.

Chapple, Geoff. "Harvest of Souls." *New Zealand Geographic*. July–August 2005. http://www.nzgeo.com/stories/harvest-of-souls.

Cherry-Garrard, Apsley. *The Worst Journey in the World*. London: Picador, 1994. First published 1922.

Chilean Antarctic Institute. "Traces of Antarctica around Punta Arenas and the Straits of Magellan." Punta Arenas: INACH, 2013. https://issuu.com/jgallardo /docs/traces_of_antarctica_web.

Chipman, Elizabeth. *Women on the Ice: A History of Women in the Far South*. Melbourne, Australia: Melbourne University Press, 1986.

Christensen, Miyase, Annika E. Nilsson, and Nina Wormbs, eds. *Media and the Politics of Arctic Climate Change: When the Ice Breaks*. New York: Palgrave Macmillan, 2013.

Clancy, Robert, John Manning, and Henk Brolsma. *Mapping Antarctica: A Five Hundred Year Record of Discovery*. Dordrecht, Netherlands: Springer Praxis, 2014.

Clark, C. W., and R. H. Lamberson. "An Economic History and Analysis of Pelagic Whaling." *Marine Policy* 6, no. 2 (1982): 103–20.

Conboy, Martin. *The Language of Newspapers: Socio-Historical Perspectives*. London: Continuum, 2010.

———. *The Press and Popular Culture*. London: Sage, 2002.

"Convention on the Regulation of Antarctic Mineral Resource Activities" (CRAMRA). June 2, 1988 (not in force). Wellington. 27 ILM 868. Accessed August 28, 2017. http://www.ats.aq/documents/recatt/Att311_e.pdf.

Cordero, Raúl, Edgardo Sepúlveda, Sarah Feron, Alessandro Damiani, Francisco Fernandoy, Steven Neshyba, Penny M. Rowe et al. "Black Carbon Footprint of Human Presence in Antarctica" *Nature Communications* 13, no. 984 (2022). https://doi.org/10.1038/s41467-022-28560-w.

Cox, Patrick L. "Charles Lindberg and Mobiloil: The New Model for Modern Celebrity Endorsement." *Journalism History* 30, no. 2 (2004): 98–106.

Craciun, Adriana. "Oceanic Voyages, Maritime Books, and Eccentric Inscriptions." *Atlantic Studies* 10, no. 2 (2013): 170–96.

Cronin, William. "The Trouble with Wilderness; or, Getting Back to the Wrong Nature." In *Uncommon Ground: Rethinking the Human Place in Nature*, edited by William Cronin, 69–90. New York: W. W. Norton, 1995.

Dahlen, Micael, Fredrik Lange, and Terry Smith. *Marketing Communications: A Brand Narrative Approach*. West Sussex: John Wiley & Sons, 2010.

Dali, Avivit Agam. "Advertising as a Semiotic System of Space: Image of the Desert in Israeli Advertising, 1967–2004." *Israel Affairs* 19, no. 2 (2013): 338–52.

Day, David. *Antarctica: A Biography*. Sydney: Random House, 2012.

Delmas, R. J., J. Beer, H.-A. Synal, R. Muscheler, J.-R. Petit, and M. Pourchet. "Bomb-test 36Cl Measurements in Vostok Snow (Antarctica) and the Use of 36Cl as a Dating Tool for Deep Ice Cores." *Tellus B* 56, no. 5 (2011): 492–98.

Dibbern, S. J. "Fur Seals, Whales and Tourists: A Commercial History of Deception Island, Antarctica." *Polar Record* 46, no. 238 (2010): 210–21.

Dillard, Annie. *Teaching a Stone to Talk*. New York: Harper Perennial, 1982.

Dodds, Klaus. *The Antarctic: A Very Short Introduction*. Oxford: Oxford University Press, 2012.

———. "The Great Trek: New Zealand and the British/Commonwealth 1955–58 Trans-Antarctic Expedition." *The Journal of Imperial and Commonwealth History* 33, no. 1 (2005): 93–114.

Dodds, Klaus, and Kathryn Yusoff. "Settlement and Unsettlement in Aotearoa/New Zealand and Antarctica." *Polar Record* 41, no. 217 (2005): 141–55.

Douglas, Mary. *Purity and Danger: An Analysis of Concepts of Pollution and Taboo*. Boston: Routledge and Keegan Paul, 1980.

Echtner, Charlotte M. "The Semiotic Paradigm: Implications for Tourism Research." *Tourism Management* 20 (1999): 47–57.

Edensor, Tim. "Performing Tourism, Staging Tourism: (Re)Producing Tourist Space and Practice." *Tourist Studies* 1, no. 1 (2001): 59–81.

Elliot, Stuart. "In Detroit, Agencies Compete to Sell City as a Creative Haven." *New York Times*, November 15, 2009. https://www.nytimes.com/2009/11/16/business/media/16adcol.html.

Elmore, Carl H. *Quit You Like Men*. New York: Scribner, 1944.

Farley, Rebecca. "'By Endurance We Conquer': Ernest Shackleton and Performances of White Male Hegemony." *International Journal of Cultural Studies* 8 (2008): 231–54.

Fiennes, Ranulph. *Captain Scott*. London: Coronet, 2003.

———. *Race to the Pole*. New York: Hyperion, 2004.

Fletcher, Richard, and Heather Crawford. *International Marketing: An Asia-Pacific Perspective*. Melbourne, Australia: Pearson, 2013.

Fox, Adrian, and Kate Bazeley. "Naming the Unnamed." *Geographical Magazine*. December 2013. http://geographical.co.uk/places/mapping/item/430-naming-the-un-named.

Fox, Stephen. *The Mirror Makers: A History of American Advertising and Its Creators*. Urbana-Champaign: University of Illinois Press, 1997.

Frew, Elspeth. "Advertising World Heritage Sites." In *Last Chance Tourism: Adapting Tourism Opportunities in a Changing World*, edited by Harvey Lemelin, Jackie Dawson, and Emma J. Stewart, 117–32. New York: Routledge, 2012.

Fricker, Helen Amanda, T. Scambos, R. Bindschadler, and L. Padman. "An Active Subglacial Water System in West Antarctica Mapped from Space." *Science* 315 (2007): 1544–48.

Gilbert, Neil. "A Continent for Peace and Science." In *Exploring the Last Continent: An Introduction to Antarctica*, edited by Daniela Liggett, Bryan Storey, Yvonne Cook, and Veronika Meduna, 327–59. Cham, Switzerland: Springer International, 2016.

Gilbert, Neil, and Alan Hemmings. "Antarctic Mythbusting." *Antarctic* 33, no. 3 (2015): 29–31.

Gilchrist, Paul. "Gender and British Climbing Histories: Introduction." *Sport in History* 33, no. 3 (2013): 223–35.

Glasberg, Elena. *Antarctica as Cultural Critique: The Gendered Politics of Scientific Exploration and Climate Change*. New York: Palgrave Macmillan, 2012.

———. "The Last Place on Earth: Antarctica and Virtual Capitalism." *Political and Legal Anthropology Review* 21, no. 1 (1998): 65–76.

———. "'Living Ice': Rediscovery of the Poles in an Era of Climate Crisis." *Women's Studies Quarterly* 39, no. 3/4 (2011): 221–46.

Goodell, Jeff. "The Larsen C Crack-Up on Antarctica: Why It Matters." *Rolling Stone*. July 12, 2017. https://www.rollingstone.com/politics/politics-features /the-larsen-c-crack-up-in-antarctica-why-it-matters-206228/.

Gramling, Carolyn. "Mysterious Antarctic Lake Will Remain out of Reach." *Science* 350, no. 6260 (2015): 494.

Greenpeace. "World Park Antarctica." Accessed August 22, 2017. http://www .greenpeace.org/australia/en/about/history/how-we-saved-antarctica.

Gregg, Emma. "Leave No Trace: Exploring the Fragile Frontiers of Antarctica and South Georgia." *National Geographic*, April 16, 2021. https://www .nationalgeographic.co.uk/travel/2021/04/leave-no-trace-exploring-the -fragile-frontiers-of-antarctica-and-south-georgia.

Griffiths, Tom. *Slicing the Silence*. Sydney: University of New South Wales Press, 2007.

Groden, Claire. "Alaskan Airlines Apologizes for Inviting Everyone to 'Meet Our Eskimo.'" *Fortune*, January 29, 2016. http://www.fortune.com/2016/01/29 /alaska-airlines-eskimo.

Grow, Jean. "Stories of Community: The First Ten Years of Nike Women's Advertising." *American Journal of Semiotics* 22, no. 1–4 (2006): 165–94.

Guly, H. R. "Medical Comforts during the Heroic Age of Antarctic Exploration." *Polar Record* 49, no. 2 (2013): 110–17.

Gunster, Shane. "'You Belong Outside': Advertising, Nature, and the SUV." *Ethics and the Environment* 9, no. 2 (2004): 4–32.

Haase, Daniela. "Tourism in the Antarctic: Modi Operandi and Regulatory Effectiveness." PhD thesis, University of Canterbury, Christchurch, 2008.

Hadley, Peter. *The History of BOVRIL Advertising*. London: Hyde Park House, 1969.

Hall, C. Michael. "The Tourist and Economic Significance of Antarctic Travel in Australian and New Zealand Antarctic Gateway Cities." *Tourism and Hospitality Research* 2, no. 2 (2000): 157–69.

Hallberg, Garth. *All Consumers Are Not Created Equal: The Differential Marketing Strategy for Brand Loyalty and Profits*. Hoboken, New Jersey: John Wiley & Sons, 1995.

Headland, Robert K. "Historical Development of Antarctic Tourism." *Annals of Tourism Research* 21 (1994): 269–80.

Hemmings, Alan D. "'Environmental Management' as Diplomatic Method: The Advancement of Strategic National Interest in Antarctica." In *Exploring Antarctic Values: Proceedings of the Workshop Exploring Linkages between Environmental Management and Value Systems: The Case of Antarctica*, edited by Daniela Liggett and Alan D. Hemmings, 70–89. Canterbury: Gateway Antarctica Special Publication Series, 2013.

Hicks, Robin. "Sustainability: Can Advertising Save the World?" *Campaignlive.co.uk*. July 15, 2005. https://www.campaignlive.co.uk/article/sustainability-advertising-save-world/486529#.

Hince, Bernadette. *The Antarctic Dictionary: A Complete Guide to Antarctic English*. Collingwood, Victoria: CSIRO, 2000.

Hodgson-Johnston, Indiah, Andrew Jackson, Julia Jabour, and Tony Press. "Cleaning Up after Human Activity in Antarctica: Legal Obligations and Remediation Realities." *Restoration Ecology* 25, no. 1 (2017): 135–39.

"How Lord Roberts Spells Bovril." Bovril. 1900. Bodleian Libraries, Oxford University. John Johnson Collection: Patent Medicines 1 (60a).

Hughes, Kevin A., and Paul D. Bridge. "Potential Impacts of Antarctic Bioprospecting and Associated Commercial Activities upon Antarctic Sciences and Scientists." *Ethics in Science and Environmental Politics* 10 (2010): 13–18.

Hughes, Kevin A., and Peter Convey. "Implications of the COVID-19 Pandemic for Antarctica." *Antarctic Science* 32, no. 6 (2020): 426–39.

Hult, John, and Neil Ostrander. *Antarctic Icebergs: A Global Fresh Water Resource*. Prepared for the National Science Foundation. Santa Monica CA: Rand, 1973.

Hunt, Linda, and Sam Ikin. "Antarctica Under Threat from Human Visitors, Australian Environmental Scientist Says." *ABC News*. Updated June 22, 2014.

http://www.abc.net.au/news/2014-06-18/antarctic-tourism-threat-to-the
-pristine-wilderness-scientist/5533252.

Huntford, Roland. *Scott and Amundsen*. London: Hodder and Stoughton, 1979. Reprinted as *The Last Place on Earth: Scott and Amundsen's Race to the South Pole*. London: Abacus, 2000.

Huxley, Leonard. *Scott's Last Expedition: The Journals of Captain R. F. Scott*. New York: Dodd, Mead, 1913.

Jackson, Andrew. *Who Saved Antarctica? The Heroic Era of Antarctic Diplomacy*. Cham, Switzerland: Palgrave Macmillan, 2021.

Jackson, Kate. *George Newnes and the New Journalism in Britain, 1880–1910: Culture and Profit*. Ashgate: Aldershot, 2001.

Jones, Max. *The Last Great Quest: Captain Scott's Antarctic Sacrifice*. Oxford: Oxford University Press, 2003.

Jones, Max, Berny Sèbe, John Strachan, Bertrand Taithe, and Peter Yeandle. "Decolonising Imperial Heroes: Britain and France." *The Journal of Imperial and Commonwealth History* 42, no. 5 (2014): 787–825.

Joyner, Christopher C. "The Evolving Minerals Regime for Antarctica." In *The Antarctic Legal Regime*, edited by Christopher C. Joyner and Sudhir K. Chopra, 129–43. Dordrecht: Martinus Nijhoff, 1988.

Keneally, Thomas. "Captain Scott's Biscuit." *Granta Magazine*. May 12, 2010. Accessed August 22, 2017. http://www.granta.com/captain-scotts-biscuit.

Kiem, Anthony S., Tessa R. Vance, Carly R. Tozer, Jason L. Roberts, Ramona Dalla Pozza, John Vikovsky, Kate Smolders, and Mark A. Curran. "Learning from the Past—Using Palaeoclimate Data to Better Understand and Manage Drought in South East Queensland (SEQ), Australia." *Journal Hydrology: Regional Studies* 29 (2020): 1–14.

Krapp, Peter. "POLAR MEDIA." *Information, Communication & Society*, 11, no. 6 (2008) 831–45. DOI: 10.1080/13691180802010675.

Lai, David C. *Pentothal Postcards*. West New York NJ: Mark Batty, 2005.

Lamers, Machiel, Eke Eijgelaar, and Base Amelung. "Last Chance Tourism in Antarctica: Cruising for Change?" In *Last Chance Tourism: Adapting Tourism Opportunities in a Changing World*, edited by Harvey Lemelin, Jackie Dawson, and Emma J. Stewart, 25–41. New York: Routledge, 2012.

Larson, Edward J. *An Empire of Ice: Scott, Shackleton, and the Heroic Age of Antarctic Science*. New Haven CT: Yale University Press, 2011.

Leane, Elizabeth. *Antarctica in Fiction: Imaginative Narratives of the Far South*. Cambridge: Cambridge University Press, 2012.

———. "Antarctic Travel Writing and the Problematics of the Pristine: Two Australian Novelists' Narratives of Tourist Voyages to Antarctica." In *Proceedings of Imaging Nature: Media, Environment and Tourism*, edited by L. Lester and C. Ellis, 1–8. Cradle Mountain, Tasmania, June 27–29, 2004.

———. "Freezing Time in Far Southern Narratives." In *Antarctica in Fiction: Imaginative Narratives of the Far South*, edited by Elizabeth Leane, 153–79. Cambridge: Cambridge University Press, 2012.

———. "Introduction: The Cultural Turn in Antarctic Studies." *Polar Journal* 1, no. 2 (2011): 149–54.

———. "The Land That Time Forgot: Fictions of Antarctic Temporality." In *Futurescapes: Space in Utopian and Science Fiction Discourses*, edited by Ralph Pordzik Rodopi, 199–223. New York: Amsterdam, 2009.

———. "The Polar Press: A Century of Australian Antarctic 'Newspapers.'" *Australian Antarctic Magazine*, no. 22 (2012): 31–35.

———. *South Pole: Nature and Culture*. London: Reaktion, 2016.

———. "Unstable Places and Generic Spaces: Thrillers Set in Antarctica." In *Popular Fiction and Spatiality: Reading Genre Settings*, edited by Lisa Fletcher, 25–44. New York: Palgrave Macmillan, 2016.

Leane, Elizabeth, and Jeffrey McGee, eds. *Anthropocene Antarctica: Perspectives from the Humanities, Law and Social Sciences*. London: Routledge, 2020.

Leane, Elizabeth, and Stephen Nicol. "Filming the Frozen South." In *Screening Nature: Cinema beyond the Human*, edited by Anat Pick and Guinevere Narraway, 127–44. New York: Bergham, 2013.

Leane, Elizabeth, and Stephanie Pfennigwerth. "Marching on Thin Ice: The Politics of Penguin Films." In *Considering Animals: Contemporary Case Studies in Human-Animal Relations*, edited by Carol Freeman, Elizabeth Leane, and Yvette Watt, 29–40. Surrey: Ashgate, 2011.

Le Blond, Elizabeth Alice Frances. *True Tales of Mountain Adventure for Non-Climbers Young and Old*. New York: E. P. Dutton, 1903.

Leiss, William, Stephen Kline, Sut Jhally, and Jacqueline Botterill. "Social Communication in Advertising." In *Media Studies: A Reader*, 3rd ed., edited by Sue Thornham, Caroline Bassett, and Paul Marris, 772–85. Edinburgh: Edinburgh University Press, 2009.

———. *Social Communication in Advertising: Consumption in the Mediated Marketplace*. New York: Taylor and Francis, 2005.

Lemelin, Harvey, Jackie Dawson, Emma J. Stewart, Pat Maher, and Michael Lueck. "Last-Chance Tourism: The Boom, Doom, and Gloom of Visiting Vanishing Destinations." *Current Issues in Tourism* 13, no. 5 (2010): 477–93.

Lewander, Lisbeth. "Women and Civilisation on Ice." In *Cold Matters: Cultural Perceptions of Snow, Ice and Cold*, edited by Heidi Hansson and Catherine Norberg, 87–102. Umeå: Umeå University and Royal Skyttrean Society, 2009.

Long, David, and Phil Matthews. *Knowing Australian Volkswagens*. New South Wales: Bookworks, 1993.

Lubick, Naomi. "DDT Levels in Antarctic Penguins Present a Complex Mystery." *Environmental Science & Technology* (2008): 3909.

Lucas, Anna, Chris Henderson, Elizabeth Leane, and Lorne Kriwoken. "A Flight of the Imagination: Mawson's Antarctic Aeroplane." *Polar Journal* 1, no. 1 (2011): 63–75.

Lukin, Valery V., and Nikolay I. Vasiliev. "Technological Aspects of the Final Phase of Drilling Borehole 5G and Unsealing Vostok Subglacial Lake, East Antarctica." *Annals of Glaciology* 55, no. 65 (2014): 83–89.

Maddison, Ben. *Class and Colonialism in Antarctic Exploration, 1750–1920*. London: Pickering & Chatto, 2014.

Maizonave, G. B., F. S. Dos Reis, J. C. M. Lima, A. J. Bombardieri, F. E. Chiapetta, G. B. Ceccon, R. R. N. Souza, R. Tonkoski, and R. W. Dos Reis. "Integrated System for Intelligent Street Lighting." *Industrial Electronics*, IEEE International Symposium, July 9, 2006: 721–26.

Manhire, Bill. *The Wide White Page: Writers Imagine Antarctica*. Wellington: Victoria University Press, 2004.

Matthews, Phil. "Antarctica 1—Volkswagens in Antarctica." *Australian Antarctic Magazine*, no. 28, June 2015. https://www.antarctica.gov.au/magazine/issue-28-june-2015/history/antarctica-1-volkswagens-in-antarctica/.

Matuozzi, Robert N. "Richard Byrd, Polar Exploration, and the Media." *Virginia Magazine of History and Biography* 110, no. 2 (2002): 209–36.

Mayer, Jim. *Shackleton: A Life in Poetry*. Oxford: Signal, 2014.

Maynard, Jeff. *Wings of Ice*. Sydney: Random House, 2010.

McClintock, Anne. "Soft-Soaping Empire: Commodity Racism and Imperial Advertising." In *Media Studies: A Reader*, 3rd ed., edited by Sue Thornham, Caroline Bassett, and Paul Marris, 747–62. Edinburgh: Edinburgh University Press, 2009.

McDonough, John, and Karen Egolf. *The Advertising Age Encyclopedia of Advertising*. Abingdon: Routledge, 2015.

McEwen, John M. "The National Press during the First World War: Ownership and Circulation." *Journal of Contemporary History* 17, no. 3 (1982), 459–86.

Messner, Reinhold. *Antarctica: Both Heaven and Hell*. Translated by Jill Neate. Wiltshire: Crowood, 1991.

Miller, Kathleen E. "Wired: Energy Drinks, Jock Identity, Masculine Norms, and Risk Taking." *Journal of American College Health* 56, no. 5 (2008): 481–90.

Morgan, Nigel, and Annette Pritchard. *Advertising in Tourism and Leisure*. Oxford: Butterworth-Heinemann, 2000.

Morrell, Margot, and Stephanie Capparell. *Shackleton's Way: Leadership Lessons from the Great Antarctic Explorer*. London: Penguin, 2001.

Morrison, Alastair M., and Heidi H. Sung. "Adventure Tourism." In *Encyclopedia of Tourism*, edited by Jafar Jafari and Honggen Xiao, 11. Cham, Switzerland: Springer International, 2010.

Moss, Sarah. *Scott's Last Biscuit: The Literature of Polar Exploration*. Oxford: Signal, 2006.

Nash, Meredith, Hanne Nielsen, Justine Shaw, Matt King, Mary-Anne Lea, Narissa Bax. "'Antarctica Just Has This Hero Factor . . .': Gendered Barriers to Australian Antarctic Research and Remote Fieldwork." *PLoS One* 14, no. 1 (2019): 1–22.

Nasht, Simon. *The Last Great Explorer: Hubert Wilkins, Australia's Unknown Hero*. Sydney: Hodder, 2005.

Neufeld, Erin, Jessica O'Reilly, Rupert Summerson, and Tina Tin. "Valuing Antarctica: Emerging Views from International Studies." In *Antarctic Futures: Human Engagement with the Antarctic Environment*, edited by Tina Tin, Daniela Liggett, Patrick T. Maher, and Machiel Mathers, 233–52. Dordrecht, Netherlands: Springer, 2014.

Never Stop Exploring. "Mission Antarctic." January 8, 2013. Accessed April 25, 2016. http://www.neverstopexploring.com/explore/mission-antarctic -overview (site discontinued).

Nielsen, Hanne. "From Shelter to Showpiece." Christchurch: COMNAP Report, 2014.

———. "Selling the South: Commercialisation and Marketing of Antarctica." In *Handbook on the Politics of Antarctica*, edited by Klaus Dodds, Alan Hemmings, and Peder Roberts, 183–98. Cheltenham: Edward Elgar, 2017.

Nielsen, Hanne, and Cyril Jaksic. "Recruitment Advertising for Antarctic Personnel: Between Adventure and Routine." *Polar Record* 54, no. 1 (2018): 65–75.

Nielsen, Hanne, and Gabriela Roldán. "Polar Policy in Practice: Tour Guiding in Antarctica." *The Yearbook of Polar Law Online* 14, no. 1 (2023): 145–66. DOI: https://doi.org/10.1163/22116427_014010008.

Noble, Anne. "Antarctica Nullius." *Now Future: Dialogues with Tomorrow 2010 Series*. Edited by Sophie Jerram and Dugal McKinnon. 2010. Accessed June 24, 2014. http://www.dialogues.org.nz (site discontinued).

Norman, Jane. "What Is the 'Holy Grail of Climate Science' and How Will Scientists Find It?" ABC *News*. Updated December 11, 2016. https://www.abc.net.au/news/2016-12-12/what-is-the-million-year-ice-core/8102552.

Nüsser, Marcus, and Ravi Baghel. "The Emergence of the Cryoscape: Contested Narratives of Himalayan Glacier Dynamics and Climate Change." In *Environmental and Climate Change in South and Southeast Asia: How Are Local Cultures Coping?*, edited by Barbara Schuler, 138–57. Boston: Brill, 2014.

Opel, Andy. "Constructing Purity: Bottled Water and the Commodification of Nature." *Journal of American Culture* 22, no. 4 (1999): 67–76.

Orheim, Olav. "Managing the Frozen Commons." In *Antarctica: Global Science from a Frozen Continent*, edited by David Walton, 273–330. Cambridge: Cambridge University Press, 2013.

O'Shaughnessy, Michael, and Jane Stadler. *Media and Society: An Introduction*, 2nd ed. Oxford: Oxford University Press, 2004.

Palmer, Catherine. "Shit Happens: The Selling of Risk in Extreme Sport." *Australian Journal of Anthropology* 13, no. 3 (2002): 323–36.

Parker, Betty J. "Exploring Life Themes and Myths in Alcohol Advertisements through a Meaning-Based Model of Advertising Experiences." *Journal of Advertising* 27, no. 1 (1998): 97–112.

Paterson, Mark. *Consumption and Everyday Life*. London: Routledge, 2006.

Pearce, Fred. "Boiled-to-Death Penguins Are Back from the Brink." *New Scientist* (February 22, 2012). http://www.newscientist.com/article/dn21501-boiled-to-death-penguins-are-back-from-the-brink.

Pearse, Guy. *Green Wash: Big Brands and Carbon Scams*. Collingwood, Victoria: Black, 2012.

Peat, Neville. *Shackleton's Whisky: The Extraordinary Story of an Heroic Explorer and Twenty-Five Cases of Unique MacKinlay's Old Scotch*. Auckland: Random House, 2013.

Perkins, Dennis N. T., Margaret P. Holtman, Paul R. Kessler, and Catherine McCarthy. *Leading at the Edge: Leadership Lessons from the Extraordinary Saga of Shackleton's Antarctic Expedition*. New York: AMACOM, 2000.

Pictures of 1912: Pall Mall Magazine Extra. London: Pall Mall, 1912. https://archive.org/details/picturesof1912pa00lond/page/n139/mode/2up.

Powell, R., S. Kellert, and S. Ham. "Antarctic Tourists: Ambassadors or Consumers?" *The Polar Record* 44 (2008), 233–41. https://doi.org/10.1017/S0032247408007456.

Pryde, James, John Conner, Frances Jack, Mark Lancaster, Lizzie Meek, Craig Owen, Richard Paterson, Gordon Steele, Fiona Strang, Jacqui Woods. "Sensory and Chemical Analysis of 'Shackleton's' Mackinlay Scotch Whisky." *Journal of the Institute of Brewing* (2011): 156–65.

Pynchon, Thomas. *V*. New York: Perennial Library, 1963.

Riffenburgh, Beau. *The Myth of the Explorer*. Oxford: Oxford University Press, 1993.

Roberts, Kevin. "Antarctica—Anything Is Possible." Address, April 29, 1998, in Christchurch, New Zealand. Accessed August 26, 2015. http://www.saatchikevin.com/speech/antarctica-anything-possible.

Roberts, Peder. "The Politics of Early Exploration." In *Antarctica and the Humanities*, edited by Peder Roberts, Lize-Marié van der Watt, and Adrian Howkins, 318–36. London: Palgrave Macmillan UK, 2016.

———. "The White (Supremacist) Continent: Antarctica and Fantasies of Nazi Survival." In *Antarctica and the Humanities*, edited by Peder Roberts, Lize-Marié van der Watt, and Adrian Howkins, 105–24. London: Palgrave Macmillan UK, 2016.

Roberts, Peder, Lize-Marié van der Watt, and Adrian Howkins. "Antarctica: A Continent for the Humanities." In *Antarctica and the Humanities*, edited by Peder Roberts, Lize-Marié van der Watt, and Adrian Howkins, 1–23. London: Palgrave Macmillan UK, 2016.

Rodger, Alan. "Antarctica: A Global Change Perspective." In *Antarctica: Global Science from a Frozen Continent*, edited by David Walton, 301–24. Cambridge: Cambridge University Press, 2013.

Rodgers, Eugene. "Richard E. Byrd's First Antarctic Expedition." *Virginia Magazine of History and Biography* 110, no. 2 (2002): 153–74.

Roldán, Gabriela. "A Door to the Ice?: The Significance of the Antarctic Gateway Cities Today." *Journal of Antarctic Affairs* 2 (2015): 57–70.

Ruddiman, William F. "The Anthropocene." *Annual Review of Earth and Planetary Sciences* 41 (2013): 45–68.

Ryan, James R. *Photography and Exploration*. London: Reaktion, 2013.

Samuel, Lawrence R. "Thinking Smaller: Bill Bernbach and the Creative Revolution in Advertising of the 1950s." *Advertising & Society Review* 13, no. 3 (2012). https://www.muse.jhu.edu/article/491080.

Sareff, Mark. "Campaign for Change." In *Westpac Stakeholder Impact 2006*. Australia: Westpac Bank, 2006.

Savolainen, Akseli. "Driving Towards a Better Future." *ABB Review* 4 (2004): 34–38.

Scarles, Caroline. "Becoming Tourist: Renegotiating the Visual in the Tourist Experience." *Environment and Planning D: Society and Space* 27 (2009): 465–88.

Shaw, Justine, Aleks Terauds, Martin Riddle, Hugh Possingham, and Steven Chown. "Antarctica's Protected Areas Are Inadequate, Unrepresentative, and at Risk." *PLoS Biology* 12, no. 6 (2014): 1–5.

Simpson-Housley, Paul. *Antarctica: Exploration, Perception and Metaphor*. London: Routledge, 1992.

Sörlin, Sverker. "Cryo-History: Ice and the Emerging Arctic Humanities." In *The New Arctic*, edited by Birgitta Evengård, Joan Nymand Larsen, and Øyvind Paasche, 327–39. Heidelberg: Spring, 2015.

Spears, Nancy, Marla Royne, and Eric van Steenburg. "Are Celebrity-Heroes Effective Endorsers? Exploring the Link between Hero, Celebrity, and Advertising Response." *Journal of Promotion Management* 19, no. 1 (2013): 17–37.

Steel, Gary D. "Extreme and Unusual: Psychology in Antarctica." In *Exploring the Last Continent*, edited by Daniela Liggett, Bryan Storey, Yvonne Cook, and Veronika Meduna, 361–77. Cham, Switzerland: Springer International, 2015.

Stonehouse, Bernard. "Ecotourism in Antarctica." In *Ecotourism: A Sustainable Option?*, edited by E. Cater and G. Lowman, 195–212. Chichester: John Wiley & Sons, 1994.

Sullivan, Nick. "In Which Robert Falcon Scott's Jacket Is Resurrected." *Esquire*. March 23, 2012. http://www.esquire.com/style/a13366/robert-falcon-scott -gieves-jacket-032312.

Talbot, Peter. "A Study of the Techniques Used by the Ross Sea Committee to Raise Funds for New Zealand's Part in the Trans-Antarctic Expedition, with Selected Comparisons of Other Expeditions." Postgraduate certificate in Antarctic Studies (PCAS) 14, University of Canterbury, 2013.

Terauds, Aleks, and Jasmine R. Lee. "Antarctic Biogeography Revisited: Updating the Antarctic Conservation Biogeographic Regions." *Diversity and Distributions* 22, no. 8 (2016): 836–40.

Thomas, Thierry. "Ecotourism in Antarctica: The Role of the Naturalist-Guide in Presenting Places of Natural Interest." *Journal of Sustainable Tourism* 2, no. 4 (1994): 204–9.

Thompson, W. P. *Handbook of Patent Law of All Countries*. London: Stevens and Sons, 1920.

Tin, Tina, Rupert Summerson, and He R. Yang. "Wilderness or Pure Land: Tourists' Perceptions of Antarctica." *Polar Journal* 6, no. 2 (2016): 307–27.

Tomaselli, Kayan G. "Consuming Nature: Antarctica, Penguins and Pollution." *Critical Arts: South-North Cultural and Media Studies* 26, no. 3 (2012): 328–52.

Trojanow, Ilija. *The Lamentations of Zeno*. London: Verso, 2016.

Tsujimoto, Megumu, Satoshi Imura, and Hiroshi Kanda. "Recovery and Reproduction of an Antarctic Tardigrade Retrieved from a Moss Sample Frozen for
Over 30 Years." *Cryobiology* 72, no. 1 (2016): 78–81.

Tungate, Mark. *Adland: A Global History of Advertising*. London: Kogan Page, 2013.

van der Watt, Lize-Marié, and Sandra Swart. "The Whiteness of Antarctica:
Race and South Africa's Antarctic History." In *Antarctica and the Humanities*,
edited by Peder Roberts, Lize-Marié van der Watt, and Adrian Howkins, 125–
56. London: Palgrave Macmillan UK, 2016.

Vaughan, David G., Josefino C. Comiso, Ian Allison, Jorhe Carrasco, Georg Kaser,
Ronald Kwok, Philip Mote, Tavi Murray, Frank Paul, Jiawen Ren, Eric Rignot,
Olga Solomina, Konrad Steffen, and Tingjun Zhang. "Observations: Cryo-
sphere." In *Climate Change 2013: The Physical Science Basis. Contribution of
Working Group I to the Fifth Assessment Report of the Intergovernmental Panel
on Climate Change*, edited by T. F. Stocker, D. Qin, G.-K. Plattner, M. Tignor,
S. K. Allen, J. Boschung, A. Nauels, Y. Xia, V. Bex, and P. M. Midgley, 317–82.
Cambridge: Cambridge University Press, 2013.

Wall, Geoffrey. "Ecotourism." In *Encyclopedia of Tourism*, edited by Jafar Jafari
and Honggen Xiao, 165. Cham, Switzerland: Springer International, 2010.

Walton, David W. H. "Discovering the Unknown Continent." In *Antarctica: Global
Science from a Frozen Continent*, edited by David W. H. Walton, 1–34. Cambridge: Cambridge University Press, 2013.

Wehi, Priscilla M., Nigel J. Scott, Jacinta Beckwith, Rata Pryor Rodgers, Tasman
Gillies, Vincent Van Uitregt, and Krushil Watene. "A Short Scan of Māori
Journeys to Antarctica." *Journal of the Royal Society of New Zealand* 52, no. 5
(2022). DOI: 10.1080/03036758.2021.1917633.

Wells, Liz. *Land Matters: Landscape Photography, Culture and Identity*. New York:
I. B. Tauris, 2011.

West, Douglas, John Ford, and Essam Ibrahim. *Strategic Marketing: Creating
Competitive Advantage*, 2nd ed. Oxford: Oxford University Press, 2012.

Wheeler, Sara. *Terra Incognita: Travels in Antarctica*. New York: Random House,
1996.

Williamson, Judith. "Unfreezing the Truth: Knowledge and Denial in Climate
Change Imagery." In *Now Future: Dialogues with Tomorrow 2010 Series*, edited
by Sophie Jerram and Dugal McKinnon. 2010. Accessed June 24, 2014. http://
www.dialogues.org.nz (site discontinued).

Wilson, David M. *The Lost Photographs of Captain Scott: Unseen Photographs from
the Legendary Antarctic Expedition*. New York: Little, Brown, 2011.

Worsley, Henry. *In Shackleton's Footsteps: A Return to the Heart of the Antarctic.* London: Virgin Books, 2011.

Yenne, Bill. *Beer: The Ultimate World Tour.* New York: Race Point, 2014.

Yusoff, Kathryn. "Visualizing Antarctica as a Place in Time: From the Geological Sublime to 'Real Time.'" *Space and Culture* 8, no. 4 (2005): 381–98.

Yusoff, Kathryn, and Jennifer Gabrys. "Climate Change and the Imagination." *WIRES Climate Change* 2 (2011): 516–34.

Index

Page numbers in italics indicate illustrations

3, 140, 163–65, 192; as seventh continent, 98, 155, 167, 177, 192
Antarctic tourism (product): branding in, xi, 20, 164–65, *164*, 167, 178–87; and celebrities, 180, 184; early chronology of, 102, 159; commercial value of "wilderness," 179, 181, 186–87; and consumer tastes, 102; inclusive model of engagement in, 103, 156–57; and leadership programs, 157, 182; and market fragmentation, 156, 163; and marketing, 165–67, 171, 175–77, 178, 180; materiality of destination in, xi, 156, 189; modes of travel represented in, 174–75, 178–79; as symbolic consumption, 168–70; as threat to pristine image, 100, 116; and types of tourism, 166–68. *See also* International Association of Antarctica Tour Operators (IAATO)
Antarctic tourists: as "Antarctic Ambassadors," 100, 165, 171; expectations of, 169–70, 186–87, 192; motivating factors to, 3, 155, 167–68, 170, 173, 178; versus explorers, 174–75
Antarctic Treaty (1959), 3, 12–14, 19, 62, 80, 108–9, 111–12, 189, 194; and territorial claims, 68, 83; and 2048 expiry myth, 14, 136
Antarctic Treaty Consultative Meeting (ATCM), 114–15, 127, 165. *See also* Antarctic Treaty System (ATS)
Antarctic Treaty System (ATS), 12–13, 23, 88, 109–12; 116, 138–40
"Antarctic Whalebone" advertisement (1895), 10, *11*
Antarctic workforce: minorities, 57, 63, 117; recruitment advertising for,

28, 185–86; scientists, 20, 21, 57, 73, 82, 107, 146, 185; tourism operators and guides, 163, 169–70, 185, 192. *See also* women in Antarctica
Antarctilyne cream, 107. *See also* skin care products
anthropogenic climate change, 23, 73, 105, 133–35, 137–38, 143, 152, 191, 195
appliances. *See* Carl Zeiss; Croton; General Electric; Rolex; Singer
Australian National Antarctic Research Expedition (ANARE), 20, 85–86, 87
aviation, 32, 101–3, 159

Belgian Geographical Society *Belgica* expedition (1897), 17, 28, *28*, 30
Bernbach, Bill, 84
bioprospecting, 14, 23, 126–31, 135
biscuits: as commemorative products, 42–46, 51; nutritional value of, 44–45
Blackmores Eco Krill advertisement (2012), 12, 128–30. *See also* icewashing
Borchgrevink, Carsten, *First on the Antarctic Continent* (1901), 17–18. *See also* Heroic Era: expeditions; official expedition narratives; sponsorships
Bovril: celebrity endorsements of, 12, 39–49, *39*, 74; and heroism, 37, 40–41 "It must be Bovril" campaign, 38–40, *39*; and nutrition, 38–40, 41, 47. *See also* food products; Shackleton, Ernest
BP (British Petroleum) sponsorships, 80, 81, 82. *See also* Commonwealth Trans-Antarctic Expedition (TAE)

brand ambassadors. *See* Antarctic tourists; celebrity explorers

Brand Antarctica: and brand values, 3, 113; and commercial value of unsung heroes, 58–59; conceptual framings of, 3–4, 20–21, 162; and connotations of purity, 23

British Airways, 101

British Services Antarctic Expedition (BSAE2012), 63–64. *See also* expeditions (charity); veterans

building materials, 22, 77–79, 92–94

Byrd, Richard E.: celebrity endorsements, 12, 84, 85, 90, 93, 118–120, 183; "hero," 35–36, 57–58, 60, 190; "This Hero Business" (1928), 57–58. *See also* Carl Zeiss; Grape-Nuts; Lifebuoy; Rinso; Veedol Motor Oil

Cape Town, South Africa. *See* Antarctic Gateway cities

Captive Minds (agency), 65–68

Carl Zeiss (company), 12, 90

celebrity endorsements, xi, 33, 36–38, 47, 51, 95

celebrity explorers, 1, 15–16, 29–34, 36–37, 45, 51, 58–61, 65, 175, 190. *See also* Byrd, Richard E.; Wilkins, Hubert

centenary reenactments, 59–63, 66–67, 174–75. *See also* Heroic Era: centenary

CFC-free aerosols, 146–48, *147*. *See also* Montreal Protocol; penguins

Chandi, Preet, 63

Cherry-Garrard, Apsley, 9, 116, 159; *The Worst Journey in the World* (1922), 92

Christchurch, New Zealand, 3, 77, 82, 94, 161–62. *See also* Antarctic Gateway cities

cinema. *See* cultural production; films

cleaning products, 116, 118–22, 126, 131

cleanliness (cult of), 116–22, 165–66. *See also* purity framing

cleanliness (domestic): 23, 109, 119–21; soap advertisements, 23, 43, 109, 118–21, 131. *See also* Antarctic fiction; purity framing

climate change: and Antarctic imagery, 7, 23–24, 133–35; and global policy changes, 137–38. *See also* Montreal Protocol

Coca-Cola, 6, 99–100

cold weather branding, 22, 77–83. *See also* extremity and performance

COLDZYME Project. *See* enzymes

commercialization of Antarctica, 5, 108, 127, 189

Commission for the Conservation of Antarctic Marine Living Resources (CCAMLR), 12–13, *13*, 109–10, 128, 130, 161

Committee for Environmental Protection (CEP), 112. *See also* Madrid Protocol

Commonwealth Trans-Antarctic Expedition (TAE), 1, 33, 80–82; *Foothold on Antarctica* (1956) film, 81; and "race to the pole," 81; sponsorship of, 81–82. *See also* Fuchs, Vivian; Hillary, Edmund; official expedition narratives

Convention for the Conservation of Antarctic Seals (1972), 109

Convention on the Conservation of Antarctic Marine Life (CAMLR) (1982). *See* Commission for the Conservation of Antarctic Marine Living Resources (CCAMLR)

films, 73, 81, 87, 97, 113, 134, 136, 149, 155, 193

food products, 10, 43, 47, 118, 126, 178, 183–84

fragility framing: and anthropogenic threats, 7, 23, 135, 137–38, 152, 155, 191; and cultural production, 3–4, 7–8, 24, 114, 133–35, 140–41, 196; and global climate systems, 7, 133–35, 138, 181; implications for branding, 141–51; mobilized by environmental NGOs, 136–40; monetized by tourism operators, 167–68, 180–81; and overlap between tourism and environmental advocacy, 180–82

Frank Hurley Photographer's Jacket (2019), 72

Franklin, John. *See* heroic sacrifice and death

frozen imagery, 140–41. *See also* ice-washing

Fuchs, Arved, Shackleton 2000 expedition, 59–60. *See also* centenary reenactments

Fuchs, Vivian, Commonwealth Trans-Antarctic Expedition (TAE), 81–82. *See also* Mechanical Age of exploration

General Bernardo O'Higgins Base, 114–15

General Electric, 90

geopolitics, 13, 40, 63, 82, 108

ghostwriters, 18–19. *See also* "hero business"; official expedition narratives

Gieves and Hawkes (clothing company), 60. *See also* centenary reenactments

Glacier 51 Toothfish, 127, 130

Glenfiddich: "Spirit of a Nation" campaign (2003), 66–68; Team Glenfiddich and *Walking with the Wounded*, 54, 64–66, 68. *See also* nationalism; nostalgia; sponsorships

Godet Antarctica Icy White advertisement (2010), 122–24, *124*; and purity trope, 122–23

GoPro "Be a Hero" campaign (2021), 36

Grape-Nuts (food company) "What's Your Mountain?" campaign (2013), 183–84

Greenpeace, 110, 111, 139

greenwashing, 140–46, 150. *See also* ice-washing

"Hatch's Sea Elephant oil" advertisement, *8, 9*

Hearst, William Randolph, 1, 32. *See also* media barons; place-naming; Wilkins, Hubert

Heinemann. *See* official expedition narratives

Heinz baked beans, 34–35. *See also* Hooper, Frederick; sponsorships

heritage business, 45, 48–50, 58, 60, 70–71, 161

hero: as concept, 37, 53–54, 61–62, 74–75, 173; definitions of, 35–37, 46, 74; and masculinity, 40–41, 46, 53–54, 56–57, 69–71, 75, 80–81, 90–91, 103–4, 120–22, 185–86, 190; and personal reputation, 18–19, 28–30, *28*, 33–37, 44, 49, 55–56, 182; in popular culture, 18–20, 27–29, 30–31, 49, 55–56, 69, 113; as shorthand for Edwardian values, 21, 29; in traditional Western

33, 53–54, 71, 75; and whiteness 56–57, 69
Massey Ferguson (tractor company), 65, 81–82. *See also* extremity and performance; Mechanical Age of exploration;
materiality, xi, 156, 189
Mawson, Douglas, 9, 17, 172; on Australasian Antarctic Expedition (1911–14), 30, 34, 48; endorsement advertising, 37, 46–49; station, 85–87, 89. *See also* Yalumba
Mawson's Huts: at Cape Denison, 34, 47–49; in Replica Museum, Hobart, 58, 161
Mawson's Huts Foundation Expedition (2000–2001), 48, *48*
McGrath Foundation "PinKtarctica" advertisement (2015), 184–85, *185*. *See also* transformation framing
McLean, Archibald. See *Adélie Blizzard* (newspaper); ghostwriters
Mechanical Age of exploration, advertisements for, 57–58, 84–85, 89–92
media: and Antarctic exploration, 1, 15–16, 18, 190; barons, 1–2, 31–32, 37, 190; global distribution of, 16–18; revolution in, 36. *See also* New Journalism
melting ice, 133–34, 138, 140, 142, 145, 148–53, 181–82, 187, 195
"Men Wanted" advertisement, 27–28, *28*, 182
Metallica "Freeze 'Em All" concert (2013), 99–101, 167
military personnel, 62–66. *See also* veterans
mineral resources, 14, 110–12, 135–36. *See also* Convention on the Regula-

tion of Antarctic Mineral Resource Activity (CRAMRA)
Montreal Protocol, 137–39, 146

Nansen, Fridtjof, 18, 30. *See also* official expedition narratives
National Antarctic Programs: activities, 19, 77, 68, 117, 160, 167, 185–86; in advertising, 85, 94–95; official suppliers to, 94–95; response to COVID-19 pandemic by, 114–15. *See also* extremity and performance
National Geographic: magazine, 73, 92, 103, 179; as tour operator, 160, 172
National Geographic Explorer (ship), *160*
nationalism: in Antarctic advertising, 54, 66–67, 71; and colonialism, 29, 67, 108; and territorial claims, 40, 57, 67–68
New Journalism, 16
Newnes, George, 1, 17–18, 174. *See also* media: barons; place-naming
newspapers, 15–18, 31, 190; produced in Antarctic, 34–35
New Zealand Antarctic Heritage Trust, 42–43, 49–50, 82, 173
New Zealand Scott Base, xii, 77, 93. *See also* Resene (paint company)
Nike "Does a Hero Know She's a Hero?" campaign (1999–2000), 36
The North Face (clothing company), 95–98; and extremity framing, 97–98
Norwegian Airlines, 59–60
nostalgia, 10–12, 41–43, 62, 67, 175
Oakite, 119, 131. *See also* cleaning products; purity framing
Oates, Lawrence, 46, 159. *See also* heroic sacrifice and death

oceanwide. *See* polar cruise travel

official expedition narratives, 18–19, 61, 169–70

Oliver, John, anti-tourism campaign (2014), 155–56, 179

Operation Deepfreeze (1955–56), 80–81, 91, 103. *See also* veterans

Operation Highjump (1946–47), 81. *See also* veterans

Oxo (soup), 12, 43. *See also* endorsement advertising

Pan Am Airline "It's easier to remember where we don't go" advertisement (1975), 101–2

Pan American Health Organization "Every Blood Donor Is a Hero" campaign (2012), 36

Pearson's Magazine. See official expedition narratives; sponsorships

penguins: and anthropogenic climate change, 9, 23–24, 116, 142–44, 146, 148; anthropomorphized in advertising, 102, 107, 123, 126, 146–48, *147*, 152; as metonym for Antarctica, 6, 77–78, 101, 142–43, 146, 178; use of stock images of, 6, 12, 127–29, 145, 167, 169, 172, 179; symbolic versatility of, 140, 145–46, 148, 151–52. *See also* ABB; ice; Resene (paint company); Westpac Banking Corp.

Pentothal anesthetic postcard campaign (1961), 98–99

photographers, 17–18, 33, 72, 79, 169. *See also* Hooper, Frederick; Hurley, Frank; Ponting, Herbert

photography, 17, 33–35, 88, 129, 144, 168–70

place-naming, 1–2, 194–95

polar bears, 6, 10, 23

polar cruise travel, 84, 159, 164–67, *164, 171–78, 185*

"Polar Impact" and minorities in polar research, 117. *See also* Antarctic workforce

Ponting, Herbert, 17, 33, 35

promotional material, 45, 50, 60, 68, 70, 172–73

protection rhetoric, 100, 130, 135, 141–44, 152–53, 164, 185

Protocol on Environmental Protection to the Antarctic Treaty (1991–98). *See* Madrid Protocol

Pseudoalteromonas antarctica, 107–8. *See also* bioprospecting

Punta Arenas, Chile. *See* Antarctic Gateway cities

Pure Altitude's Pure Antarctica serum, 107. *See also* purity framing; skin care products

purity and contamination: and drilling of subglacial lakes, 90, 114–16; and "pure science," 108–31; and waste management practices, 108, 136

purity framing, 107, 113–14, 130–31; Antarctica as a *tabula rasa*, 108; association with natural products, 109, 122, 125, 127–28; women as target audience, 120–21. *See also* whiteness (of Antarctica); wilderness

Quark Expeditions "Explorers Wanted" campaign (2024), 174

race: to the pole (1911), 30–33, 42, 45, 55, 81; for science, 33; for news, 31–33

Ray-Ban (sunglasses) advertisement (1959), 12, 103–4. *See also* extremity framing; women in Antarctica

sponsorships, 15, 22, 29–30, 33–34,
37–38, 45, 54, 58–68, 73–74, 118,
174–75, 184
Stanley, H. M., 40, 43
stock images, 10, 88, 129, 144
stories, commercial and reputational
value of, 18–19, 35–36
Süd Polaire Antarctic Dry Gin advertisement (2016), 122–26
Supernova Cushion shoes advertisement (2004), 176–77
TAE. See Commonwealth Trans-
Antarctic Expedition
technology 79, 81–82, 88, 98, 104, 115,
142–43
Terra Australis Incognita, 3, 25
transformation framing, xi, 24, 156–
58, 182–84, 187
tropes: Antarctic hero, 29, 36, 41, 57, 66,
74–75, 122, 190; as used in Antarctica, 91, 104; types of, 21, 92, 130–31,
170–71, 193; extremity, 18, 92, 104–5,
137; fragility, 181; man versus nature,
29–30, 69, 75, 92, 104–5; masculinity, 53, 105; purity, 108, 122–23,
125–27, 179; race to the pole, 30–32,
42, 45, 55, 81; transformation, 157
Tucker Sno-Cat. See extremity and
performance; Mechanical Age of
exploration
UAE Iceberg Project, 14
United Nations Convention on the Law
of the Sea (UNCLOS) (1982), 111, 139
Ushuaia, Argentina. See Antarctic
Gateway cities

Veedol Motor Oil, 85. See also extremity and performance; Mechanical
Age of exploration
veterans, 22, 63–65, 68
Vickers airplane, 37
Victoria University of Wellington
Antarctic Expedition, 2
Visco-Static Motor Oil, 20; "The Men
of Mawson" advertisement (1956),
85–86
Volkswagen (vw) "First car in Antarctica" campaign (1960s), 87–89
Walking with the Wounded (2013), 54,
61, 64–66, 68. See also veterans
watches and time, 6, 22, 79, 90–92,
104
Westpac Banking Corp. "Equator Principles" campaign (2003, 2008),
135, 144–48
whisky. See Glenfiddich; Mackinlay's
whiteness: of Antarctica, 73–74, 104,
113–114, 118, 121–23, 191; of explorers, 54, 56–57, 65, 67, 69–70, 108
wilderness, 23–24, 30, 88, 100–101,
107–13, 124, 127, 130, 168, 179
Wilkins, Hubert, 1, 32, 58, 87, 195
Wolfes Schnapps, 34–35
women in Antarctica, 54, 80, 89, 102–
3, 156, 184
World Wildlife Fund (wwf), 111, 128
Worsley, Henry, 61–62, 69, 174–75, 179
Xander Creative, 128–29
Yalumba (wine), 37, 51; "Southward
Ho! with 'Yalumba'" advertisement
(1930), 46–49, 48

IN THE POLAR STUDIES SERIES

*Brand Antarctica: How Global Consumer Culture
Shapes Our Perceptions of the Ice Continent*
Hanne Elliot Fønss Nielsen

To order or obtain more information on these or other University of Nebraska Press titles, visit nebraskapress.unl.edu.

Printed in the USA
CPSIA information can be obtained
at www.ICGtesting.com
LVHW091918011123
762773LV00002B/5